STRENGTH AND CONDITIONING FOR YOUNG ATHLETES

Strength and Conditioning for Young Athletes offers an evidence-based introduction to the theory and practice of strength and conditioning for children and young athletes. Drawing upon leading up-to-date research in all aspects of fitness and movement skill development, the book adopts a holistic approach to training centred on the concept of long-term athletic development and the welfare of the young athlete.

While other textbooks focus on a single aspect of youth trainability, this book explores every key topic in strength and conditioning as applied to young people, including:

- talent identification
- motor skill development
- strength, power and plyometrics
- speed and agility
- metabolic conditioning
- mobility and flexibility
- periodization
- weightlifting myths
- overtraining and injury prevention
- nutrition.

Written by a team of leading international strength and conditioning experts and paediatric sport scientists, every chapter includes programming guidelines for youths throughout childhood and adolescence to show how the latest scientific research can be applied by coaches to optimize young athletic potential. This is an essential resource for all students of strength and conditioning or paediatric exercise science, as well as any coach or athletic trainer working with children and young people.

Rhodri S. Lloyd is Lecturer in Sport and Exercise Physiology at Cardiff Metropolitan University, UK.

Jon L. Oliver is Senior Lecturer in Exercise Physiology at Cardiff Metropolitan University, UK.

STRENGTH AND CONDITIONING FOR YOUNG ATHLETES

Science and application

Edited by Rhodri S. Lloyd
and Jon L. Oliver

Routledge
Taylor & Francis Group

LONDON AND NEW YORK

First published 2014
by Routledge
2 Park Square, Milton Park, Abingdon, Oxon OX14 4RN

Simultaneously published in the USA and Canada
by Routledge
711 Third Avenue, New York, NY 10017

Routledge is an imprint of the Taylor & Francis Group, an informa business

British Library Cataloguing in Publication Data
A catalogue record for this book is available from the British Library

Library of Congress Cataloging in Publication Data
Strength and conditioning for young athletes : science and application / edited by Rhodri S. Lloyd and Jon L. Oliver.
pages cm
1. Physical fitness for children. 2. Physical fitness for youth. 3. Exercise for children. 4. Exercise for youth. I. Lloyd, Rhodri S.
GV443.S775 2013
613.7'042--dc23
2013003449

ISBN: 978–0–415–69487–2 (hbk)
ISBN: 978–0–415–69489–6 (pbk)
ISBN: 978–0–203–14749–8 (ebk)

Typeset in Bembo
by GreenGate Publishing Services, Tonbridge, Kent

Printed and bound in Great Britain by
TJ International Ltd, Padstow, Cornwall

Dedicated to Rhia and Oliver
Rhodri S. Lloyd

For Melissa, Isla and Ivy
Jon L. Oliver

CONTENTS

ILLUSTRATIONS

Figures

Tables

ABOUT THE CONTRIBUTORS

Rhodri S. Lloyd is Lecturer in Sport and Exercise Physiology at Cardiff Metropolitan University. Previously he earned his doctorate at the University of Wales Institute Cardiff, examining the development of plyometric ability in male youths. He is a fully accredited strength and conditioning coach with the UK Strength and Conditioning Association (UKSCA), and holds certified strength and conditioning status with distinction from the National Strength and Conditioning Association (NSCA). He serves on the Board of Directors for the UKSCA and is the inaugural convener of the UKSCA Youth Training Special Interest Group. He is also an Executive Council Board Member for the NSCA Youth Training Special Interest Group. His main research interests surround strength and power development in young athletes and long-term athletic development modelling.

Jon L. Oliver is Senior Lecturer in Exercise Physiology at Cardiff Metropolitan University. He completed his doctorate at the Children's Health and Exercise Research Centre at the University of Exeter in 2006. He previously served as convenor of the British Association of Sport and Exercise Science Paediatric Exercise Science Interest Group. He has conducted extensive research on childhood and long-term athlete development and translated much of this knowledge to aid practitioners. His work in youth sport has included collaborations in elite youth soccer, rugby union and athletics. He is primarily interested in the development of speed and explosives activities during childhood, together with the long-term monitoring of development, training and performance.

Abbe Brady presently works at the University of Gloucestershire where she is Course Leader for the MSc in Sports Coaching. Her work with children and young people in sport extends across a range of contexts as an educator, coach, sport scientist, researcher, youth worker, coach educator and mentor. As an accredited sport psychologist working in high-performance settings, she has gained insights to discourse, praxis and varied experiences of young athletes, parents and coaches. This awareness has fuelled her research interest to understand athlete well-being in sport and promote athlete-centred practices.

John B. Cronin is Professor in Strength and Conditioning within the Division of Sport and Recreation at AUT University in New Zealand. He also holds an Adjunct Professorial position with Edith Cowan University in Perth. He has research interests in human movement research particularly around the strengthening of muscle, these themes spanning high-performance sport to long-term athlete development.

Duncan N. French is Senior Strength and Conditioning Coach with the English Institute of Sport and Technical Lead of Strength and Conditioning for the North West region. He is currently the National Lead Strength and Conditioning Coach to Great Britain's Taekwondo Olympic programme, prior to which he was Head Strength and Conditioning Coach to Newcastle United FC and National Lead Strength and Conditioning Coach to Great Britain Basketball. He is Senior Lecturer at Northumbria University and gained his PhD in 2004 from the University of Connecticut, USA. He has served on the United Kingdom Strength and Conditioning Association Board of Directors since 2008, and currently holds the esteemed position as Chair of the association.

David H. Fukuda is currently Assistant Professor in the programme of Sport and Exercise Science at the University of Central Florida. His research interests include the development of performance-based testing methodologies, the analysis of physiological profiles in athletes, and the assessment of adaptations to exercise training and nutritional interventions in varying populations.

Paul Gamble has worked in high-performance sport for over a decade. He began his career in professional rugby union with English Premiership side London Irish and has since worked with elite athletes in a diverse array of sports, notably serving as National Strength and Conditioning Lead for Scottish Squash. Since completing his PhD in 2005, he has published three textbooks as sole author, and has also authored a number of book chapters and articles in peer-reviewed journals. He is one of a select few practitioners from the UK to hold High Performance Sport Accreditation with the British Association of Sport and Exercise Sciences (BASES), and is the only person to hold it for the specialism of strength and conditioning. He recently relocated to New Zealand where he has developed the Informed Practitioner in Sport website and e-learning resources for practitioners working with sports injuries.

Paul Green is currently a doctoral student at Cardiff Metropolitan University, studying the impact of age, maturation and training on the development of fundamental movement skills in youth. Accredited with the UK Strength and Conditioning Association, he has previously worked as a strength and conditioning coach for Falkirk Football Club senior squad, and with the club's community youth players.

G. Gregory Haff is Senior Lecturer and Senior Strength Scientist at Edith Cowan University, Perth. He is the 2011 NSCA William J. Kraemer Sport Scientist of the Year Award Winner. He has served as the Vice President of the NSCA, is a Certified Strength and Conditioning Specialist with Distinction, a founding Fellow of the NSCA, and an accredited member of the UK Strength and Conditioning Association. He is a Level 3 Australian Weightlifting Association Coach and a USA Weightlifting Regional Level Coach, and has served as an outside scientist with the United States Olympic Training Centers Performance Enhancement Teams for track cycling and weightlifting.

Robert P. Hetrick is currently a fitness consultant and serves as a personal trainer at Fitness One in Norman, Oklahoma. His research interests include the analysis of sports and metabolic performance as well as the effects of nutritional interventions on body composition and exercise.

Patria Hume is Professor of Human Performance at AUT University's Sport Performance Research Institute New Zealand (SPRINZ). A former international rhythmic gymnast (1980–1986) and coach of Olympic, Commonwealth and World Championships gymnasts (1987–1992), she is now a provider of sport science service, research and education to elite sport in New Zealand. She delivers as a lecturer on IOC courses, and received an IOC diploma for contribution to Olympic sport in 2001. She is on the editorial boards for *Sports Medicine* and *Sports Biomechanics*, and has published over 150 scientific research papers. Her research focuses on improving sport performance using sports biomechanics and sports anthropometry, and on reducing sporting injuries by investigating injury mechanisms and injury prevention methods and using sports epidemiology analyses. She is also a Fellow of the International Society of Biomechanics in Sports.

Ian Jeffreys is Senior Lecturer in Strength and Conditioning at the University of Glamorgan, where he directs all of the university's strength and conditioning activities, and is also the Proprietor and Performance Director of All-Pro Performance based in Brecon. A board member of the UKSCA since its inception, he is the Editor of the UKSCA journal *Professional Strength and Conditioning* and is on the Editorial Board for the NSCA's *Strength and Conditioning Journal* and the *Journal of Australian Strength and Conditioning*. He has authored three books as well as numerous book chapters and peer-reviewed articles. He has coached and delivered numerous keynote presentations and coaching workshops internationally. He was recognized as the NSCA's High School Professional of the Year in 2006, and was made a fellow of the NSCA in 2009.

Thomas Jones is currently a doctoral student at Northumbria University completing his PhD in exercise physiology. His research is focused on the physiological and performance responses to concurrent strength and endurance training. He holds a Masters degree from Nottingham Trent University, and alongside his studies provides strength and conditioning support to the Rugby Football Union, working with both junior and senior female rugby players.

Kristina L. Kendall is currently Assistant Professor in the Department of Health and Kinesiology at Georgia Southern University. She is the Director of the Human Performance Laboratory and her interests include the investigation of the effects of nutritional interventions on body composition and performance.

William J. Kraemer is a Full Professor in the Department of Kinesiology in the Neag School of Education working in the Human Performance Laboratory at the University of Connecticut. He also holds an appointment as a Full Professor in the Department of Physiology and Neurobiology and an appointment as a Professor of Medicine at the UCONN Health Center/School of Medicine. He is a Fellow in the American College of Sports Medicine and is a past president of the National Strength and Conditioning Association (NSCA). He is the current Editor in Chief of the *Journal of Strength and Conditioning Research*, and Associate Editor of both *Medicine and Science in Sports and Exercise* and the *Journal of Applied Physiology*.

Jeni McNeal is Professor in Exercise Science at Eastern Washington University. She is the Lead Strength and Conditioning Consultant for USA Diving, where she conducts research, training and performance testing, as well as provides coaches' education. She also serves as the Vice-Chair of Research for the US Elite Coaches Association for Women's Gymnastics. Her primary research focus is on performance aspects of acrobatic sports.

Cesar Meylan currently works as the lead sport scientist for the Canadian women's national soccer team and is also near completion of a PhD examining the development and trainability of power output during childhood and adolescence. In his current role he is responsible for the physical development of both junior and senior soccer players. He has worked with youth athletes for a number of years, particularly in youth soccer. He previously ran the physical talent identification programme at the National Talent Centre in New Zealand and has consulted with New Zealand Football on the development of the National Player Framework.

Satoshi Mizuguchi is Assistant Professor in the Department of Exercise and Sport Sciences at East Tennessee State University and works with the Center of Excellence for Sport Science and Coach Education. He has worked with numerous sports including soccer, volleyball, softball, football and weightlifting as a strength and conditioning coach or sport scientist. He is also a competitive weightlifter.

Jeremy A. Moody is currently Director of the MSc in Strength and Conditioning degree at Cardiff Metropolitan University and Chief Operations Officer for Welsh Judo. Previous to this he has served as Performance Manager for UK Athletics and has worked for the English Institute of Sport (EIS) as a Senior Strength and Conditioning Coach and Regional Lead. He has also been a Head Coach and Performance Director at Paralympic level attending the Sydney and Athens Paralympic Games respectively. He has served as a Board Director and recently Chair of the UK Strength and Conditioning Association from 2010 to 2012, and continues to act as an assessor and coach educator for the association.

Fernando Naclerio is Principal Lecturer and Programme Leader of the MSc Strength and Conditioning degree at the Centre of Sports Science and Human Performance at the University of Greenwich. He has authored or co-authored several scientific manuscripts and book chapters related to sports sciences and nutrition. He has served as a strength and conditioning coach for a number of elite level athletes from sports including skiing, boxing, martial arts, bodybuilding, rugby and soccer.

Kyle C. Pierce is currently Professor in the Kinesiology and Health Science Department at Louisiana State University in Shreveport (LSUS) and the Director of the USA Weightlifting Center for High Performance and Development at LSUS. His work has provided the opportunity to publish weightlifting and strength training articles and to teach children the sport of weightlifting and coach them throughout their careers to World Championships and Olympic Games. He has also been a coach for the United States at such events. He was the United States National Junior Women's Coach from 2004 to 2006 and the Junior Men's Coach from 2007 to 2008. He has been a member of the IWF Coaching and Research Committee since 2000 and a Vice President of the Pan American Weightlifting Federation since 2008. In 2005 he won the United States Olympic Committee's 'Doc' Counsilman Science Award for a coach that utilizes scientific techniques and equipment as an integral part of his or her coaching methods or has created innovative ways to use sport science.

Michael W. Ramsey is Chair of the Department Exercise and Sport Science at East Tennessee State University. He received his PhD in Exercise Physiology from Texas A&M University and holds a bachelor's degree from Sam Houston State University in Psychology/Kinesiology with an emphasis in Elementary Physical Education. He has worked with various youth sports including cycling, volleyball and basketball.

Michael C. Rumpf currently works as a Sport Scientist to both youth and senior teams through the Excellence Football Project at Aspetar in Qatar. He has worked with developing football players for a number of years and was previously the lead Sport Scientist for New Zealand Football National Centres, providing support from grass roots through to the national teams. He completed his PhD at Auckland University of Technology, examining sprint running kinetics and kinematics in youths.

Keith Russell is Professor at the College of Kinesiology, University of Saskatchewan, Canada and is an associate member of Anatomy and Cell Biology, College of Medicine. He is the former Canadian Men's National Coach and coach of two Canadian Olympians. A life member of the Canadian Gymnastic Federation in 1993, he received the 3M Canadian Male Coach of the Year award in 1995, and was the recipient of the 2010 Lifetime Achievement Award by the Coaching

Association of Canada. He is currently the President of the Scientific Commission of the International Gymnastics Federation (FIG), and author of major components of both the Canadian and the FIG's Coach Education Programmes. He has taught the scientific components of 45, seven-day FIG Coaching Academies in 25 countries and presents regularly at international conferences on scientific applications in high-level competitive sports. His main topic of interest is the effects of intensive sport training on growing tissues.

William Sands is Professor in the Department of Exercise and Sport Science at East Tennessee State University. He is the former Recovery Center Leader, Head of Sport Biomechanics and Engineering and Senior Physiologist for the US Olympic Committee in Colorado Springs. He has over 40 years of experience in Olympic sports. He has served as Associate Professor at the University of Utah, Co-Director of the Motor Behavior Research Laboratory with adjunct appointments in Bioengineering and Physical Therapy, Director of Research and Development for USA Gymnastics, and a member of the Scientific Commission of the International Gymnastics Federation.

Margaret E. Stone is Director of the Center of Excellence for Sport Science and Coach Education at East Tennessee State University. A two-time Olympian competing in the discus for Great Britain, she has previously held strength and conditioning positions at the University of Arizona, Texas Tech and Appalachian State University where she has coached many players in the NBA, NFL and MLB. Additionally, she has served as the National Track and Field Coach for Scotland, and as the Coaching Manager for the United States Olympic Committee. Recently she was presented with the prestigious 'Legends in the Field Award' by the College Strength Coaches Association and was made a fellow of the National Strength and Conditioning Association. In 2009, she received the honour of winning the National Strength and Conditioning Association's Lifetime Achievement Award.

Michael H. Stone is currently Professor in the Department of Exercise and Sport Science at East Tennessee State University. He is the Exercise and Sport Science Laboratory Director and PhD Coordinator. His research interests deal with studying methods of strength training and fatigue management among athletes. He has coached several sports including throws and weightlifting.

Jeffrey R. Stout is currently Associate Professor in the programme of Sport and Exercise Science at the University of Central Florida. He has published over 200 research studies and presentations that have focused on nutrition, exercise performance, muscle function and body composition in young and elderly populations. Furthermore, he has co-authored and co-edited eight books and eight book chapters on sports nutrition and body composition.

Gareth Stratton is Professor of Paediatric Exercise Science and Director of the Applied Sport Technology Exercise Medicine (A-STEM) Research Centre at Swansea University. He is also founder and Chair of the Research in Exercise Activity and Children's Health (REACH) Group, and Adjunct Professor at the University of Western Australia. Previous to this he held a chair at the Research Institute of Sports and Exercise Sciences at Liverpool John Moores University. He led the first British Association of Sports and Exercise Sciences (BASES) Guidance on Children, Young People and Resistance Exercise, chaired the National Institute of Health and Clinical Excellence Group that wrote *Physical Activity Guidance for Children and Young People* in 2009, and chaired the Children and Young People's section of Start Active, Stay Alive, guidelines on healthy levels of physical activity. He is also Principal Investigator of the Sportslinx programme that won the European Childhood Obesity Group award in 2011. He is also a fellow of the British Association of Sport and Exercise Sciences (BASES).

Craig A. Williams is Professor of Paediatric Exercise and Health and Director of the Children's Health and Exercise Research Centre (CHERC) at the University of Exeter. His research interests are within the areas of children's talent development, fatigue, exercise tolerance and muscle metabolism. He regularly works with professional Premiership youth football and rugby teams, as well as having consultant roles with organizations such as British Cycling, British Gymnastics, the Lawn Tennis Association and the English Cricket Board.

PREFACE

During recent times, the importance placed on strength and conditioning for athletic development has increased to such an extent that it is now recognized as one of the most significant disciplines within the field of sports sciences. Recently there has been an evident rise in profile of strength and conditioning provision for young athletes in a bid to enhance performance and prevent injury. Despite the dramatic rise in popularity of youth training, it is essential that those involved in the development process have the requisite knowledge and expertise to ensure that children and adolescents can improve their physical capacities in a safe and effective manner. Consequently, as editors we deemed it necessary to draw together some of the most well-respected researchers and practitioners in the field to help produce *Strength and Conditioning for Young Athletes: Science and Application.*

Part 1 provides chapters devoted to key underpinning concepts surrounding young athlete development, examining the influence of growth and maturation on physical performance, talent identification and long-term athletic development strategies. These chapters are extremely important for the remaining sections of the textbook and provide a vital grounding in key concepts associated with strength and conditioning provision for paediatric populations.

Part 2 is dedicated to the effects of natural development and training on the development of key fitness qualities, including physical literacy, strength, power, agility, speed, mobility and metabolic conditioning. In every chapter the contributing authors have provided an overview of the scientific literature examining the effects of natural growth, maturation and training on the development of specific fitness components, and propose practical guidelines for coaches to consider when prescribing training to develop specific physical qualities.

Part 3 offers an insight into key contemporary issues, which are often overlooked within youth strength and conditioning. The section provides expert insights into periodization and nutritional strategies for young athletes, the myths associated with resistance training for this unique population and, importantly, chapters devoted to the prevention of overuse injuries and athlete welfare and well-being.

Thanks to our expert panel of contributing authors, we are confident that this textbook will be the first of its kind to attempt to provide a comprehensive overview of all issues surrounding the holistic development of young athletes. We envisage that this textbook will provide strength and conditioning coaches, technical coaches, parents, undergraduate and postgraduate students and the athletes themselves with the latest information surrounding strength and conditioning provision for young athletes. By bridging the gap between scientific principles and practical application, we hope that this textbook can help promote the safe and effective development of youths for many years to come.

Rhodri S. Lloyd and Jon L. Oliver

ACKNOWLEDGEMENTS

We would like to thank a number of people who have been instrumental in the completion of this book.

First, our thanks must go to Simon Whitmore, Joshua Wells and all other personnel at Routledge who have helped us bring this book from its initial conception to the final print.

An edited book is only as strong as its contributors, and for *Strength and Conditioning for Young Athletes: Science and Application* we have been fortunate to secure the services of an array of truly world-class coaches and scientists who continue to develop ideas and practices in paediatric exercise science and youth strength and conditioning. We are extremely grateful to our team of contributors for their tireless efforts in editing drafts, working to deadlines and, ultimately, for delivering exceptional content.

In addition to those directly involved in the completion of this book, we would also like to take this opportunity to thank the coaches, athletes, scientists and educators we have worked with who have helped us form our views and beliefs in what is such an important topic.

Rhodri S. Lloyd and Jon L. Oliver

PART 1
Fundamental concepts of youth development

1

THE IMPACT OF GROWTH AND MATURATION ON PHYSICAL PERFORMANCE

Gareth Stratton and Jon L. Oliver

Introduction

'Give the boy until he is seven and I will give you the man.' This Jesuit maxim highlights the importance of growth and development during the early years where the interaction of the environment and genotype on the phenotype is expressed through an evolving body composition, shape and size. An understanding of growth and development in relation to human performance is essential for those working with youth athletes. There is significant individual variability in factors that affect the pathway of growth, development and maturation from infancy through childhood to adolescence and on to adulthood, which in turn have an impact on physical performance and health-related issues. The strength and conditioning coach needs an awareness of how factors that affect current and future growth, development and maturation interact with different training stimuli. This will allow developmentally appropriate training programmes to be constructed that help to meet training objectives throughout childhood and adolescence.

Basic theoretical concepts

Defining growth development and maturation

The terms growth, development and maturation are used interchangeably when describing the pathway from birth to adulthood. There is much debate over the definition of these terms but each refers to specific biological activities. Generating operational definitions for these terms will help clarify the subsequent discussion and debate.

Growth is the most significant biological activity during the first 20 years or so of life, starting from conception to full maturity. Tissue growth occurs within body parts and results in a quantitative increase in body mass and stature. These changes are a result of a combination of hyperplasia, hypertrophy and accretion leading to an increase in cell number, size and cellular material respectively. Hyperplasia, hypertrophy and accretion are significant cellular processes that drive growth. These processes are not linear, for example the number of cells (hyperplasia) is largely determined during the pre-natal period whereas hypertrophy follows a non-linear pathway through childhood to adulthood.

Maturation is the process of becoming mature. The timing and tempo of maturation varies between biological systems. For example, sexual maturity is defined as a fully functional reproductive system, compared to skeletal maturity which refers to a fully ossified skeleton; the timing and tempo of both can differ significantly. Timing defines 'when' a particular maturation process occurs whereas tempo is the 'rate' at which maturation progresses. As we will note later the timing and tempo of stature are highly individual and are also different between girls and boys. In essence, growth is a quantitative increase in stature or size at any given time, compared to maturity which is the rate of progress to full adult stature or mature state. Clearly growth and maturity are inextricably linked and are processes that are measurable and directional.

Development is a broader concept than growth and maturation. It is generally viewed as qualitative, involves differentiation of tissues and is both biological and behavioural. The biological differentiation of cells to form specific tissues, organs and body systems occurs in the embryonic and fetal stages of the pre-natal environment and differentiation of a tissue is complete when it becomes functional. This development continues in the post-natal environment as the function of the body systems and tissues becomes refined. Behavioural development reflects a period of change in the psychomotor (fitness, skills), cognitive (knowledge, understanding) and affective (social, relationships) domains. As children interact with society their ability to express themselves in these domains becomes refined and their intellectual, physical, social and moral competencies mature.

The strength and conditioning coach should not only consider the physical consequences of the interaction of training with growth, maturation and development, but also the important impact of behavioural development and whether training provides a positive educational experience for youths.

Defining chronological age

Chronological age is used to define a time framework with the clock set at zero on a child's date of birth. Chronological age is measured at a single time point away from the date of birth. The first year of life is referred to as 'infancy' with childhood beginning at the end of infancy and ending at the start of adolescence. Childhood is generally split into three stages. Early childhood involves the pre-school years age 1.0–4.99 years, mid-childhood 5.0–7.99 years and late childhood age 8.0 years to the start of adolescence. Adolescence is a much more difficult period to define by chronological age. It begins with the onset of puberty where changes in the neuro-endocrine system stimulate the development of secondary sexual characteristics alongside a rapid increase in stature. The period of adolescence ends at maturity where full adult stature is attained. This period ranges from 8–19 and 10–22 years of age in girls and boys respectively. These chronological ages are generally defined by school entry or public health cohorts and are used purely for organizational purposes.

Defining biological age

Whereas chronological age is predictable and easily assessed, biological age is significantly more problematic, less predictable and more difficult to assess. There is a large inter-individual variation in the timing and tempo of the adolescent growth spurt. Moreover, there are a number of methods of assessing maturation status, none of which are the absolute gold standard.

The types of measures of maturity generally match the biological system under consideration. Common measures of biological maturation are skeletal, sexual and somatic and these measures are reasonably well related (Tanner, 1990). Other developmental milestones of interest are the ages of sitting and walking, with more detailed measures including nerve conduction velocity as well as other measures related to the psychomotor, affective and cognitive domains (Haywood and Getchell, 2008). The focus of this chapter will be on stages of biological maturity and the application of psychomotor measures of motor skill and fitness related to these.

Skeletal age

Perhaps the best measure of maturity status is a radiograph of the skeleton. The progress of the skeleton from cartilage to bone occurs in all healthy individuals. A hand–wrist radiograph and subsequent assessment of bones against standardized images allows an assessment of the degree of ossification of the anatomical area. There are three main approaches to quantifying skeletal age (SA) by assessing the hand–wrist radiograph. The Greulich-Pyle (1959), Tanner-Whitehouse (1975) and Fels (Roche *et al.*, 1988) methods vary in the approach used to assess the radiograph but all produce a composite score of SA. Each method has its limitations, not least the radiation dose of an X-ray as well as the need for experienced assessors of radiographs. The future for more widespread assessment of SA probably depends on lower dose radiation scans (such as dual energy X-ray absorptiometry) and automated computer analysis of the image.

Sexual age

The transition from childhood to adulthood is characterized by the development of secondary sexual characteristics, maturation of the reproductive system and rapid increases in growth. Additionally, this phase is accompanied by complex psychosocial and behavioural changes that affect physical activity, health and sports performance. The assessment of secondary sexual characteristics involves an assessment of breast development, age at menarche and pubic hair development for girls, and penis, testes and pubic hair development in boys (Tanner, 1990). The assessment of sexual maturity would accurately be carried out by a trained health professional or paediatrician using standardized photographs. Because of the invasive nature of the measure self-assessment procedures have been validated in athletic and overweight populations. Youths are generally good at estimating their sexual maturity, although boys generally overestimate and girls typically underestimate their status (Williams *et al.*, 1988; Leone and Comtois, 2007).

Somatic age

As the processes of growth are difficult to study, indirect measures have been used to assess their overall outcome. These are commonly indirect measures of body size and proportion. Anthropometry defines the methods used to take measures of the human body and these are extremely robust if undertaken by skilled assessors. There are numerous measures of body size that are commonly grouped in breadths (widths), lengths and circumferences. Overall body size is most often assessed using measures of body mass or stature. Other measures such as skinfolds are used to estimate adiposity and, if combined with stature, body mass and bone widths, can be used to describe somatotype. Recently measures of ratios and proportions have been more commonly used in sport and exercise. The ratio of sitting height to sub-ischial (leg length) has been used to predict maturity (Mirwald *et al.*, 2002; Sherar *et al.*, 2005) and second to fourth digit ratio to predict athletic talent (Manning, 2002). Anthropometric measures are probably the most widely available method for the assessment of maturity status. Perhaps the most expedient approach involves regular measures of stature and body mass. Three monthly intervals may be a suitable time period over which to monitor growth of mass and stature; providing a balance between regular monitoring while allowing enough time to detect changes in body size with reasonable confidence. This data is then plotted against time and growth curves produced. Growth charts for stature are shown in Figure 1.1.

Figure 1.1 illustrates growth patterns over time for two boys, Child A and Child B. Child A's growth line starts just below the 50th centile line and accelerates by the age of 11 when his stature begins to exceed that of Child B. Child A remains taller than Child B for over three years, at which point Child B's rate of growth accelerates his stature. By full maturation both children revert back to their pre-peak height velocity centiles. During the earlier accelerated growth Child A may start to outperform his later-maturing peer, who will more than likely catch up later. This has implications for both talent identification and development, which will be covered in Chapter 2 and 3, respectively.

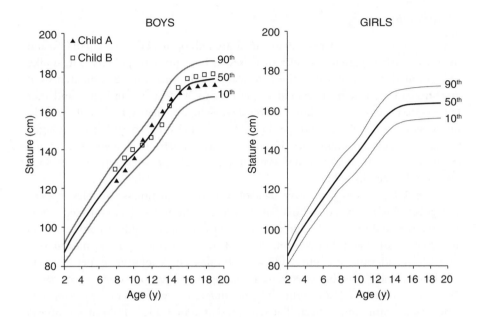

FIGURE 1.1 Growth charts showing the 10th, 50th and 90th percentiles for male (left panel) and female (right panel) stature (growth curve data available from www.cdc.gov/growthcharts). Data for two boys are plotted on the male chart

Body composition, maturation and effects on performance

In boys, body composition changes significantly throughout childhood and adolescence with increases in fat-free mass (FFM) and decreases in fat mass (FM). Patterns of change in body composition are similar in girls and boys pre-puberty, after which post-pubertal proportional differences between males and females emerge. Body fat patterning also changes around peak height velocity (PHV) with extremity trunk skinfold thickness increasing at a greater rate than trunk skinfold thicknesses in females. Increases in boys' arm girth exceed those of girls while changes in calf girth are similar between the sexes (Malina *et al.*, 2004). Increases in bone mineral content also peak in conjunction with PHV (Pérez-López *et al.*, 2010). Further biacromial (shoulder) increases in breadth are greater in boys than girls, whereas bicristal (hip) breadths are similar. Girls' hips are about 70 per cent of shoulder breadth compared to boys whose hip breadth decreases from 70 to 65 per cent of shoulder breadth between childhood and adulthood. These differences are driven by a significant increase in circulating androgens in boys compared to girls, resulting in rapid increases in FFM, small increases in FM and overall decreases in fat percentage. At the end of the adolescent growth spurt, boys' FFM is 25–30 per cent greater than girls', and their per cent body fat about half that of girls'.

Motor performance

For boys, a curvilinear increase in maximal strength occurs between childhood and maturity. Girls experience similar increases to boys prior to puberty but, unlike boys, strength then plateaus in the years leading up to maturity. Sex differences in grip strength increase from around 10 per cent to 30–40 per cent before and after puberty respectively, with boys' scores always higher than girls', similarly girls' jump distances are about 5–10 per cent less than boys' before puberty (e.g. aged 9 years) increasing to more than 15 per cent after puberty (e.g. aged 14–15 years) (Stratton *et al.*, 2004; Catley and Tomkinson, 2012). These patterns of development can be seen in Table 1.1.

Table 1.1 provides normative data on a number of fitness variables in boys and girls, which is based on analysis of a large volume of data collected across 15 studies examining the health and fitness of Australian children between 1985 and 2009 (Catley and Tomkinson, 2012). Boys outperform girls in measures of strength (handgrip), strength endurance (push-ups), explosive upper (basketball throw) and lower-body exercise (standing broad jump), sprint performance (50 m) and endurance (1.6 km run). Gender differences widen with increasing age, reflecting a maturational effect. The data presented in Table 1.1 also demonstrates the use of percentiles to represent performance that may be considered average (50th percentile), high (90th percentile) and low (10th percentile) relative to age. Such information can be used for benchmarking and may help the strength and conditioning coach identify children who are at the top and bottom ends of the performance continuum.

A problem with the data in Table 1.1 is that it is presented according to chronological age and subsequently masks the variation in maturation within each age group. Much of the variation in scores may be attributed to differences in maturation stage at the same chronological age. As an example, Figure 1.2 demonstrates the influence of maturation on vertical jump performance in boys. Longitudinal data presented in Figure 1.2a shows the velocity of gains in vertical jump performance relative to the timing of the adolescent growth spurt, with the rate of improvement aligned around PHV. There is a clear pattern of acceleration and deceleration in jump performance around PHV. The exact pattern of the rate of improvement experienced is dependent on the motor task; in boys measures of strength and power (arm pull, vertical jump) occur 6–12 months after PHV, whereas increases in flexibility (sit and reach) occur 6 months prior to PHV, and limb speed (shuttle run) 18–24 months before PHV (Beunen *et al.*, 1988). Consequently, considering test scores in relation to chronological age alone is problematic. Figure 1.2b shows the impact of early, average and late maturation on performance of the vertical jump in relation to chronological age; clearly performance of 14-year-old boys will be markedly different if comparing early- and late-maturing individuals. From a follow-up of their original study tracking fitness development in adolescent boys, Beunen *et al.* (1997) found that not only did late-maturing boys eventually catch up the

TABLE 1.1 Percentile scores for 9–15-year-old boys and girls across a range of performance tests

Percentile	Handgrip strength (kg)[a]			Basketball throw (m)[b]			Push-ups (no.)[c]			50m sprint (s)			Standing broad jump (cm)			1.6km run (s)		
	10th	50th	90th	10th	50th	90th	10th	50th	90th	10th	50th	90th	10th	50th	90th	10th	50th	90th
Boys																		
9 yr	12.5	16.4	20.8	2.5	3.3	4.1	6	12	20	10.2	9.1	8.3	113	138	161	684	522	423
10 yr	14.3	19.0	23.9	2.8	3.6	4.5	6	13	21	10.1	9.0	8.2	117	143	168	666	511	420
11 yr	15.9	21.2	26.8	3.1	4.0	5.0	6	13	20	10.0	8.9	8.1	121	149	174	646	500	416
12 yr	17.0	22.7	28.7	3.4	4.5	5.6	6	13	20	9.8	8.7	7.9	126	156	182	621	485	408
13 yr	19.3	25.8	32.8	3.8	5.0	6.2	7	14	22	9.4	8.4	7.7	136	166	194	587	465	395
14 yr	22.9	30.7	39.1	4.2	5.5	6.9	8	16	23	9.0	8.1	7.4	146	178	206	556	446	382
15 yr	27.1	36.5	46.5	4.6	6.0	7.4	10	18	25	8.6	7.7	7.1	157	189	219	531	432	373
Girls																		
9 yr	10.8	14.4	18.4	2.3	3.0	3.7	3	9	16	11.3	10.0	9.0	102	126	150	769	609	499
10 yr	12.6	17.1	21.8	2.6	3.3	4.1	3	9	16	10.7	9.5	8.6	108	133	158	759	600	494
11 yr	13.9	18.8	23.9	2.8	3.6	4.5	3	8	16	10.3	9.2	8.3	114	140	166	741	586	483
12 yr	16.0	21.4	26.9	3.1	4.0	4.9	2	7	15	10.0	8.9	8.1	118	145	171	726	575	474
13 yr	18.0	23.6	29.5	3.3	4.3	5.3	2	7	15	9.8	8.8	8.0	123	150	176	716	569	469
14 yr	19.7	25.4	31.3	3.4	4.4	5.4	2	6	15	9.7	8.7	7.9	127	154	180	711	567	468
15 yr	21.3	26.9	32.7	3.6	4.5	5.5	2	6	14	9.6	8.6	7.9	129	156	181	710	570	469

Source: adapted from Catley and Tomkinson, 2012.

Notes
a Handgrip strength is the mean score across both hands.
b Basketball throw was performed as per the Australian Council for Health, Physical Education and Recreation (1996) guidelines.
c Push-ups are the number of push-ups completed in 30s.

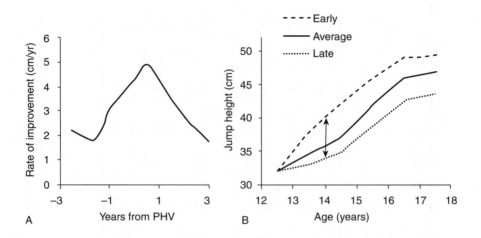

FIGURE 1.2 Development of vertical jump performance in boys in relation to maturation. Figure A shows the rate of growth of vertical jump performance aligned around the adolescent growth spurt (adapted from Beunen *et al.*, 1988), with gains peaking shortly after PHV (likely coinciding with peak weight velocity). Figure B shows the performance of early-, average- and late-maturing boys (adapted from Malina *et al.*, 2004), with the arrow demonstrating potential differences in maturation and subsequent performance of boys with a chronological age of 14 years

performance of their early-maturing peers, they went on to significantly out-perform the early maturers in functional and explosive strength in adulthood. This suggests some possible long-term performance benefit of late maturation in boys.

Longitudinal monitoring around adolescence has also been used to present growth-related changes in the motor performance of Canadian girls (Little *et al.*, 1997), illustrating an inconsistent advantage in motor performance according to maturation group. There were small advantages in arm and back strength during PHV for early-maturing girls, however, in contrast to boys, early-maturing girls performed more poorly in vertical jump, shuttle run, flexed arm hang and 20 m dash at age 14. Research on early-, average- and late-maturing boys and girls clearly highlights differences in performance related to maturation and how these affect the motor performance of children independent of chronological age. Thus, it is essential that all professionals involved in the development of motor performance in youth account for such differences in the application of their practice.

Anaerobic function and metabolism

Children produce significantly less absolute power at all exercise durations compared with adults. This is a result of a combination of biochemical and biomechanical factors that are discussed in detail elsewhere (Van Praagh, 1998). Power output per unit of thigh muscle cross-sectional area increases significantly in girls and boys between 8 and 20 years of age (Saavedra *et al.*, 1991). This indicates a significant increase in economy of muscle fibre recruitment as well as more efficient biochemical energy production, although much is still unknown about the mechanisms of anaerobic power output by developmental age. The development of anaerobic power is central to programmes aimed at improving this aspect of fitness in young people. In this sense it is important that children and youth are not seen as miniature adults, rather as qualitatively different individuals who require bespoke anaerobic programmes that reflect the development of these components as well as differences between adults and children.

Cardiopulmonary system

Growth in the cardiopulmonary system is driven by a 20-fold increase in heart size from birth to adulthood (from $40\,cm^3$ to $600-800\,cm^3$), and body surface area correlates closely with left ventricular mass (LVM) during the growing years (Rowland, 1996). Resting heart rates also decrease for boys and girls throughout childhood and adolescence. Stroke volume increases nearly 10-fold from birth to late childhood (4–40 ml) and 15-fold from birth to adulthood (4–60 ml). Blood composition also changes during puberty with haematocrit increasing from about 30 per cent in the infant to 40–45 per cent in adult males and 38–42 per cent in adult females. Haematocrit also increases up to about 40 per cent of red blood cell volume in both girls and boys and haemoglobin follows a similar path increasing from around 10 during childhood, to 14 and 16 g/dl in adult females and males respectively.

As with cardiac tissue, the lungs also grow rapidly from 65 g at birth to 1.3 kg at maturity. Further, the number of alveoli increase from 20 to 300 million and breaths/min decrease from 22 to 16 between infancy and maturity. These changes also result in an increase in maximal ventilatory volume from 50 to over 100 litres between age 5 and maturity. Further ventilatory equivalent (minute ventilation/oxygen uptake) decreases almost linearly with age. These differences have a significant effect on aerobic exercise performance with changes particularly noticeable during the adolescent growth spurt. A combination of changes in anatomical, metabolic and haematological factors as well as developmental improvements in running economy (through reduced co-contraction of exercising muscle and lower oxygen cost per stride) and thermoregulation result in the cardiopulmonary system being able to cope with progressively increasing exercise workloads. These changes manifest themselves in laboratory and field measures of endurance performance and aerobic fitness.

Between the ages of 8 and 12 aerobic power increases by almost 50 per cent (1.4 to 2.1 litres/min^{-1}). Boys then experience further large increases with peak oxygen consumption (VO_2) reaching 3.5 litres/min^{-1} at maturity. Girls' VO_2peak slightly trails that of boys before puberty but then decreases slowly into early adulthood. There is however significant debate around the analysis of data related to body size. Armstrong and Welsman (1994) have strongly advocated that the use of allometric scaling as a number of studies by their group suggest that larger children's VO_2peak scores are deflated and smaller children's scores inflated when ratio scaling (per kilogram body mass) is used. However, there has been a significant lack of consistency in the literature resulting in most scientists continuing to report their data using simple ratio scaling (Rowland, 1996). More recent work also suggests that there may be less of an effect of maturity in girls' growth-related VO_2 than boys (McNarry et al., 2011). The Saskatchewan longitudinal growth study tracked VO_2max in 83 boys aged between 8 and 16 years (Bailey et al., 1978). These growth velocity curves report absolute VO_2 and illustrate little change in aerobic fitness during childhood. Just prior to puberty there was a small decrement in VO_2 followed by an exponential increase which mirrored increases in lean body mass changes.

Relative age effect

As opposed to maturation, the relative age effect (RAE) refers to a biased distribution of birth dates within an age grouped cohort. For example, identical twins born on 31 December at 23:50pm and 1 January 00:15am would only be eligible for participation in either of two adjacent calendar years. Being born early or late in their calendar year may have a positive and negative effect on the future success of either twin. Further, there is strong evidence that being born early or late in a selection year can influence performance in sport, academic achievement and employment. The literature suggests that the RAE varies according to sports, age-group, sex and level of performance (Delorme et al., 2010a, b; Williams and Reilly, 2000). The RAE has been studied in elite sport for some time, yet many studies demonstrate that the RAE is still widely prevalent across sport, games and athletes participating in major games. There is significant evidence from early studies in baseball and ice hockey that an RAE exists (Thompson et al., 1991; Boucher and Mutimer, 1994). Most of the evidence exists for boys where the RAE is prevalent across most sports but there is some evidence that the RAE also exists in girls. More recent studies have focused attention on international competitors across Senior and Youth Olympic games (Hoffmann et al., 2012; O'Neill et al., 2012) analysing the birth dates of thousands of elite athletes. In the Youth Olympic Games an RAE was evident for both males and females, although only males were overrepresented in the Olympics. Recently, O'Neill and Cotton (2012) demonstrated an RAE for track and field athletics across two Olympic Games.

In relation to motor performance tests, a significant RAE has been found in the 20 m shuttle-run test performance in 15,000 9–12-year-old children, even after controlling for somatic maturity (Roberts et al., 2012). Examples of sport-specific RAE data have been collated and presented in Table 1.2. The data presented in Table 1.2 is consistent with the wider literature, showing a consistent RAE in both senior and junior male athletes but a less consistent age advantage in female

TABLE 1.2 Examples of the relative age effect across sport and gender, showing the percentage distribution of birth dates across different quartiles of the competitive season

Sport	Sex	n	Age	Q1%	Q2%	Q3%	Q4%	Author
Baseball	M	837	Senior	29	25	23	23★	Thompson et al. (1991)
Baseball	M	682	Senior	29	27	23	21★	Thompson et al. (1991)
Ice hockey	M	884	Senior	34	31	20	15★	Boucher and Mutimer (1994)
Ice hockey	M	951	Junior	37	28	23	12★	Boucher and Mutimer (1994)
Soccer	M	2,768	Junior	43	27	18	11★	Del Campo et al. (2010)
Soccer	M	735	Junior	39	26	20	15★	Helsen et al. (2005)
Soccer	F	804	Junior	26	26	25	23	Vincent and Glamser (2006)
Tennis	F	239	Junior	31	25	28	17★	Edgar and Donoghue (2005)

Notes
★ Significant RAE (P<0.05).
M = male; F = female; Q = birth quartile.

sports (although conclusions on female sport are limited by the lack of studies on the RAE in this population). The lower prevalence of an RAE in girls is mainly attributed to a lower number of elite junior sport systems that start from a young age with the possible exception of gymnastics, dance and ballet. A 10 cm difference in stature of 9–12-year-old girls born early or late in their respective year or a 4 kg year-on-year difference in body mass of 8–11-year-old boys provides clear evidence of distinct size advantage in stature and mass by children born early in the selection year. It should be noted that for some sports, such as gymnastics, a shorter stature is advantageous, as opposed to a sport such as tennis where greater stature is an advantage.

Practical applications

As previously stated, anthropometric measures are probably the most widely available for the assessment of maturity status. Consequently, this section will focus on the anthropometric techniques available to a practitioner to provide accessible means with which to assess growth and maturation. From a longitudinal perspective, regular monitoring (every three months) of stature and body mass will provide growth curves and identify peak growth periods. However, this method requires longitudinal monitoring which is not always possible and only identifies peak growth rates after they have occurred. Where access to young athletes is limited to a one-off occasion, or there is a desire to try and predict future growth and maturation, prediction equations are available.

Predicted adult stature

Being able to predict adult stature and the per cent of adult stature achieved at any time point is important in elite junior sport, especially where stature is a significant predictor for successful performance. Sports such as gymnastics, trampolining, basketball and volleyball rely on a narrow range of either tall or short participants. There is less reliance in sports such as football, cricket, cycling and sailing, although playing positions and categories within these sports may require taller or shorter participants. Likewise for sports where there are body mass classifications such as boxing and judo, stature may also be an important predictor of performance.

Anthropometric techniques probably provide the most expedient and ethical approach to estimating maturity. Further, these techniques can also be used to estimate final adult stature of healthy children. Parental stature also provides a guide to estimating final adult stature of offspring. If the stature of both biological parents is available then the mid-parent stature can be used to estimate final adult stature (Tanner *et al.*, 1970), based on an average difference in stature of 13 cm (or 5 inches) between men and women. Calculations are shown below in centimetres, where 13 cm is added to (boys) or subtracted from (girls) the combined parental height and the result then divided by two:

Males
$$\text{Boys' mid-parental height} = \frac{(\text{mother's height} + \text{father's height} + 13)}{2}$$

Females
$$\text{Girls' mid-parental height} = \frac{(\text{mother's height} + \text{father's height} - 13)}{2}$$

Further work by Sherar *et al.* (2005) used longitudinal growth data to generate prediction equations for adolescent girls and boys. The method requires measurement of body mass, stature and sitting stature to take maturity status into account (see automated calculation: http://taurus.usask.ca/growthutility/phv_ui.cfm?type=2). Predicting adult stature using anthropometric approaches is accurate to within 5–8 cm in boys and 3–8 cm in girls in 95 per cent of cases. The percentage of predicted adult stature is used as a measure of somatic maturity.

Peak height velocity

Whereas final adult stature and size are important variables to estimate throughout childhood, the tempo of growth varies considerably, most notably during adolescence. The age at the maximum rate of growth is the most commonly used marker of somatic maturity; it is reported in cm/yr and centred around PHV. PHV occurs around the age of 12 in girls and 14 in boys, although there is considerable variation around these ages (Tanner, 1990). Similar to producing a growth chart (see Figure 1.1), stature can be recorded every three months but then the change in stature used to calculate the current rate of growth. Figure 1.3 illustrates a height (stature) velocity by age curve and shows the rate of change in height of girls and boys over time. From this measure of somatic maturity events can be identified that help to mark the start of adolescence (start of the growth spurt) and cessation of maturation/start of adulthood (no further growth). Closer inspection of Figure 1.3 shows that growth spurts in boys start later and are both longer and more intense than in girls, and this explains why girls are on average 13 cm shorter than boys at maturity. PHV can vary between 10 and 15 years and 12 and 16 years in girls and boys respectively (Preece and Bains, 1978).

Peak weight velocity (PWV) is also sometimes used as a measure of growth but is more susceptible to environmental influences. PWV trails PHV and values are higher in boys than girls. Thus PWV and PHV can be monitored longitudinally by taking regular measures over time. Where longitudinal measures of stature are not available, age, body mass, height and sitting height can be taken at a single point in time and used to estimate the years a child is from the time of PHV (Mirwald *et al.*, 2002):

Boys
Maturity offset = $-29.769 + 0.0003007 \times$ leg length and sitting height interaction $- 0.01177 \times$ age and leg length interaction $+ 0.01639 \times$ age and sitting height interaction $+ 0.445 \times$ leg by height ratio.

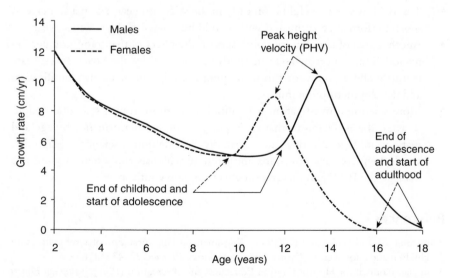

FIGURE 1.3 Rate of growth of stature in boys and girls throughout childhood and adolescence, with important events relative to rate of growth identified

Girls
Maturity offset = −16.364 + 0.0002309 × leg length and sitting height interaction + 0.006277 × age and sitting height interaction + 0.179 × leg by height
ratio + 0.0009428 × age and weight interaction.

The above equations rely on the differential growth rates of the legs and trunk,
with the long bones of the leg experiencing peak growth before the short bones of
the trunk. The equations above have a standard error of approximately six months
(Mirwald *et al.*, 2002). Estimating maturation may be useful for a number of reasons, including during talent identification and selection processes. For example,
estimating time from PHV in a group of boys will help account for the advantage
early-maturing individuals are likely to gain over their late-maturing counterparts.

Key points

*   The effect of maturation on performance during childhood and adolescence
    can be summarized in three main areas. First, changes in motor performance
    are dependent on the task or exercise performed. Second, patterns of change
    in motor performance are dependent on maturation. Third, there is a sex and
    maturation interaction for some components of motor performance.
*   Changes in growth patterns result in significant differences in shape and size
    and performance between girls and boys. Moreover, changes in body size and
    proportion during adolescence have a significant effect on physical perfor-
    mance that in turn can cause significant practical problems in the organization
    of youth sport.
*   The RAE is where a child born early in the selection year has an advantage in
    sports performance compared with a child born later in the selection year.
*   Another area of concern for youth sport is the effect of maturation on perfor-
    mance. Simple non–invasive methods can be used by the coach to estimate
    maturity and account for this in training prescription or talent identification
    and development programmes.
*   More scientific investigation is required using more robust scientific designs
    to assess the mechanisms that underpin growth and performance by age and
    maturation stage. No one study currently has a definitive scientific design that
    would help coaches and sports and exercise scientists apply better systems to
    manage the RAE and maturation effects in elite youth sport.

References

Armstrong, N. and Welsman J.R. (1994) 'Assessment and interpretation of aerobic fitness in
   children and adolescents', *Exercise and Sports Science Reviews*, 22: 435–476.
Australian Council for Health, Physical Education and Recreation (1996) *Australian Fitness
   Education Awards: User's Manual and Curriculum Ideas*, Adelaide: Australian Council for
   Health, Physical Education and Recreation.

Bailey, D.A., Ross, W.D., Mirwald, R.L. and Weese, C. (1978) 'Size dissociation of maximal aerobic power during growth in boys', *Medicine in Sport*, 11: 140–151.

Beunen, G., Malina, R.M., Van't Hof., M.A., Simon, J., Ostyn, M., Renson, R. and Van Gerven, D. (1988) *Adolescent Growth and Motor Performance: A Longitudinal Study of Belgian Boys*, Champaign, IL: Human Kinetics.

Beunen, G., Ostyn, M., Simons, J., Renson, R., Claessens, A.L., Vanden Eynde, B., Lefevre, J., Vanreusel, B., Malina, R.M. and Van't Hof, M.A. (1997) 'Development and tracking in fitness components: Leuven longitudinal study on lifestyle, fitness and health', *International Journal of Sports Medicine*, 18: S171–178.

Boucher, J.L. and Mutimer, B.T. (1994) 'The relative age phenomenon in sport: A replication and extension with ice-hockey players', *Research Quarterly in Exercise and Sport*, 65: 377–381.

Catley, M.J. and Tomkinson, G.R. (2012) 'Normative health-related fitness values for children: Analysis of 85347 test results on 9–17-year-old Australians since 1985', *British Journal of Sports Medicine*, e-pub, March.

Del Campo, D.G.D., Vicedo, J.C.P., Villora, S.G. and Jordan, O.R.C. (2010) 'The relative age effect in youth soccer players from Spain', *Journal of Sports Science and Medicine*, 9: 190–198.

Delorme, N., Boiche, J. and Raspaud, M. (2010a) 'Relative age and dropout in French male soccer', *Journal of Sports Sciences*, 28: 717–722.

Delorme, N., Boiche, J. and Raspaud, M. (2010b) 'Relative age effect in female sport: A diachronic examination of soccer players', *Scandinavian Journal of Medicine and Science in Sports*, 20: 509–515.

Edgar, S. and O'Donoghue, P. (2005) 'Season of birth distribution of elite tennis players', *Journal of Sports Sciences*, 23: 1013–1020.

Greulich, W.W. and Pyle, S.I. (1959) *Radiographic Atlas of Skeletal Development of the Hand and Wrist*, Stanford, CA: Stanford University Press.

Haywood, K.M. and Getchell, N. (2008) *Lifespan Motor Development*, 5th Edition, Champaign, IL: Human Kinetics.

Helsen, W.F., Winckel, J.V. and Williams, A.M. (2005) 'The relative age effect in youth soccer across Europe', *Journal of Sports Sciences*, 23: 629–636.

Hoffmann, A., Wulff, J., Büsch, D. and Sandner, H. (2012) *Relative Age Effect in Olympic Sports: A Comparison of Beijing 2008 and Singapore 2010*, European College of Sports Sciences Congress, Bruges, July.

Leone, M. and Comtois, A.S. (2007) 'Validity and reliability of self-assessment of sexual maturity in elite adolescent athletes', *Journal of Sports Medicine and Physical Fitness*, 47: 361–365.

Little, N.G., Day, J.A.P. and Steinke, L. (1997) 'Relationship of physical performance to maturation in perimenarcheal girls', *American Journal of Human Biology*, 9: 163–171.

McNarry, M.A., Welsman, J.R. and Jones, A.M. (2011) 'Influence of training and maturity status on the cardiopulmonary responses to ramp incremental cycle and upper body exercise in girls', *Journal of Applied Physiology*, 110: 375–381.

Malina, R.M., Bouchard, C. and Bar-Or, O. (2004) *Growth, Maturation, and Physical Activity*, 2nd Edition, Champaign, IL: Human Kinetics.

Manning, J.T. (2002) 'The ratio of 2nd to 4th digit length and performance in skiing', *Journal of Sports Medicine and Physical Fitness*, 42: 446–450.

Mirwald, R.L., Baxter-Jones, A.D.G., Bailey, D.A. and Beunen, G.P. (2002) 'An assessment of maturity from anthropometric measurements', *Medicine and Science in Sports and Exercise*, 34: 689–694.

O'Neill, K.S. and Cotton, W.G. (2012) *Factors Influencing the Development of Australian Olympic Athletes: The Impact of Relative Age Effect and Early Specialization*, International Convention on Science, Education and Medicine in Sport, Glasgow, July.

Pérez-López, F.R., Chedraui, P. and Cuadros-López, J.L. (2010) 'Bone mass gain during puberty and adolescence: Deconstructing gender characteristics', *Current Medical Chemistry*, 17: 1–14.

Preece, M.A. and Bains, M.J. (1978) 'A new family of mathematical models describing the human growth curve', *Annals of Human Biology*, 5: 1–24.

Roberts, S.J., Boddy, L.M., Fairclough, S.J. and Stratton, G. (2012) 'The influence of relative age effects on the cardio-respiratory fitness levels of children age 9 to 10 and 11 to 12 years of age', *Pediatric Exercise Science*, 24: 72–83.

Roche, A.F., Chumlea, W.C. and Thissen, D. (1988) *Assessing the Skeletal Maturity of the Hand-Wrist: Fels Method*, Springfield, IL: Charles C Thomas.

Rowland, T. (1996) *Developmental Exercise Physiology*, Champaign, IL: Human Kinetics.

Saavedra, C., LaGasse, P., Bouchard, C. and Simoneau, J.A. (1991) 'Maximal anaerobic performance of the knee extensor muscles during growth', *Medicine and Science in Sports and Exercise*, 23: 1083–1089.

Sherar, L.B., Mirwald, R.L., Baxter-Jones, A.D. and Thomis, M. (2005) 'Prediction of adult height using maturity-based cumulative height velocity curves', *Journal of Pediatrics*, 147: 508–514.

Stratton, G., Reilly, T., Williams, A.M. and Richardson, D. (2004) *Youth Soccer: From Science to Performance*, London: Routledge.

Tanner, J.M. (1990) *Foetus into Man: Physical Growth from Conception to Maturity*, Cambridge, MA: Harvard University Press.

Tanner, J.M., Goldstein, H. and Whitehouse, R.H. (1970) 'Standards for children's height at ages 2–9 years allowing for heights of parents', *Archives of Disease in Childhood*, 45: 755–762.

Tanner, J.M., Whitehouse, R.H., Marshall, W.A., Healy, M.J.R. and Goldstein, H. (1975) *Assessment of Skeletal Maturity and Prediction of Adult Height (TW2 Method)*, New York: Academic Press.

Thompson, A., Barnsley, R. and Stebelsky, G. (1991) 'Born to play ball: The relative age effect and major league baseball', *Sociology of Sport Journal*, 8: 146–151.

Van Praagh, E. (ed.) (1998) *Pediatric Anaerobic Performance*, Champaign, IL: Human Kinetics.

Vincent, J. and Glamser, F.D. (2006) 'Gender differences in the relative age effect among US Olympic development program youth soccer players', *Journal of Sports Sciences*, 24: 405–413.

Williams, A.M. and Reilly, T. (2000) 'Talent identification and development in soccer', *Journal of Sports Sciences*, 18: 657–667.

Williams, R.L., Cheyne, K.L., Houtkooper, L.K. and Lohman, T.G. (1988) 'Adolescent self-assessment of sexual maturation: Effects of fatness classification and actual sexual maturation stage', *Journal of Adolescent Health Care*, 9: 480–482.

2

TALENT IDENTIFICATION

Cesar Meylan and John B. Cronin

Introduction

The talent identification process usually involves screening anthropometric, physiological and/or technical attributes of current performers in order to identify individuals with potential to succeed in a designated sport. It needs to be emphasized early in this treatise however, that even though this definition of talent identification provides the focus of this chapter, a one-dimensional approach to talent identification based on anthropometric and physiological parameters can be misguided. Given that excellence in sport is not dependant on one standard set of skills but can be achieved through different combinations of abilities, a multidisciplinary approach addressing sociological, psychological and cognitive-perceptive skills (e.g. anticipation or decision-making) as well as anthropometric, physiological and technical predictors is an intuitively appealing and all-encompassing approach to identifying talent (Vaeyens *et al.*, 2008). Identifying and developing talent is a complicated process, as it is genetically determined (nature) but *also* influenced by environmental conditions (nurture), and it is perhaps for these reasons that there is really no consensus as to the theory and methodology behind talent identification.

It also needs to be noted that talent identification is different to talent detection, selection and development. Talent detection refers to the discovery of potential performers not involved in the sport in question, whereas talent selection involves the ongoing identification of athletes with the prerequisite levels of performance already involved in a sport. Talent development involves providing support and infrastructure to develop the detected, selected or identified talent. Little attention is given to talent detection, selection and development in this chapter, however in the real world there would be integration between these three components and talent identification. Rather, this chapter will discuss some of the issues implicit in talent identification and thereafter identify sports that may benefit from talent identification. Typically these will be sports in which anthropometric and physiological parameters play a decisive role, as these qualities are easier to measure and talent subsequently easier to identify.

Basic theoretical concepts: misconceptions in talent identification

Entrance into various academies and selection to national or state representative junior squads are often regarded as important stages in an athlete's development. The athletes selected in these programmes are exposed to highly qualified coaches and national and international competitions. The 'coach driven' method of talent identification rests in a multifaceted intuitive knowledge comprised of socially constructed 'images' of the ideal athlete. When a coach selects talent, they usually have the feeling of doing something self-evident, logical and inevitable as they distinguish between different talented athletes without being explicit about the generative principles that guide their observation. Choices of gifted athletes are therefore made on personal preferences, knowledge and expertise and this process is viewed as legitimate by coaches. However, such an approach is highly subjective and can lead to repetitive misconceptions in talent evaluation (Christensen, 2009).

During childhood and adolescence, differences in maturity can be extensive, even among individuals of the same chronological age (Malina et al., 2004). Athletes who are born early in the selection year often have the advantage of being bigger, stronger, faster and having greater longevity in their sport (Musch and Grondin, 2001; Sherar et al., 2007; Delorme and Raspaud et al., 2009). Consequently, they may be more successful than their younger counterparts, resulting in greater motivation and commitment. Younger and less-mature players may be regarded as having less talent during the selection process (Sherar et al., 2007), and may drop out of their chosen sport because of low perceived competence and lack of success (Delorme and Raspaud, 2008). This phenomenon creates a bias in the birth date distribution of selected players and is referred to as the relative age effect (RAE) (Musch and Grondin, 2001). That is, the children born in the first 3–4 months from cut-off dates are overrepresented in athletes' selection for various sports (Musch and Grondin, 2001; Cobley et al., 2009). The RAE is present across youth teams, from club to national level with a progressive increased incidence with level of play (from club to national representative), sport popularity (e.g. ice hockey in Canada or soccer in Europe) and age (up to U18) (Cobley et al., 2009). The RAE provides a problem regarding the selection process and the coaches' view of gifted players. Unsurprisingly, the RAE is not apparent in sports where physical attributes are unimportant and other parameters, such as motor skills, are more important (e.g. dancing, gymnastics, golf) (Côté et al., 2006; van Rossum, 2006).

Considering the above comments, birth date distribution cannot alone be used to indicate a tendency to discriminate younger players or less-mature players in talent identification. Also, early maturers of the third or fourth quartile can be as physically mature as late maturers of the first two quartiles (Carling *et al.*, 2009). In this context, an indication of maturity status would appear more relevant to this issue as maturity may play a crucial role in the coaches' view on youth athletes' potential and the chance of a young athlete to succeed. The physical advantages afforded by age and advanced maturity status during adolescence are largely transient and are reduced or reversed in young adulthood (Beunen *et al.*, 1997). Late maturers may be dismissed on the basis of their physical characteristics and not on their adult potential. Alternatively, youth 'talented' players may fail to meet adult expectations as their late-maturing peers who persist in the sport catch up in size, endurance, speed, strength and power. For instance, this hypothesis is confirmed by the reduced RAE in senior professional soccer players compared to elite youth players (Mujika *et al.*, 2009). If physical and physiological characteristics may be appealing for initial talent identification, their ability to successfully predict a subsequent professional career is debateable considering the multidimensional characteristics of high-performance sports (Vaeyens *et al.*, 2008).

In many cases, elite adult athletes have anthropometric and physiological characteristics specifically suited to their sport. Consequently athletic profiling is valuable in terms of providing a useful database upon which talented athletes may be compared and oriented towards a sport or position in the team. Those involved in the identification and developments of gifted athletes need to be aware of the contributions of growth and maturation in relation to the various demands of the sport (i.e. physical, technical, tactical and psychological). Given these issues, the physical assessment of young players should be interpreted alongside maturational status to conduct a more objective talent identification process (Malina *et al.*, 2004). Initial classification between late, average and early maturers within the same age category is a valuable method to ensure talent is identified that may previously have been overlooked. Therefore, multiple objective criteria are necessary when screening for gifted athletes.

Practical applications

Anthropometric and physiological profiling for talent in youth

Research in specific sports has identified a number of 'key markers' of potential success, which may guide the development of talent identification models for the detection and tracking of potentially successful athletes in the designated sport. Since the aim is to predict future accomplishments, the distinction between performance levels at the time of testing and the capacity an individual has to develop is essential. Also, when observing young athletes, certain anthropometric and physiological factors may be more determinant to success at a youth compared to an elite level (Abbott and Collins, 2002). Therefore, a sport-specific talent identification model should always bear in mind the demands of the elite level and subsequently develop an age-appropriate testing battery. Age-specific normative data should then be created to benchmark athletes, conduct gap analysis and track athletes' progress. However, based on previous comments, maturity status should always be central to the young athletes' evaluation.

Based on these comments, at least four statistically and theoretically based criteria must be satisfied to develop an effective talent identification model (Abbott and Collins, 2002):

1 *Discriminability*: anthropometry and physical tests must be sensitive enough to discriminate (successful or unsuccessful) athletes on the parameter measured.
2 *Appropriate norms*: sport-specific representative normative data must be created to meaningfully interpret data (e.g. soccer player 10 m sprint time).
3 *Appropriate algorithms and weightings*: relative importance attributed to specific testing measures within a sport must be appropriately correlated with the sport performances (e.g. power in weightlifting).
4 *Relative performance stability on selection criteria*: relative testing values in youth should transfer into adulthood (e.g. height in basketball).

In order to meet these specific criteria, particular attention must be paid to the selected tests, the measurement error associated with such tests and subsequent data analysis. The following sections highlight the considerations associated with core anthropometric and physiological measures that are being used to monitor young athletes.

Anthropometry

A wide variety of measures are available to quantify the anthropometric characteristics of an individual and can include: height, weight, the sum of skinfolds and/or percentage body fat, girth measurements and a variety of indexes, e.g. body mass index (BMI), brachial and crural indexes, etc. While the general nature of the protocols used for assessing anthropometry in youth is similar to that of adults, it should be realized that multi-component, criterion-referenced equations that account for age, gender and maturational stages have been developed (Eston *et al.*, 2009).

There is no doubt that anthropometry affects sporting performance. Gymnasts and divers are typically the smallest and lightest of all sports people with shorter than average lower-limb lengths, which is advantageous for tumbling and turning in the air. Tall linear physiques are advantageous for tennis, basketball and volleyball players, swimmers, rowers and cricket fast bowlers for example, where longer levers offer specific mechanical advantages for their sport. Weight and power lifters, on the other hand, typically have shorter than average upper and lower-limb lengths as well as shorter distal segments (Hume and Stewart, 2010). It can be surmised that these skeletal structures are strongly influenced by genetic influences and therefore can be predicted with some accuracy using some of the methods cited previously. Furthermore, there are many examples of sports (netball, basketball and volleyball) that screen players for height or predicted height on the premise that, with three or four years of training, players will be sufficiently skilled to compete at the highest level. However, stature cannot be trained and a range of other anthropometric factors (i.e. weight, percentage fat mass and lean muscle mass, etc.) are environmentally determined and responsive to training and diet. Using such factors to identify talent is fraught with difficulty and likely of little practical benefit. Table 2.1 provides an overview of sports where anthropometric and/or physiological variables may be beneficial for the process of talent identification.

Strength

Strength is defined as the maximal force or torque generated by a muscle or muscle group either during a single maximal voluntary effort or in response to electrical stimulation. In practice, it can also be referred to the maximal one-repetition (1RM) during a lift. 1RM testing on adapted machinery (Faigenbaum *et al.*, 2004) and isokinetic dynamometers (De Ste Croix, 2007) has been found to be reliable to assess strength in youths.

Considerable physiological changes associated with growth and maturation are likely to influence strength in youths, such as an increase in muscle cross-sectional area (Jones and Round, 2008). The adolescent spurt in strength starts about 1.5 years prior to peak height velocity (PHV) and attains a peak 0.5–1.0 year after PHV, which is more coincident with peak weight velocity (PWV) (Beunen and Malina, 1988). The

TABLE 2.1 Summary of sports that may benefit from anthropometric and/or physiological profiling for talent identification

Sport	Anthropometry	Specialization	Physiological
Gymnasts, divers	Small and light, smaller than average lower-limb lengths	Early	Flexibility, strength, power and speed
Weight lifters, power lifters	High ratio of sitting height to stature, shorter than average upper and lower-limb lengths, low CI and BI	Late	Strength and power
Distance runners	Short and light, relatively short lower limbs and high CI and low BI	Mid	Aerobic fitness
Discus and javelin throwers	Tall, high BI	Late	Power and speed
Jumpers	High relative lower-limb length and high CI	Late	Leg power and speed

Notes
CI = Cormic index and is calculated as the ratio of sitting height to standing height; BI = Brugsch index and is calculated as the ratio of chest circumference to standing height.

evidence indicates that during adolescence young athletes are first stretched (spurt in stature) and then filled-out (spurt in muscle mass, weight and strength). However, strength gains related to neuromuscular activation and control are still likely to occur in pre-adolescence. In this sense, strength can be considered as a factor to distinguish elite from non-elite youth players (Hansen *et al.*, 1999) and future professionals from future amateurs (le Gall *et al.*, 2010). Yet, as strength is largely influenced by maturation and can only be trained fully from late adolescence, it should not be considered as a selection factor in youth. In addition, if maximal strength is related to performance, the ability to produce force at high velocity (power) might be more relevant to most sports and therefore power capability needs to be taken into consideration. This issue is further discussed in the power section (below).

Speed

Over-ground sprint ability is a critical success factor in many sports and therefore many sporting codes place a great deal of emphasis on identifying athletes with 'true speed'. Sprint ability can be defined and therefore measured in a number of ways. First step quickness, as the name suggests, is the ability of an individual to cover the first 2.5–5 m in as short a time as possible and is important in sports such as volleyball and badminton. Acceleration can be defined as the time to maximum velocity or the time to 5–20 m and is fundamental to tennis and football codes. Maximum velocity or the time to 20–40 m is important for the football codes, sprinters and gymnast vaulters. Finally, most field sports require repeated sprint ability so developing sport-specific repeated sprint-ability tests to identify talent is also important. Linear speed is assessed with timing lights for both adults and children, however, age-specific distance to maximal speed has to be considered since coordination may become impaired in excessive sprint distances in children.

Many practitioners believe sprint ability to be one of the most difficult qualities to change, especially once athletes have matured. Given this information many sports screen players for speed ability (e.g. football codes) on the premise that other qualities, such as technical, tactical and physiological, are more trainable and will improve from a quality long-term athlete development programme. Previous studies (Beunen and Malina, 1988; Viru *et al.*, 1999) have highlighted the earlier performance spurt in high-velocity movement (pre-PHV) compared to leg power or strength (mid/post-PHV). Optimal velocity seems to also be the changing factor in peak power during pre-adolescence, while force becomes the main determinant of peak power during and after puberty (Martin *et al.*, 2004, 2003; Santos *et al.*, 2002). Therefore, when speed is being considered, scouts should investigate the ability to produce high-velocity movement and good running mechanics, as these appear to be determined prior to puberty and are harder to develop following full maturation of the neuromuscular system.

Power

In many sports (e.g. track and field events, soccer, basketball, ice hockey and volleyball), neuromuscular power is regarded as a major physical attribute of elite players/athletes. A variety of throws for the upper body and vertical and horizontal jumps for the lower body are the most widely used movements to assess power because of their simplicity. These tests are also considered as some of the most 'explosive' tests due both to their very short duration and the high intensity involved. Power output is the product of force and velocity and is defined and limited by the force–velocity relationship. Establishing the force–velocity–power profile of a young athlete may have the ability to distinguish the different muscular capabilities that might be relevant to sport performance and long-term development. Incremental loading during safe ballistic movement allows the determination of the force–velocity–power relationships (Samozino et al., 2012). Cycling force–velocity–power profiles in youths have been found to be reliable (Dore et al., 2003) but the validity of such a test for field sport athletes is questionable (Van Praagh, 2008). Force is directly proportional to the muscle cross-sectional area (Jones and Round, 2008) which increases during growth and therefore contributes to increased power output. The maximal shortening velocity is dependent on the length of the myofibrils and the fibre type composition (Schiaffino and Reggiani, 1996). Both factors are believed to change with growth and increases in shortening velocity might be expected to influence the velocity-dependent force and power relationship (Van Praagh and Dore, 2002). On average, the adolescent performance spurt in power development (i.e. vertical jump) starts about 1.5 years prior to PHV and reaches a peak approximately 0.5–1.0 year after PHV (Beunen and Malina, 1988). Power as such should not be used as a determinant factor for talent identification until late adolescence considering the impact of growth and maturation on this variable, especially the force-dependant factors. Instead, velocity-dependant factors may warrant attention at a younger age, as a spurt in maximum velocity performance in speed tests (shuttle run and plate tapping) occurs before PHV (Beunen and Malina, 1988).

Agility

According to the deterministic model proposed by Young et al. (2002) agility is comprised of perceptual decision-making factors and change of direction (COD) factors. This COD ability is in turn influenced by technique, anthropometry, straight sprinting speed and leg strength factors. To assess agility potential and/or ability, therefore, an assessment battery needs to take into account all these factors and needs to be event- or sport-specific.

Identifying talent based on agility assessments would seem problematic given the multi-factorial nature of this component. The perceptual decision-making component is no doubt influenced by age and the experiences of the athlete. Most of the COD factors are influenced by physique, as discussed previously, and therefore the physical maturity of the athlete. Given this information, an agility assessment would most likely be poor predictors of a child's potential, however, COD performance has been shown to be one of the main distinguishing factors in a multidisciplinary talent identification battery in youth soccer players (Reilly et al., 2000).

Aerobic fitness

Aerobic endurance performance is determined by VO_2max, the lactate threshold and running economy (Pfeiffer et al., 2008), which are important for many individual sports (e.g. athletics, swimming) and team sports (e.g. soccer, Australian rules football) athletes. The most accurate method for measuring VO_2max, the lactate threshold and running economy is via treadmill testing (Pfeiffer et al., 2008). Several sport-specific field tests are available for estimating VO_2max and simulate metabolic stress encountered in a game. Some of these tests include the Yo-Yo Intermittent Recovery Test levels 1 and 2 (Bangsbo et al., 2008), the University of Montreal Track Test (Leger and Boucher, 1980), the 30–15 Intermittent Fitness Test (Buchheit, 2008) as well as sport-specific endurance tests (e.g. Hoff Track in soccer) (Hoff et al., 2002).

These field tests have been used to distinguish elite from non-elite youth soccer players (Vaeyens et al., 2006) as well as discriminating future professional and amateur players (Roescher et al., 2010). It is noteworthy that the role of maturity was accounted for either statistically (Vaeyens et al., 2006) or by the longitudinal approach (Roescher et al., 2010) since absolute VO_2max (L·min^{-1}) shows a clear adolescent spurt. On average, VO_2max begins to increase several years before PHV and continues to increase after PHV. Conversely, VO_2max per unit of body mass (mL O_2·kg^{-1}·min^{-1}), generally begins to decline one year before PHV and continues to decline after PHV (Pfeiffer et al., 2008). Changes in relative aerobic power during adolescence probably reflect alterations in body size and composition and not changes in aerobic function, which increases at this time (Beunen and Malina, 2008). Considering the relative trainability in this area from a young age (Pfeiffer et al., 2008) and the discriminative (Vaeyens et al., 2006) and predictive (Roescher et al., 2010) ability of playing level from these tests once maturity is taken into account, aerobic endurance tests can be used to identify athletes in sports that require a high aerobic endurance capability (e.g. running, Australian rules football, soccer).

Anaerobic fitness

Anaerobic endurance has mainly been measured with the Wingate tests in adults and children (Inbar and Chia, 2008). In contrast to maximal aerobic power (VO_2max), relative anaerobic endurance (Watts-kg^{-1}) in children as compared to adults is low (i.e. 81.3 per cent and 91.6 per cent for males and females, respectively), which places them at a relative functional disadvantage compared to adults when performing strenuous activities that last 5–60s (Inbar and Chia, 2008). It is speculated that the metabolic pathways involved in anaerobic endurance exercise and the tolerance to acidosis (lactate acid production) are not fully mature until after the adolescent growth spurt and perhaps into early adulthood (Inbar and Chia, 2008). Therefore, anaerobic endurance capability should not be used as a determinant factor for talent identification until late adolescence even though it might be crucial in sports that involve high–intensity exercise (e.g. 400 m, football codes).

Flexibility

The range of motion around a single or multiple joints is used to measure flexibility and can be quantified in linear (sit and reach) or angular (shoulder rotation) units. Flexibility can be measured using a variety of equipment (goniometers, inclinometers, flexometers and tape measures), which can be used on both adult and youth populations. However, consideration needs to be given to the choice of test, as assessments such as the sit and reach will be influenced by different growth rates of the lower limbs and trunk around adolescence (Malina *et al.*, 2004).

Flexibility can be developed at any age, given the appropriate training. During childhood, it is questionable whether children need to stretch at all, due to low risk of injury and the compliance of their tissues. If a window of trainability for flexibility exists, it was reported for subjects in pre–PHV status (Beunen and Malina, 1988) around 8–10 years of age for girls and 10–12 for boys. However, given the relative trainability throughout the life span, flexibility should not be used as a measure to identify talent, even though extreme flexibility would be desirable in sports such as the martial arts and gymnastics.

Summary on testing batteries

The generic testing battery for talent identification can in its simplest form comprise of easily administered tests to assess the ability to run, jump and throw. An example of how this data could be presented within a radar plot is presented in Figure 2.1. The tests would be administered over a number of years (e.g. aged 8–16), and results could be compared to performance standards that are event- and age-specific. Alongside the physiological testing battery, maturation and anthropometric measurements need to be taken to direct athletes towards events they would likely succeed in.

A more sport specific approach would use tests that simulate the demands of the sport (i.e. validity) and match the abilities of the young players in order to accurately select players and monitor specific training effects. The timing of testing is important, and unfortunately many tests to determine ability are only performed at the beginning of the season. Inter-season and intra-season variability are both important especially as players can increase substantially in size and weight over a single sporting season. However, it needs to be noted that few of these testing batteries are able to discriminate elite from sub-elite players and future national team level from future professional club level players. A comprehensive approach should be multidimensional, including psychological questionnaires (psycho–behavioural

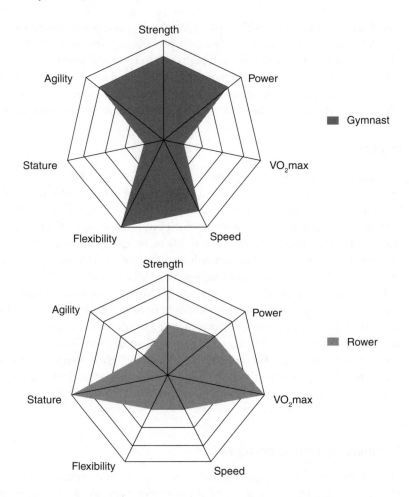

FIGURE 2.1 Theoretical athletic profile of young athletes from different sports

skills: goal setting, motivation, anxiety control), cognitive-perceptive assessments (e.g. computer game simulation) and open-environment assessments (e.g. game-like situation) in addition to the aforementioned testing battery. In addition, during scouting days, players could be organized according to individual size, birth date or maturity status so that comparisons are fair and equitable.

Key points

- In many sports talented athletes are the product of genetics as well as environmental influences, implying that the required body structure for each sport needs to be present at birth and that the required training and support needs to be in place in order to achieve sporting success.

- Identification of 'talented' individuals based on proficiency of performing age-based physical and performance tests (e.g. strength or aerobic tests) is problematic since research has established a direct link between performance and physique, and therefore the physical maturity of a child. Hence such tests are typically poor predictors of a child's future potential to excel.
- The RAE is present in many sports where mature players are likely to dominate the game physically at youth level due to greater body size, strength, speed, power and endurance. Considering the differences in timing and tempo of maturation, coaching staff should not select players based on the short-term outcome (i.e. youth competitions) but rather emphasize a long-term development approach as this physical advantage may not transfer to the top senior level and technically skilled, yet less-mature players, may be overlooked in the selection process due to maturity associated limitations in their physical and functional capacities (i.e. smaller size, or less strength, power and speed).
- Considering the differences in timing and tempo of maturation, anthropometric characteristics of players/athletes and maturation status should be measured and accounted for when physiological ability is interpreted (i.e. scaling and statistical control). Non-invasive methods for estimating maturity status may allow youth programmes and coaches to interpret physical, physiological and technical testing data with a better understanding of human growth.
- The importance of psychosocial behaviours when identifying the future potential of an individual within sport should not be overlooked. Many believe these features to be of greater importance than the physique and physiology of an individual when predicting future potential.
- An earlier onset and higher volume of discipline-specific training and competition, and an extended involvement in institutional talent promotion programmes during adolescence are in many cases not associated with greater success in senior elite sport. Alternative methods such as 'talent recycling' and 'mature-age talent identification', which have recently been employed in the field, seem to be successful in delivering additional world-class performers in certain sports.

References

Abbott, A. and Collins, D. (2002) 'A theoretical and empirical analysis of a "state of the art" talent identification model', *High Ability Studies*, 13: 157–178.

Bangsbo, J., Iaia, F. M. and Krustrup, P. (2008) 'The Yo-Yo Intermittent Recovery Test: A useful tool for evaluation of physical performance in intermittent sports', *Sports Medicine*, 38: 37–51.

Beunen, G. and Malina, R. M. (1988) 'Growth and physical performance relative to the timing of the adolescent spurt', *Exercise and Sport Science Reviews*, 16: 503–540.

Beunen, G. and Malina, R. M. (2008) 'Growth and biologic maturation: Relevance to athletic performance', in H. Hebestreit and O. Bar-Or (eds) *The young athlete*, Malden: Blackwell Publishing Ltd.

Beunen, G., Ostyn, M., Simons, J., Renson, R., Claessens, A. L., Vanden Eynde, B., Lefevre, J., Vanreusel, B., Malina, R. M. and van't Hof, M. A. (1997) 'Development and tracking in fitness components: Leuven longtudinal study on lifestyle, fitness and health', *International Journal of Sports Medicine*, 18, Suppl 3: S171–178.

Buchheit, M. (2008) 'The 30–15 intermittent fitness test: Accuracy for individualizing interval training of young intermittent sport players', *Journal of Strength and Conditioning Research*, 22: 365–374.

Carling, C., le Gall, F., Reilly, T. and Williams, A. M. (2009) 'Do anthropometric and fitness characteristics vary according to birth date distribution in elite youth academy soccer players?' *Scandinavian Journal of Medicine & Science in Sports*, 19: 3–9.

Christensen, M. K. (2009) '"An eye for talent": Talent identification and the "the practical sense" of top-level soccer coaches', *Sociology of Sport Journal*, 26: 365–382.

Cobley, S., Baker, J., Wattie, N. and McKenna, J. (2009) 'Annual age-grouping and athlete development: A meta-analytical review of relative age effects in sport', *Sports Medicine*, 39: 235–256.

Côté, J., Macdonald, D. J., Baker, J. and Abernethy, B. (2006) 'When "where" is more important than "when": Birthplace and birthdate effects on the achievement of sporting expertise', *Journal of Sports Sciences*, 24: 1065–1073.

De Ste Croix, M. (2007) 'Advances in paediatric strength assessment: Changing our perspective on strength development', *Journal of Sports Science and Medicine*, 6: 292–304.

Delorme, N. and Raspaud, M. (2008) *Influence of the relative age effect on the dropout of sports activities.* Paper presented at the 13th Annual Congress of the ECSS: European College of Sport Science, Estoril.

Delorme, N. and Raspaud, M. (2009) 'The relative age effect in young French basketball players: A study on the whole population', *Scandinavian Journal of Medicine & Science in Sports*, 19: 235–242.

Dore, E., Duche, P., Rouffet, D., Ratel, S., Bedu, M. and Van Praagh, E. (2003) 'Measurement error in short-term power testing in young people', *Journal of Sports Sciences*, 21: 135–142.

Eston, R., Hawes, M., Martin, A. and Reilly, T. (2009) 'Human body composition', in R. Eston and T. Reilly (eds) *Kinanthropometry and exercise physiology laboratory manual: Tests, procedures and data*, Oxon: Routledge.

Faigenbaum, A., Milliken, L. and Wescott, W. (2004) 'Maximal strength testing in healthy children', *Journal of Strength and Conditioning Research*, 17: 162–166.

Hansen, L., Bangsbo, J., Twisk, J. and Klausen, K. (1999) 'Development of muscle strength in relation to training level and testosterone in young male soccer players', *Journal of Applied Physiology*, 87: 1141–1147.

Hoff, J., Wisloff, U., Engen, L. C., Kemi, O. J. and Helgerud, J. (2002) 'Soccer specific aerobic endurance training', *British Journal of Sports Medicine*, 36: 218–221.

Hume, P. and Stewart, A. (2010) 'Use of kinanthropometry in youth sports for talent development and improving sports performance', in M. Chia, J. Wang, G. Balasekaran and N. Chatzisarantis (eds) *International Conference of Physical Education and Sports Science*, Singapore: National Institute of Education.

Inbar, O. and Chia, M. (2008) 'Development of maximal anaerobic performance: An old issue revisited', in H. Hebestreit and O. Bar-Or (eds) *The young athlete*, Malden: Blackwell Publishing Ltd.

Jones, D. A. and Round, J. M. (2008) 'Muscle development during childhood and adolescence', in H. Hebestreit and O. Bar-Or (eds) *The young athlete*, Malden: Blackwell Publishing Ltd.

le Gall, F., Carling, C., Williams, M. and Reilly, T. (2010) 'Anthropometric and fitness characteristics of international, professional and amateur male graduate soccer players from an elite youth academy', *Journal of Science and Medicine in Sport*, 13: 90–95.

Leger, L. and Boucher, R. (1980) 'An indirect continuous running multistage field test: The Université de Montréal track test', *Canadian Journal of Applied Sports Sciences*, 5: 37–84.

Malina, R., Bouchard, C. and Bar-Or, O. (2004) *Growth, maturation, and physical activity*, Champaign, IL: Human Kinetics.

Martin, R. J., Dore, E., Hautier, C. A., Van Praagh, E. and Bedu, M. (2003) 'Short-term peak power changes in adolescents of similar anthropometric characteristics', *Medicine and Science in Sports and Exercise*, 35: 1436–1440.

Martin, R. J., Dore, E., Twisk, J., Van Praagh, E., Hautier, C. A. and Bedu, M. (2004) 'Longitudinal changes of maximal short-term peak power in girls and boys during growth', *Medicine and Science in Sports and Exercise*, 36: 498–503.

Mujika, I., Vaeyens, R., Matthys, S. P., Santisteban, J., Goiriena, J. and Philippaerts, R. (2009) 'The relative age effect in a professional football club setting', *Journal of Sports Sciences*, 27: 1153–1158.

Musch, J. and Grondin, S. (2001) 'Unequal competition as an impediment to personal development: A review of the relative age effect in sport', *Developmental Review*, 21: 147–167.

Pfeiffer, K., Loberlo, F., Ward, D. and Pate, R. (2008) 'Endurance trainability of children and youth', in H. Hebestreit and O. Bar-Or (eds) *The young athlete*, Malden: Blackwell Publishing Ltd.

Reilly, T., Bangsbo, J. and Franks, A. (2000) 'Anthropometric and physiological predispositions for elite soccer', *Journal of Sports Sciences*, 18: 669–683.

Roescher, C. R., Elferink-Gemser, M. T., Huijgen, B. C. and Visscher, C. (2010) 'Soccer endurance development in professionals', *International Journal of Sports Medicine*, 31: 174–179.

Samozino, P., Rejc, E., Di Prampero, P. E., Belli, A. and Morin, J. B. (2012) 'Optimal force-velocity profile in ballistic movements. Altius: Citius or fortius?' *Medicine and Science in Sports and Exercise*, 44: 313–322.

Santos, A., Welsman, J. R., De Ste Croix, M. and Armstrong, N. (2002) 'Age- and sex-related differences in optimal peak power', *Pediatric Exercise Science*, 14: 202–212.

Schiaffino, S. and Reggiani, C. (1996) 'Molecular diversity of myofibrillar proteins: Gene regulation and functional significance', *Physiological Reviews*, 76: 371–423.

Sherar, L. B., Baxter-Jones, A. D., Faulkner, R. A. and Russell, K. W. (2007) 'Do physical maturity and birth date predict talent in male youth ice hockey players?' *Journal of Sports Sciences*, 25: 879–886.

Vaeyens, R., Lenoir, M., Williams, A. M. and Philippaerts, R. M. (2008) 'Talent identification and development programmes in sport: Current models and future directions', *Sports Medicine*, 38: 703–714.

Vaeyens, R., Malina, R. M., Janssens, M., Van Renterghem, B., Bourgois, J., Vrijens, J. and Philippaerts, R. M. (2006) 'A multidisciplinary selection model for youth soccer: The ghent youth soccer project', *British Journal of Sports Medicine*, 40: 928–934; discussion 934.

Van Praagh, E. (2008) 'Testing anaerobic performance', in H. Hebestreit and O. Bar-Or (eds) *The young athlete*, Massachusetts: Blackwell Publishing Ltd.

Van Praagh, E. and Dore, E. (2002) 'Short-term muscle power during growth and maturation', *Sports Medicine*, 32: 701–728.

van Rossum, J. H. (2006) 'Relative age effect revisited: Findings from the dance domain', *Perceptual and Motor Skills*, 102: 302–308.

Viru, A., Loko, J., Harro, M., Volver, A., Laaneaots, L. and Viru, M. (1999) 'Critical periods in the development of performance capacity during childhood and adolescence', *European Journal of Physical Education*, 4: 75–119.

Young, W. B., James, R. and Montgomery, I. (2002) 'Is muscle power related to running speed with changes of direction?' *Journal of Sports Medicine and Physical Fitness*, 42: 282–288.

3

TALENT DEVELOPMENT

Craig A. Williams, Jon L. Oliver and Rhodri S. Lloyd

Introduction

Talent development of young athletes is a very complex, multidimensional and unpredictable concept. Despite this fact, sporting organizations in their pursuit of nurturing young talented athletes have spent considerable time, resources and finances in developing programmes that can guarantee success. Unfortunately to date, most programmes lack a framework and empirical evidence to support their implementation, if indeed a theoretical framework is provided at all. There is still considerable debate about whether it is possible to have one overarching strategy that encompasses an aim to increase youth sports participation while at the same time preparing young athletes for elite performance (Green, 2007). Or whether these two aims are unachievable under one strategy and need to be disentangled. These dilemmas are understandable given the difficulty, in the first instance of identifying talented athletes (see Chapter 2) and then planning ahead to develop and enhance their talents. In this chapter talent development is defined as the procedure or provision of the environment that realizes an athlete's potential. This definition is in contrast to talent identification which is a process of recognizing an athlete's potential to succeed (Russell, 1989).

A major weakness of all talent-development programmes is that the empirical evidence used to support them is usually cross-sectional. Recent debates about the Long Term Athlete Development Plan (see 'basic theoretical concepts' below) in the UK have accelerated the growing concerns that the cross-sectional data upon which to base such programmes is outdated and ignores the multidimensional and dynamic nature of young athlete's development (Bailey *et al.*, 2010; Ford *et al.*, 2011). Most paediatric literature, either physiological or psychological, is cross-sectional and rectifying this problem is technically challenging, expensive and time consuming. The opportunity to longitudinally measure youngsters throughout childhood and adolescence is a daunting prospect and is not sufficiently acknowledged in the adult literature where, of course, the majority of growth and maturation has ceased, and training and learning effects are likely to be smaller in magnitude.

The consequences of growth and maturation are fundamental to the study of paediatric exercise science and are a key differentiator between young athletes and adult athletes. The assumption that an important characteristic of success found in adult athletes can be extrapolated back to young athletes has as much validity as expecting a successful young athlete possessing that characteristic to retain it into adulthood. Generally, there has been little debate by adult and junior coaches as to their expectations about how to translate or transition these junior characteristics into successful performance in adulthood. An effect of growth and maturation is observed in the relative age effect, a phenomenon first reported in adult ice hockey players in the mid-1980s (Barnsley et al., 1985). Barnsley and colleagues showed that the majority of players were born in the first half of the year. This study was followed up for three years in young junior ice hockey players in Canada with strikingly similar results (Barnsley and Thompson, 1988). Since that time the relative age effect has been confirmed across a variety of both individual and team sports. This skewing of the birth distribution data for selection is a reflection of those youngsters gaining an advantage not only in relation to increased exposure to sports training and coaching time, but also as a reflection that chronological age does not mirror biological age. Hence, early-maturing children who gain advantages in height, weight, speed and strength are often selected ahead of late maturers in team sports. Conversely in those sports where it favours late maturers (e.g. dance, gymnastics) the relative age effect (RAE) is reversed because these characteristics can be detrimental to sports performance. For an extensive literature review on the RAE see Cobley et al. (2009).

Basic theoretical concepts

Although all talent-development programmes currently in use lack longitudinal data to establish their validity, this does not mean they are worthless. In the first instance any model must be proposed and then tested. Subsequent data emerging from the model should then be used to verify or modify the theoretical framework and this is where a number of models are currently placed. Several of the more well-discussed models will now be described, although it should be reiterated that there is no one model that adequately accounts for talent development in youth sport.

Differentiated Model of Giftedness and Talent (DMGT)

A model of talent development often proposed is the Differentiated Model of Giftedness and Talent (DMGT) based on the work of Gagné (1993). Gagné makes an important distinction between those individuals that are 'gifted' whether this relates to abilities of memory, creativity, intelligence or physical strength (the constituent domains) versus talent, which he defined as the systematic development of their giftedness or aptitude. This distinction is important to acknowledge as it allows practitioners to be reminded of the process of developing the gifted individual rather than just relying on their immediate inherent and observable ability. Gagné further defined gifted as those individuals in the top 10 per cent of their same-age peers, while talent was the demonstration of systematically acquired abilities to a level that the individual is placed in the 10 per cent of their peers active in that domain, i.e. top 10 per cent of sprinting ability in the world. Gagné originally devised this model in education where gifted and talent programmes (e.g. in mathematics and science) have been more extensively studied.

Recently a number of researchers began to examine the model in the context of sport (Tranckle et al., 2006; Van Rossum and Gangé, 2005). The four main domains related to sensorimotor, creative, socio-affective and intellectual have struck a chord because of the complex and interactive interplay of the many variables in operation within sports. For example, youth players coming up against a team who are equally or perhaps even superior in physical ability would have to show ability to problem solve, to be creative in their execution of technical skills and even show greater awareness of leadership and team cohesion, if they are to succeed in beating their opponents. Indeed, Gagné recognizes that rather than focusing on the level of ability at that moment in time, a key pre-occupation of many coaches, particularly allied to individual physical ability, is to consider the rate of learning. What was meant by this was the rate of learning could be an indicator of giftedness rather than a particular level of ability. This example is easiest to highlight in the context of learning with an individual practising a new physical skill. According to Ericsson, the level of attainment of any skill is positively related to the accumulated practice and in order to acquire an expertise at the elite level a minimum of 10 years or 10,000 hours is required (Ericsson et al., 1993; Ericsson, 1996; Ericsson and Lehmann, 1996). There are a number of questions that remain unanswered about the 10-year rule and its acceptance has largely gone unchallenged. First, it should be noted that what exactly encompasses the 10,000 hours, i.e. the environment needed, support networks, frequency, time and duration of the practice that lead to becoming an expert are all unresolved. Second, if a sport like football or even marathon running is selected, the age at which 'peak performance' is observed is often not until late 20s or even early 30s. This observation is longer than the 10-year rule that a professional runner or football player would have been involved in that sport. Therefore, care must be taken that the 10-year rule does not become enshrined as fact when clearly there are many contexts in which it will not apply.

Developmental model of sports participation

The model of sports participation as proposed by Côté and Hay (2002) and Côté et al. (2007) advocates early, playful and non-specific specialization up to six years of age. From the age of 6–12 years there is a promotion of a variety of sports without a focus of any particular specialization. From the age of 13–15 years a reduced variety of sports are played, and from 16 years onwards there is a greater investment in a single sport. In particular for team sports, players are encouraged not to engage in any one specific sport until at least the 13–15 years. The model also highlights the particular role of the potential interactive influences of coaches, parents, schools and peers. While many coaches might recognize these paths as similar to ones their young athletes are already taking, its obvious weakness is that it is not suitable to apply to such sports as gymnastics, diving and figure skating, where specialization and sporting achievement occurs at an early age. By contrast, in sports where performance achievement and late specialization occurs later, i.e. triathlon, marathon running and rowing, the programme would be suitable.

Long Term Athlete Development

The Long Term Athlete Deveopment (LTAD) framework, established by Istvan Balyi, is a sports development framework from Canada focused on the athlete and centred on growth and maturation time points rather than chronological age determined points (Balyi and Hamilton, 2000). The six-component framework starts between three and six years old, beginning with 'FUNdamentals' emphasizing basic movement skills, followed by 'Learning to play', then 'Training to train', 'Training to compete', 'Training to win' and 'Retainment'. The framework was intended to produce a long-term approach to maximize individual potential and involvement in sport, although it was subsequently criticized for an over-reliance on unsubstantiated evidence for 'optimal windows of trainability' on young athletes (Bailey et al., 2010).

The ideas of 'critical or optimal windows' probably originated from the work of McGraw in the mid-1930s related to critical periods of learning in children. McGraw (1935) was convinced that maturation placed a primary determinant in these critical periods in which McGraw cited earlier work in the 1920s by Hall (1921) and Gesell (1928). Later, Magill and colleagues (1982) summarized these findings and labelled them as a 'growth-readiness' model of learning. Since that time aspects of the model related to learning in the cognitive domain have found their way into learning within the motor domain. In the context of the motor domain, the use of the term 'optimal window' implies that training occurs with greater efficiency at one specific time point compared to another, however, the evidence for this proposition is weak. A critical aspect to the optimal windows of trainability is determining *when* the athlete is *ready and able* to train most effectively. The descriptors highlighted by italics emphasize the importance of readiness both in terms of maturation and prior experiences. Both of these factors cannot, however, be independently responsible for determining a readiness to train because it fails to acknowledge one more factor, that of motivation. Therefore, the opportunity to achieve the greatest efficiency in training at any one time is when these three factors are at an optimum point. To date there is no method that has consistently been able to pinpoint this time period. It is certainly likely to be individual and also task specific.

The LTAD drew further criticism for being one-dimensional regarding the focus on physiological aspects of performance rather than considering other psychological, social or academic factors (Ford *et al.*, 2011). The model did, however, create a lot of debate among sporting organizations, some of whom adopted the framework while others began to realize that greater organization, planning and research for the youth athlete was needed.

Youth Physical Development model

The Youth Physical Development (YPD) model is a contemporary model for developing physical abilities throughout childhood (Lloyd and Oliver, 2012). Similar to Balyi's LTAD model the YPD highlights the importance of considering training with respect to the maturational status of children, identified via the timing of peak height velocity (PHV). However, the YPD moves away from the concept of windows of opportunity to the position that the majority of evidence available suggests that most components of fitness are trainable throughout childhood, although the mechanisms that underpin training adaptations are likely to change with maturation. Lloyd and Oliver (2012) suggest that, prior to adolescence, training adaptations will have a predominantly neural basis, whereas once puberty is reached adaptations may also be attributed to morphological changes stimulated by the increase in circulating androgens interacting with training stimuli. The YPD also extends beyond the narrow focus of physical development presented in Balyi's LTAD model to include other important qualities of human performance, including agility, power and mobility and making the distinction between strength and hypertrophy. Consequently Lloyd and Oliver believe that the YPD will provide strength and conditioning coaches, sports coaches, physical educators and parents with an overview of total physical development.

Figures 3.1 and 3.2 show the YPD model for both boys and girls, respectively. The models highlight that all components of fitness are trainable to some degree throughout childhood, with font size indicating the importance of each component during different periods of childhood. Central to the model is a large emphasis on the development of muscular strength and movement competency throughout both childhood and adolescence, which challenges previous LTAD theory (Balyi and Hamilton, 2004). Muscular strength development via resistance training has previously been associated with physical performance enhancement (Faigenbaum *et al.*, 2009), improving markers of health and well-being (Benson *et al.*, 2006; Shaibi *et al.*, 2006) and reducing the risk of sport-related injury (Valovich McLeod *et al.*, 2011). Furthermore, motor skill competency has previously been associated with higher physical activity levels and improved well-being (Lubans *et al.*, 2010). Consequently, these qualities are viewed as the major fitness commodities within the YPD model (Lloyd and Oliver, 2012).

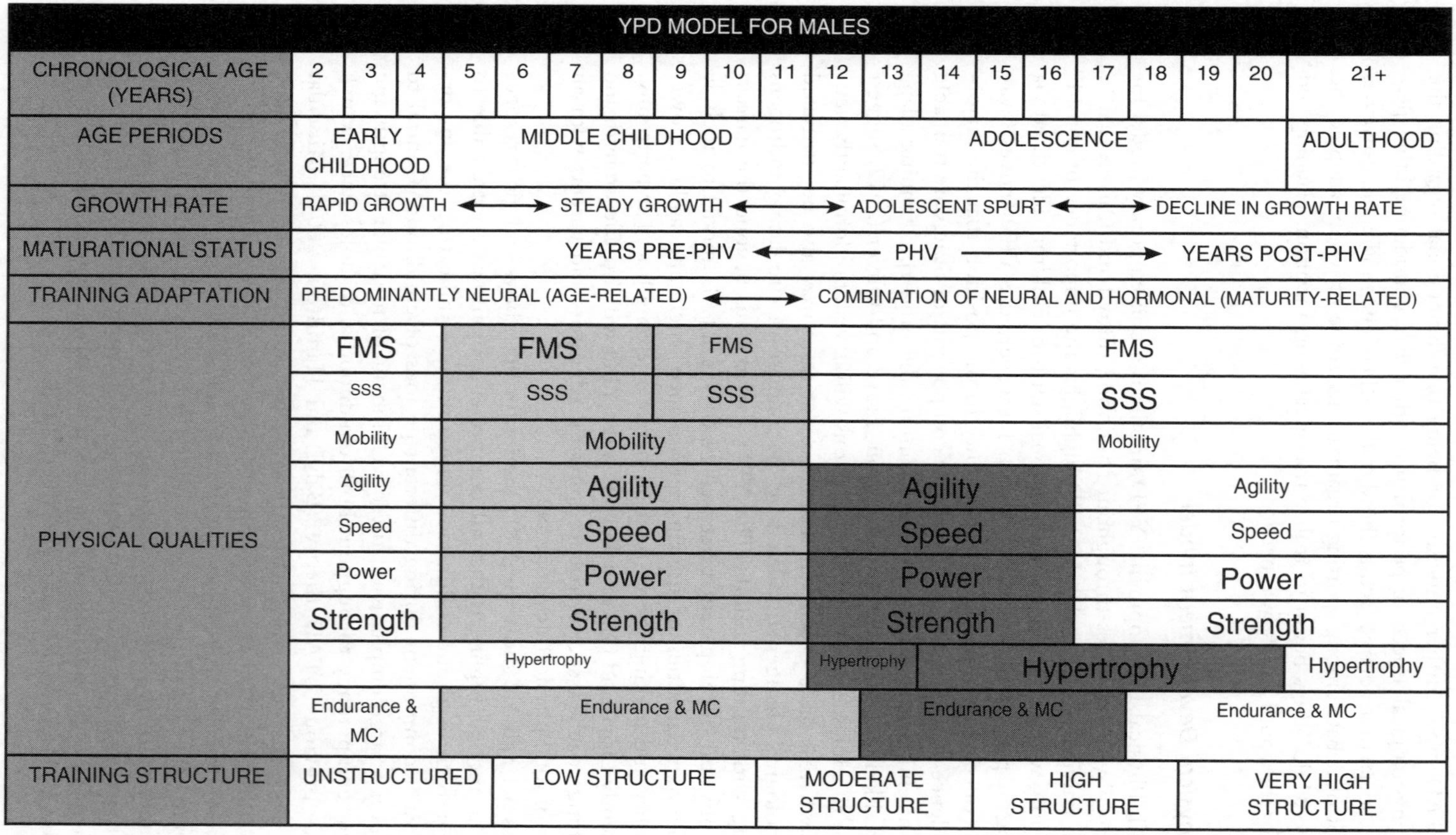

YPD MODEL FOR MALES

CHRONOLOGICAL AGE (YEARS)	2	3	4	5	6	7	8	9	10	11	12	13	14	15	16	17	18	19	20	21+
AGE PERIODS	EARLY CHILDHOOD				MIDDLE CHILDHOOD						ADOLESCENCE									ADULTHOOD
GROWTH RATE	RAPID GROWTH ←→				STEADY GROWTH ←→						ADOLESCENT SPURT ←→						DECLINE IN GROWTH RATE ←→			
MATURATIONAL STATUS	YEARS PRE-PHV ←→										PHV ←→			YEARS POST-PHV ←→						
TRAINING ADAPTATION	PREDOMINANTLY NEURAL (AGE-RELATED) ←→										COMBINATION OF NEURAL AND HORMONAL (MATURITY-RELATED) ←→									
PHYSICAL QUALITIES	FMS				FMS				FMS		FMS									
	SSS				SSS				SSS		SSS									
	Mobility				Mobility						Mobility									
	Agility				Agility						Agility									
	Speed				Speed						Speed									
	Power				Power						Power									
	Strength				Strength						Strength									
	Hypertrophy				Hypertrophy						Hypertrophy			Hypertrophy						
	Endurance & MC				Endurance & MC						Endurance & MC						Endurance & MC			
TRAINING STRUCTURE	UNSTRUCTURED				LOW STRUCTURE						MODERATE STRUCTURE			HIGH STRUCTURE			VERY HIGH STRUCTURE			

FIGURE 3.1 The Youth Physical Development (YPD) model for males

Source: Lloyd and Oliver, 2012.

Notes: font size refers to importance; light shaded boxes refer to pre-adolescent periods of adaptation, dark shaded boxes refer to adolescent periods of adaptation; PHV = peak height velocity; FMS = fundamental movement skills; SSS = sport-specific skills; MC = metabolic conditioning.

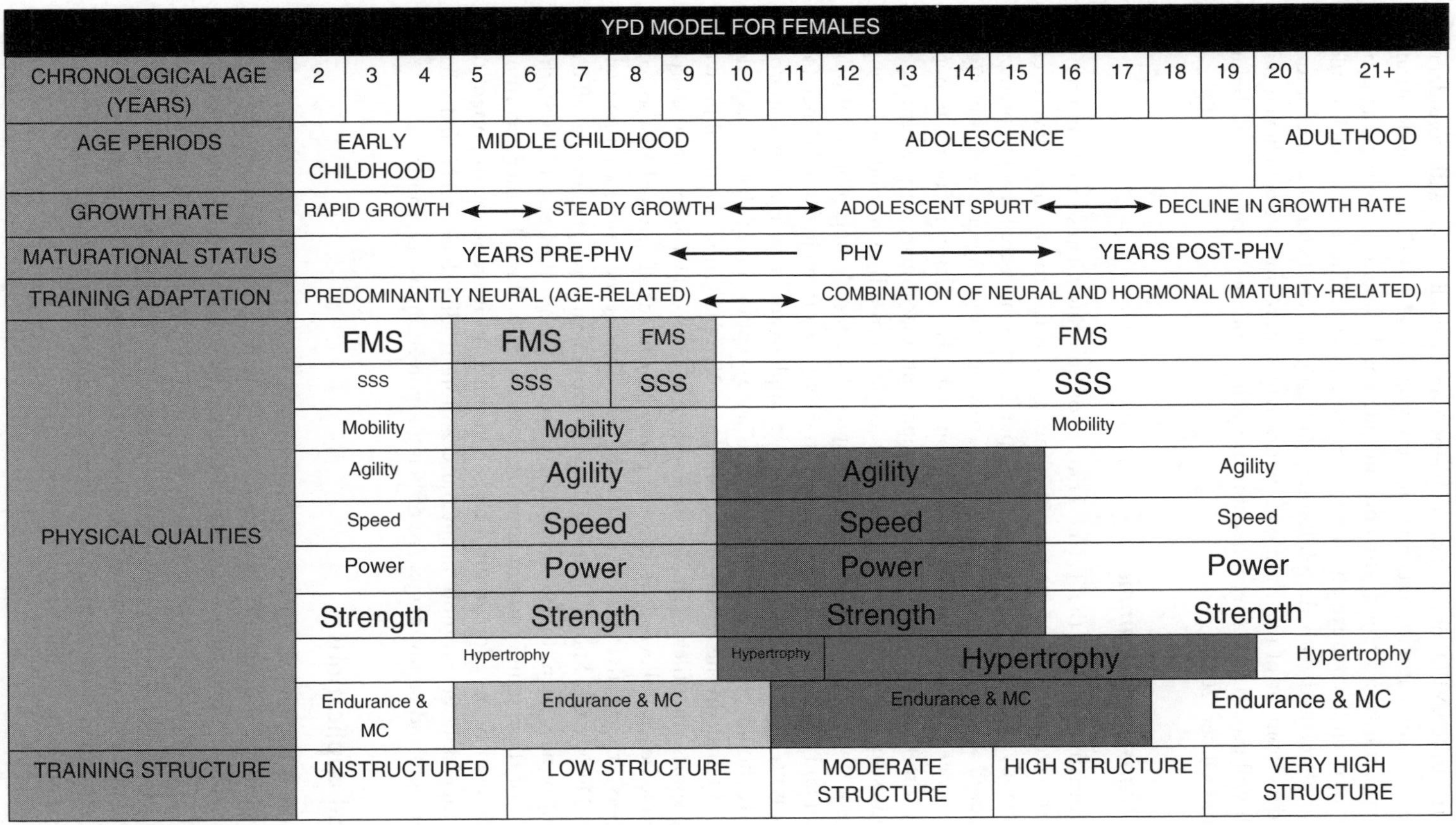

YPD MODEL FOR FEMALES

CHRONOLOGICAL AGE (YEARS)	2	3	4	5	6	7	8	9	10	11	12	13	14	15	16	17	18	19	20	21+
AGE PERIODS	EARLY CHILDHOOD			MIDDLE CHILDHOOD							ADOLESCENCE							ADULTHOOD		
GROWTH RATE	RAPID GROWTH ←→			STEADY GROWTH ←→							ADOLESCENT SPURT ←→						DECLINE IN GROWTH RATE →			
MATURATIONAL STATUS	YEARS PRE-PHV →										PHV →			YEARS POST-PHV →						
TRAINING ADAPTATION	PREDOMINANTLY NEURAL (AGE-RELATED) ←→									COMBINATION OF NEURAL AND HORMONAL (MATURITY-RELATED) ←→										
PHYSICAL QUALITIES	FMS			FMS			FMS			FMS					FMS					
	SSS			SSS			SSS			SSS					SSS					
	Mobility			Mobility			Mobility			Mobility					Mobility					
	Agility			Agility			Agility			Agility					Agility					
	Speed			Speed			Speed			Speed					Speed					
	Power			Power			Power			Power					Power					
	Strength			Strength			Strength			Strength					Strength					
	Hypertrophy			Hypertrophy			Hypertrophy			Hypertrophy					Hypertrophy					
	Endurance & MC			Endurance & MC			Endurance & MC			Endurance & MC					Endurance & MC					
TRAINING STRUCTURE	UNSTRUCTURED			LOW STRUCTURE						MODERATE STRUCTURE					HIGH STRUCTURE			VERY HIGH STRUCTURE		

FIGURE 3.2 The Youth Physical Development (YPD) model for females

Source: Lloyd and Oliver, 2012.

Notes: font size refers to importance; light shaded boxes refer to pre-adolescent periods of adaptation, dark shaded boxes refer to adolescent periods of adaptation; PHV = peak height velocity; FMS = fundamental movement skills; SSS = sport-specific skills; MC = metabolic conditioning.

Also central to the YPD model is the concept of individualization, with consideration given to age, maturation, gender and training age. All of these considerations will impact on how a strength and conditioning coach designs a safe training programme to try and maximize physical talent development. The YPD model should also be implemented with the philosophy of being athlete centred and promoting the development of the child over performance outcomes. It is believed this approach will provide long-term benefits and will encourage a sense of well-being (Lloyd and Oliver, 2012).

Talent Transfer programmes

Recent initiatives such as the Talent Transfer or Sporting Giants programmes by UK Sport have met with some success, although it is fair to say these have been predominantly in closed sports rather than open sports which are harder to predict. These closed sports, such as track cycling, rowing, canoeing and weightlifting, have often been targeted because the environment plays a lesser influence in performance and there are probably fewer components that impact on performance. Case studies such as Rebecca Romero who came from a background of rowing (winning a silver medal at the 2004 Olympics) to track cycling (double World champion and double Olympic champion in 2008) are often cited as evidence for talent transfer, but of course these types of examples cannot be evaluated appropriately. It should be noted that Rebecca is an exception given that she is only the second female in the history of the Summer Olympic Games to medal in two different sports. In other examples of transferring new talent into other sports, for example beach volleyball (usually tall players) or handball (particularly football goalkeepers), the relative success is more likely a case of increasing a limited talent pool. Despite UK Sports claiming their Sporting Giants programme has added 4 per cent of new talent to the overall UK Olympic squads (UK Sport, 2008), the full effect of these transfer programmes remains to be evaluated either according to medals won or on a longitudinal basis. On this basis it would be important to know which skill sets promote talent transfer more readily than others, and what the advantages and disadvantages are of being involved in diverse sports.

Practical applications

One of the problems for coaches working with youngsters is how to translate the above theoretical models and information into practice. Currently, there are very few examples to highlight, therefore data that has been collected on a longitudinal basis but within an academy or club basis will be discussed. The following sections will highlight three important practical aspects: the first one related to the measurement of discrete variables, e.g. speed; the second, an educational approach through coaching; and the third aspect is overtraining, particularly important so as to prevent talent development going wrong.

Monitoring sprint performance

The measurement of discrete variables – most notably physiological, but also some psychological ones – has dominated talent identification and development programmes. However, the key issue that remains to be rectified is not the measurement of a particular variable in a one-off 'snap shot' fashion, but the magnitude of change over time. This is the real value in monitoring and measuring for it relates information back to the coach and support teams about the rate of progress. Take for example sprinting. Sprint times have consistently been reported to provide reliable measures of speed in children (Drinkwater *et al.*, 2007; Rumpf *et al.*, 2011). Coefficients of variation for children's sprinting distances of between 10 m and 40 m have been reported to be in the region of 0.8–2.1 per cent (Drinkwater *et al.*, 2007; Rumpf *et al.*, 2011). The coefficient of variation represents the amount of random noise in the measurement and the reported values reflect a good level of reliability. The changes in sprint speed that may be observed with growth or following training interventions in children (Rumpf *et al.*, 2012) are normally greater than this level of noise, indicating that sprint tests are sensitive to detecting real changes in performance in childhood. To put sprint gains into perspective, Williams *et al.* (2011) calculated that improvements of 1 per cent would have meaningful influence on the performance of youth soccer players. It appears single sprint tests are sensitive to detect changes close to this small level and that training regimes can induce gains in excess of this in children (Rumpf *et al.*, 2012). Rumpf and colleagues also noted similar training gains in the region of 1–3.5 per cent for different training modalities, e.g. plyometrics and strength training.

In a longitudinal study tracking the sprint performance of youth male soccer players, Williams *et al.* (2011) reported that across an age range of 11–16 years, the 10 m sprint time improved at a rate of 3.1 per cent per year, and 30 m sprint time by 2.7 per cent per year. This is similar to rates reported in the general population for children not involved in organized sport (Papaiakovou *et al.*, 2009). These rates of progression may be useful for predicting future performance and evaluating the successfulness of training. Gains in sprint speed that are consistently above these values would suggest a successful long-term training or talent development programme. The findings of Williams *et al.* (2011) are based on the observation of linear relationships between increasing age and speed, which was supported by collection of group data. However, individual players within the study would not have followed such a predictable pattern of development. This means that there is a need for a long-term individualized approach to monitoring speed development. Over a long period, gains in speed may approximate to those given by Williams *et al.* (2011), or better if training has been more successful. However, over briefer periods individual development may be more undulating, with periods of little development combined with periods of rapid improvements, which will be influenced by the interaction of training with growth and maturation. For instance, the coach, if practical, should also monitor growth rates, particularly of the lower limbs (sitting height), to be able to identify initiation of any growth spurt and raise awareness of a possible period of adolescent awkwardness. Identification of such a period can then inform training to reinforce technical aspects of sprinting to assist a child in learning to coordinate their longer limbs.

An educational approach

A significant factor in all the discussion so far about talent development is how does a PE teacher, sports specialist coordinator, coach or organization know when to progress the young athlete onto the next stage or level? To date the intuition of the person in charge of the programme has played a major part in deciding when the player is ready for the next stage of training or competition. The measurement of some physical, physiological and psychological factors have also played a part in determining the progression. Therefore, a long-term player development approach should aim to keep as large a number of gifted players together and provide them with the same opportunity and quality of training and competition. This is important since younger players are likely to be as successful, if not more so, when they are selected into a programme. Therefore, young players should be encouraged to try the sport without any pressure and training and competition may be adjusted to take into account physical size or biological maturity status. However, if such an approach is relevant, the psychological and social implications associated with asking players to train or compete with older or younger peers should be kept in mind. For example, early maturers may not be able to cope with the emotional or cognitive demands associated with competing with their older peers. Likewise, late maturers may perceive it as degrading to play with younger players and drop out of the sport.

An education programme, whether delivered as part of in-service training or qualification based is fundamental to the relative success of the talent development programme and it must be a requisite component to any coaches' education wishing to work with youth players. Similarly, educational sessions must also be dedicated to explaining the procedures and philosophy of such programmes to the young athletes and their parents to help overcome some of these issues.

Specifically, it should be established that coaching and/or support staff need to:

- help early maturers keep success in perspective as late maturers will often catch up with them in terms of performance and success will be harder to achieve;
- be creative and keep late maturers involved in their sport as they often give up because of low perceptions of competence and self-esteem due to little early success.

Overtraining

Considering the number of young athletes training, there is surprisingly little written about overtraining in the context of the young athlete's talent development programme. Therefore, this is one very important reason why talent-development programmes must be seen to be based on empirical evidence. Raglin *et al.* (2000) investigated the prevalence of overtraining across four different countries (Japan, USA, Sweden and Greece) in a group of adolescent swimmers (14.8 ± 1.4y) and found that 35 per cent had overtrained at least once. Similarly, Kentta *et al.* (2001) examined Swedish age group athletes (*n* = 272; mean age 17.9y) found that 37 per cent of the athletes had been overtrained at least once in their sports careers. More recently, Gustafsson *et al.* (2007) found that approximately 10 per cent of competitive adolescent athletes (*n* = 980; mean age 17.5 ± 0.1y) reported high burnout scores. Most recently a study of UK young athletes (*n* = 376, 131 girls and 245 boys; age 15.1 ± 2.0y) across club to international standard in 19 different sports reported overtraining prevalence rates (Matos *et al.*, 2011), where 110 athletes (29 per cent) reported having been overtrained at least once. The incidence was significantly higher in individual sports, low-physically demanding sports, in females, and at the elite level. Interestingly, training load was not a significant predictor of being overtrained, however competitive level and gender accounted for a small (4.7 per cent and 1.7 per cent, respectively) but significant explanatory variance of being overtrained. The researchers concluded that approximately one-third of the young athletes surveyed have experienced overtraining, making this an issue for parents and coaches to recognize. Overtraining was not solely a training-load-related problem with both physical and psychosocial factors identified as important contributors.

The above study of Matos and colleagues is interesting from the perspective that their holistic approach to investigating overtraining includes many of the physiological, psychological, social, educational and environmental factors that should encompass a well-developed talent-development model. In fact, many of the issues relating to overtraining were of a non-physiological nature. The overtrained young athletes reported that sport was the most important thing in their life and that the amount of time dedicated to other activities outside their sport is very limited. Kentta *et al.* (2001) found that 20 per cent of overtrained athletes devoted less than five hours a week to activities outside their sport, and around 40 per cent had nothing else to do apart from their sport. The negative consequences of concentrating on sport too intensely, especially at a young age, can translate into the development of a one-dimensional identity that does not allow a buffering of the negative effects of stressful events. In addition, the overtrained athletes reported a lack of ability to cope between the demands from school and/or work, and the tiredness derived from training, which has previously been reported as a contributing factor to the development of overtraining. As most young athletes are involved in compulsory education, the physical and time demands of their training schedule may negatively affect their school-based work. These were just a few of the factors that impacted on their lives as they sought to realize their sporting potential. Therefore, ensuring young athletes are involved in the decision-making processes, on both a micro and macro scale, is imperative and opportunities for these discussions to occur should be given.

Summary

To date few organizations have implemented a talent-development programme that has a sound theoretical framework. Most programmes have had to make do with an ad-hoc approach to player development. These programmes have invariably focused on a few variables, mostly physiologically related, which are thought to be predictive of future performance. Increasingly it is being recognized by practitioners in youth sports that a child/adolescent focused model must be adapted and one which is supported empirically by research. The complexity and multidimensional aspects to talent development make the measurement, monitoring and evaluation of talent development exceedingly difficult, however, by definition, bringing together a variety of multidisciplinary approaches, a more holistic approach will be created. This approach can only be for the good of the young athlete.

Key points

- A number of different models of talent development exist, each with a predisposition towards a particular scientific domain. A multidisciplinary approach that considers physiological, psychological and sociological contributors to developing talent may be the most difficult but most rewarding approach.
- The YPD model suggests that all components of physical fitness are trainable to some extent throughout childhood. Consequently, the strength and conditioning coach can have a positive influence on developing physical abilities throughout the entire span of childhood.
- Talent-development programmes should ideally seek to retain as large a pool of gifted athletes as possible while providing all those athletes with the same opportunity and quality of training and competition.
- The large influence maturation can play on sports selection during childhood needs to be recognized and every effort taken to provide early-, mid- and late-maturing children with talent development opportunities. To facilitate this, coach education should be a key consideration for sports organizations.
- Overtraining can be an undesirable consequence of talent development, with approximately 30 per cent of child athletes reporting episodes of being overtrained. Coaches should be aware of potential risk factors, symptoms and positive actions to minimize the risk of a child athlete becoming overtrained.

References

Bailey, R., Collins, D., Ford, P., MacNamara, A., Toms, M. and Pearce, G. (2010) *Participant development in sport: An academic review*, Leeds: SportsCoach UK.

Balyi, I. and Hamilton, A. (2000) 'Key to success: Long-term athlete development', *Sports Coach*, 3: 30–32.

Barnsley, R. H. and Thompson, A. H. (1988) 'Birthdate and success in minor hockey: The key to the NHL', *Canadian Journal of Behavioral Science*, 20: 167–176.

Barnsley, R. H., Thompson, A. H. and Barnsley, P. E. (1985) 'Hockey success and birthdate: The relative age effect', *Canadian Association of Health, Physical Activity, Exercise, and Recreation Journal*, 51: 23–28.

Benson, A. C., Torode, M. E. and Singh, M. A. (2006) 'Muscular strength and cardio-respiratory fitness is associated with higher insulin sensitivity in children and adolescents', *International Journal of Pediatric Obesity*, 1: 222–231.

Cobley, S., Baker, J., Wattie, N. and McKenna, J. (2009) 'Annual age-grouping and athlete development: A meta-analytical review of relative age effects in sport', *Sports Medicine*, 39: 235–256.

Côté, J. and Hay, J. (2002) 'Children's involvement in sport: A developmental perspective', in J. M. Silva and D. Stevens (eds) *Psychological foundations of sport*, Boston, MA: Merrill.

Côté, J., Baker, J. and Abernethy, B. (2007) 'Practice and play in the development of sport expertise', in G. Tenebaum and R. C. Eklund (eds) *Handbook of sport psychology* (3rd edn), Hoboken, NJ: Wiley.

Drinkwater, E. J., Hopkins, W. G., McKenna, M. J., Hunt, P. H. and Pyne, D. B. (2007) 'Modelling age and secular differences in fitness between basketball players', *Journal of Sports Science*, 25: 869–878.

Ericsson, K. A. (1996) *The road to excellence: The acquisition of expert performance in the arts, and sciences, sports and games*, Mahwah, NJ: Lawrence Erlbaum Associates.

Ericsson, K. A. and Lehmann, A. C. (1996) 'Expert and exceptional performance: Evidence of maximal adaptation to task constraints', *Annual Reviews of Psychology*, 5: 25–57.

Ericsson, K. A., Krampe, R. T. and Tesch-Romer, C. (1993) 'The role of deliberate practice in the acquisition of expert performance', *Psychology Review*, 100: 363–406.

Faigenbaum, A. D., Kraemer, W. J., Blimkie, C. J., Jeffreys, I., Micheli, L. J., Nitka, M. and Rowland, T. W. (2009) 'Youth resistance training: Updated position statement paper from the national strength and conditioning association', *Journal of Strength and Conditioning Research*, 23: S60–79.

Ford, P., De Ste Croix, M., Lloyd, R., Meyers, R., Moosavi, M., Oliver, J., Till, K. and Williams, C. A. (2011) 'The Long-Term Athlete Development model: Physiological evidence and application', *Journal of Sport Sciences*, 29: 389–402.

Gagné, F. (1993) 'Constructs and models pertaining to exceptional human abilities', in K. A. Heller, F. J. Monks and A. H. Passow (eds) *International handbook of research and development of giftedness and talent*, Oxford: Pergamon Press.

Gesell, A. (1928) *Infancy and human growth*, New York: Macmillan.

Green, M. (2007) 'Olympic glory or grassroots development? Sport policy priorities in Australia, Canada and the United Kingdom, 1960–2006', *The International Journal of the History of Sport*, 24: 921–953.

Gustafsson, H., Kentta, G., Hassmen, P. and Lundqvist, C. (2007) 'Prevalence of burnout in competitive adolescent athletes', *The Sports Psychologist*, 21: 21–37.

Hall, G. S. (1921) *Aspects of child life and education*, New York: Appleton.

Kentta, G., Hassmen, P. and Raglin, J. (2001) 'Training practices and Overtraining Syndrome in Swedish age-group athletes', *International Journal of Sports Medicine*, 22: 460–465.

Lloyd, R. S. and Oliver, J. L. (2012) 'The Youth Physical Development Model: A new approach to long-term athletic development', *Strength and Conditioning Journal*, 34: 61–72.

Lubans, D. R., Morgan, P. J., Cliff, D. P., Barnett, L. M. and Okely, A. D. (2010) 'Fundamental movement skills in children and adolescents', *Sports Medicine*, 40: 1019–1035.

McGraw, M. B. (1935) *Growth: A study of Johnny and Jimmy*, New York: Appleton-Century.

Magill, R. A. (1982) 'Critical periods: Relation to youth sports', in Smoll, F. L., Magill, R. A. and Ash, M. (eds) Children in Sport (2nd edn), Champaign, IL: Human Kinetics, pp. 38–47.

Matos, N., Winsley, R. J. and Williams, C. A. (2011) 'Prevalence of non-functional overreaching/overtraining in young English athletes', *Medicine and Science in Sports and Exercise*, 43: 1287–1294.

Papaiakovou, G., Giannakos, A., Michailidis, C., Patikas, D., Bassa, E., Kalopisis, V., Anthrakidis, N. and Kotzamanidis, C. (2009) 'The effect of chronological age and gender on the development of sprint performance during childhood and puberty', *Journal of Strength and Conditioning Research*, 23: 2568–2573.

Raglin, J., Sawamura, S., Alexiou, S., Hassmen, P. and Kentta, G. (2000) 'Training practices and staleness in 13–18–year-old swimmers: A cross-cultural study', *Pediatric Exercise Science*, 12: 61–70.

Rumpf, M. C., Cronin, J. B., Oliver, J. L. and Hughes, M. (2011) 'Assessing youth sprint ability: Methodological issues, reliability and performance data', *Pediatric Exercise Science*, 23: 442–467.

Rumpf, M. C., Cronin, J. B., Pinder, S. D., Oliver, J. L. and Hughes, M. (2012) 'Effect of different training methods on running sprint times in male youth', *Pediatric Exercise Science*, 24: 170–186.

Russell, K. (1989) 'Athletic talent: From detection to perfection', *Science Periodical in Research and Technology Sport*, 9: 1–6.

Shaibi, G. Q., Cruz, M. L., Ball, G. D., Weigensberg, M. J., Salem, G. J., Crespo, N. C. and Goran, M. I. (2006) 'Effects of resistance training on insulin sensitivity in overweight Latino adolescent males', *Medicine and Science in Sports and Exercise*, 38, 1208–1215.

Tranckle, P. and Cushion, C. J. (2006) 'Rethinking giftedness and talent in sport', *Quest*, 58: 265–282.

UK Sport (2008) London 2012: It could be you. Talent identification and confirmation: The hunt for London 2012 talent. Available from: http://www.eis2win.co.uk/pages/talent_identification.aspx (accessed 25 January 2012).

Valovich McLeod, T. C., Decoster, L. C., Loud, K. J., Micheli, L. J., Parker, J. T., Sandrey, M. A. and White, C. (2011) 'National Athletic Trainers' Association position statement: Prevention of pediatric overuse injuries', *Journal of Athletic Training*, 46: 206–220.

Van Rossum, J. H. A. and Gagné, F. (2005) 'Talent development in sports', in F. A. Dixon and S. M. Moon (eds) *The handbook of secondary gifted education*. Waco, TX: Prufrock Press.

Williams, C. A., Oliver, J. and Faulkner, J. (2011) 'Seasonal monitoring of sprint and jump performance in a soccer youth academy', *International Journal of Sports Physiology and Performance*, 6: 264–275.

PART 2

Development of physical fitness qualities in youths

4

MOTOR SKILL DEVELOPMENT IN YOUTHS

Jeremy A. Moody, Fernando Naclerio, Paul Green and Rhodri S. Lloyd

Introduction

Many physiological changes related to growth and maturation occur at a rapid rate during childhood and adolescence (Malina *et al.*, 2004). Healthy youths show noticeable gains in stature, mass and measures of physical and physiological fitness during the developmental years, regardless of the inclusion of a structured conditioning programme. For example, muscular strength normally increases during childhood, and subsequently accelerates through adolescence (Malina *et al.*, 2004). Childhood is also a time where regions of the human brain, mainly the sensorimotor cortex, naturally develop at an accelerated rate (Casey *et al.*, 2005). Therefore, it is generally accepted that childhood offers a key time frame in which to learn and improve fundamental movement patterns and develop neuromuscular coordination; which, when combined with increased muscular force production, will lead to overall motor skill proficiency.

Of concern, a growing number of children are now presenting with insufficient levels of motor skill competency (Malina, 2008). For the general population this is typically due to the increasing sedentariness of youth, which, if not reversed, will ultimately lead to severe reductions in moderate to vigorous physical activity (MVPA), poor weight status and an increased likelihood of lifelong pathological processes, such as diabetes and cardiovascular disease (Faigenbaum and Myer, 2012; Lubans *et al.*, 2010; Stodden *et al.*, 2008). However, for young athletes, a leading antecedent of low motor skill proficiency is likely to be caused by early sport specialization, where a bias is directed towards sport-specific activity at the expense of global motor skill training developed via age-appropriate strength and conditioning programmes. Consequently, the implementation of integrative neuromuscular training (INT) programmes that incorporate a variety of essential motor skills (locomotion, stabilization and manipulation) and concomitant opportunities to develop strength and power, are deemed an essential strategy from which children can enrich their motor learning experience and maximize motor skill proficiency (Faigenbaum *et al.*, 2011; Myer *et al.*, 2011b). Targeting motor skill training during a child's developmental journey will enable them to take full advantage of the promoted natural windows for learning, and with the correct educational processes, help them progress and develop appropriate motor skill foundations (Myer *et al.*, 2011a). Environments enriched with this type of integrative training may not only assist youths in overcoming any genetic limitations (Cooper and Zubek, 1958), but may also help to achieve a level of motor performance that is beyond their expected adult potential (Myer *et al.*, 2011b). Of note for the strength and conditioning coach, previous research has also identified that the holistic mastery of fundamental movement skills (FMS) has injury-reducing potential for young athletes (Faigenbaum *et al.*, 2009; Granacher *et al.*, 2011).

Effective motor skill execution is governed by the efficient combination of cognitive processing, correct fundamental movement patterns and muscular force production. The development of muscular strength is covered in depth in Chapter 5; therefore, while reference will be made to the importance of muscular strength for motor skill function throughout, the primary focus of this chapter is the development of FMS in youth athletes, inclusive of locomotion, stabilization and manipulative skills.

Basic theoretical concepts

To assist in the further understanding of the content of this chapter, it is necessary to establish a clear definition for motor skill proficiency, and its relationship to FMS and functional sports skills (FSS) in the athletic development of youths. For the purposes of this chapter, motor skill proficiency will be viewed as the learning, practice and development of FMS and FSS in combination with sufficient muscular force production, resulting in efficient and effective movement across a multitude of physical activities and sporting activities.

Previous developmental literature suggests that early childhood offers a vital time frame in which to learn, practise and develop the key foundations of FMS to enhance motor skill competency, and maximize the chances of efficient FSS development at a later stage of maturity (Myer *et al.*, 2011a). Recently, authors have specifically suggested that strength and conditioning provision during early childhood should focus primarily on FMS and muscular strength development to ensure that children possess a broad array of generic movement qualities, but importantly have the requisite strength levels to ensure those movements are sufficiently robust (Lloyd and Oliver, 2012). The authors then suggest that as children enter adolescence, a greater emphasis should be placed on FSS and further strength and power development, but with a caveat of routinely revisiting FMS to avoid regression of key fundamental movements that may break down as a consequence of adolescent awkwardness (Lloyd and Oliver, 2012). As a result of this approach, it is expected that an individual will become 'physically literate' and therefore able to adjust and utilize a breadth of motor skills in response to the environment in which they are training or performing. Physically literate individuals would hopefully gain motor skill competency for a range of environments and surfaces, including on the ground, in the water and in the air.

In order to maximize the chances of developing a physically literate young athlete with a high level of motor skill proficiency, a number of simple movement capacities (such as trunk stability, balance, proprioceptive awarenesss and movement at different speeds and levels) will initially need to be mastered, which will in turn facilitate a faster and more effective transfer to combined and more complex capacities (such as rhythmical, inter-limb coordination, agility movements, multidirectional strength and power movements). The intended outcome is that a physically literate athlete would be able to achieve higher levels of athletic performance in comparison with their 'physically illiterate' counterparts who have not engaged in appropriate INT programmes.

The influence of growth and maturation on motor skill development

The natural development of motor skills

Throughout childhood and adolescence there are critical periods of time during which youths seem to have a high sensitivity for physical training and neuromuscular conditioning (Viru et al., 1999). While there is no single gene that codes for motor skill performance, there are nervous system limitations that differentiate between each individual's ability to exploit critical maturational thresholds for the development of motor skills (Davids and Baker, 2007; Rosengren et al., 2003). These skill-related tasks are more likely to be an accumulation of developed skills, and are driven by the interaction between genes and the environment in which they are subjected (Figure 4.1).

During childhood, the central nervous system (CNS) matures at an accelerated rate, and it is during this stage of development that the greatest potential for skill acquisition exists due to the heightened neural plasticity commensurate with this age group (Borms, 1986; Rabinowickz, 1986). For children, repeated exposure to a breadth of experiences results in the development of faster decision-making abilities and heightened proprioceptive awareness due to the strengthening of synaptic pathways and synaptic pruning of motor control strategies (Casey et al., 2005). The importance of ensuring children are exposed to a breadth of experiences in which to develop motor skills is underlined by Baker and colleagues (2003) who highlight that exposure to a variety of activities where common pattern recognition, hand–eye coordination and cognitive skills can be tested and developed, should aid in motor skill development and reduce the need for early specialization in a single sport. Such a holistic view to motor skill development is further reinforced

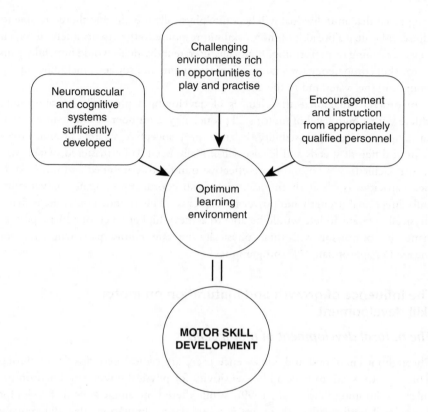

FIGURE 4.1 The process of accumulating developed motor skills via the interaction between genes and the environment in which they are subjected

by Abernethy *et al.* (2005), who suggested that exposure to a range of physical activities may indeed result in selective transfer of pattern recall skills and eventual facilitation of expert performance.

From the perspective of a youth strength and conditioning coach, childhood therefore offers the opportunity to ensure that foundational movement patterns are developed at the earliest possible age to prepare the athletes for more advanced forms of training at a later stage (Lloyd and Oliver, 2012). This would ensure that adolescent athletes have an established 'training age', thus enabling them to commence more advanced training strategies and loading schemes (Myer *et al.*, in press). However, in order to prepare children for advanced training methods such as weightlifting, high-intensity plyometrics and sport-specific speed and agility exercises, it is recommended that specific athletic motor skill competencies (AMSCs) should be integrated within the INT programmes of children (see Figure 4.2). The AMSCs depicted in Figure 4.2 are at some point in time present within global movement patterns. For example, unilateral lower-limb movements are present within running actions, therefore, INT programmes should incorporate exercises

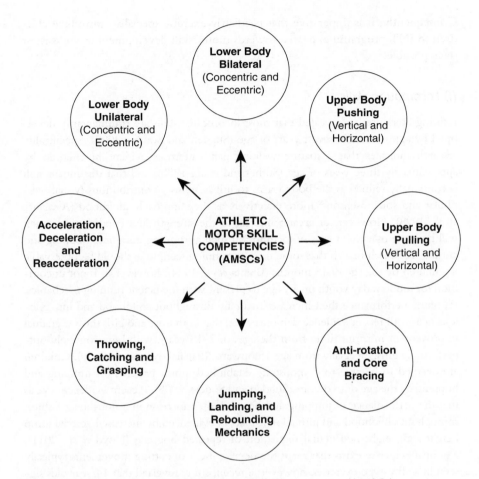

FIGURE 4.2 Components of Athletic Motor Skill Competencies (AMSCs)

that reinforce correct technical performance and muscular strength expression within such motor skills. It is speculated that such targeted INT prescription should help maximize performance and reduce injury.

Of note, it would appear that, irrespective of chronological or biological age, both children and adolescents could make noteworthy improvements in locomotive skills. However, research suggests that there exists a non-linear decrease in the volume of grey matter in the brain with age, especially following the onset of puberty as the process of synaptic pruning takes place (Gogtay *et al.*, 2004), thus making the ability to learn new motor skills more challenging as children become older. Therefore while pre-pubertal children may exhibit immature pre-frontal activation for cognitive control resulting in greater variation in motor control execution (Bunge *et al.*, 2002), their susceptibility for creating new synaptic pathways (synaptogenesis) is greater than adolescents and adults (Sowell *et al.*, 2001).

Consequently, it is imperative that paediatric exercise specialists introduce children to INT programmes geared towards motor skill development at the earliest stage possible.

(i) Locomotion skills

Existing literature has revealed that most locomotive skills are rudimentarily developed by approximately seven years of age (Sugden and Soucie, 2008). Specifically, research indicates that a mature walking gait pattern is evident in children by approximately three years of age (Sutherland *et al.*, 1980), and that this motor skill is continually refined as the body learns to utilize sensory contributions (visual, vestibular and somatosensory) more effectively as they approach adulthood (Assaiante *et al.*, 1998). However, of greater interest to the strength and conditioning coach will be more dynamic forms of locomotion such as running, jumping, hopping and cutting. Research reveals that some form of running technique should be observable in children by the age of 18 months (Branta *et al.*, 1984), however, it is not uncommon for modern day youth of any age to present with inefficient running mechanics. Running performance then increases naturally throughout childhood and into adolescence, with recent evidence demonstrating that both boys and girls show a gradual improvement in sprint times from the ages of 7–18 years, with boys routinely outperforming girls, especially from age 15 onwards (Papaiakovou *et al.*, 2009). Children are deemed to be able to demonstrate established motor patterns for jumping and hopping by the age of two years (Sugden and Soucie, 2008). Recent evidence reveals that the performance of jumping and hopping then increase in a non-linear fashion throughout childhood and into adolescence, as evidenced by increased vertcial jump height and heightened neural regulation of repeated hopping (Lloyd *et al.*, 2011). Minimal evidence exists that maps the development of cutting movements typically seen in agility-type exercises, however, a recent study revelaed that 14 year olds significantly outperformed 12 year olds in a variety of change of direction speed tasks (Jakovljevic *et al.*, in press), indicating a potential age or maturation effect.

(ii) Stabilization skills

The skills of balance and core stability are central to stabilization, and are both vital motor skills that have to be mastered by children prior to the achievement of higher levels of skill development (Karlsson and Frykberg, 2000; van Beurden *et al.*, 2002). Balance is the ability to stabilize the body in order to maintain posture during both static and dynamic situations. The process of balance relies on integrating information from the visual, vestibular and proprioceptive systems in order to elicit appropriate muscular responses to produce postural adjustments so that the body's centre of gravity is maintained over its base of support. As discussed previously, the most significant transitions in motor skill development occur in the first decade of life, with balance control usually established by the age of 8–10 years (Granacher *et al.*, 2011).

Despite the contribution of balance to overall motor skill proficiency, very few studies have investigated postural stability and control in otherwise healthy children. Mickle *et al.* (2011) observed increased levels of poor dynamic and static balance in a group of nine-year-old boys compared with girls. The authors suggested that maturation of the neurological, visual, vestibular and proprioceptive systems could occur earlier in girls such that they can perform, for example, the task of balancing on one leg more efficiently than boys. Previous studies in adults have reported that those with a pronated foot orientation, similar to a flatter foot, display reduced postural control compared to those adults with a neutral foot type (Tsai *et al.*, 2006). As foot position is a key factor for maintaining balance, the flatter foot structure – typically observed by boys compared with girls of the same age – may contribute to the explanation of reduced balance (Pfeiffer *et al.*, 2006). In addition it appears that proficiency in dual limb balance tasks may be obtained by the time children are around nine years of age (Haywood and Getchell, 2009), with no additional improvements reported when comparing ten-year-old children to their 11- or 12-year-old counterparts (Mickle *et al.*, 2011).

(iii) Manipulation skills

Manipulation skills such as grasping, throwing, catching and kicking typically improve with age as children's motor control strategies and levels of muscular strength improve (Sugden and Soucie, 2008). Additionally, manipulative skills will also require high levels of hand–eye coordination and an ability to perceive the depth and trajectory of projectiles (Haywood and Getchell, 2009). Grasping typically improves through the first two years of life and is an established motor skill by the age of 12–18 months (Sugden and Soucie, 2008). The skill of grasping continues to develop throughout childhood, with children displaying similar proficiency to adults by the age of 8–10 years (Schneiberg *et al.*, 2002). Of greater importance to the young athlete and those coaches implementing INT programmes will often be the ability to throw, kick and catch, and these skills become more proficient as children age. Studies examining manipulative development in children reveal that a proficient throwing technique (throwing with a forward step of the opposite leg with trunk rotation) is normally evident by approximately six years of age (Butterfield and Michaelloovis, 1993). Throwing performance, as measured by ball velocity, is reported to improve yearly from childhood to early adolescence, with boys consistently outperforming girls (Halverson *et al.*, 1982; Thomas *et al.*, 2010).

The trainability of motor skills

Existing developmental literature has demonstrated that locomotive skills (running, jumping and hopping), stabilization skills (balance and core stability) and manipulative skills (throwing and catching) can be enhanced when both children and adolescents participate in age-appropriate strength and conditioning programmes (Behringer *et al.*, 2011; Christou *et al.*, 2006; Faigenbaum *et al.*, 2007,

2011; Faigenbaum and Mediate, 2006; Granacher *et al.*, 2011; Ledebt *et al.*, 2005; Myer *et al.*, 2007; Thomas *et al.*, 2009). In most cases, these training interventions have included a combination of motor skill exercises, and some form of muscular strength and power development. For the purposes of this chapter, the trainability of each classification of motor skill will be reviewed independently.

(i) Locomotion skills

Previous research has shown that locomotive activities including running, jumping, cutting and hopping can be enhanced when children follow age-appropriate training programmes. For example, strength training (Buchell *et al.*, 2010; Lephart *et al.*, 2005), plyometric training (Thomas *et al.*, 2009), combined strength and power training (Faigenbaum *et al.*, 2007) and integrative neuromuscular training (Faigenbaum *et al.*, 2011) have all resulted in youths significantly improving their ability to perform various locomotive activities, such as running and jumping. Owing to the fact that greater relative ground reaction forces positively contribute to propulsion during locomotion (Cordova and Armstrong, 1996) and that strength is deemed a very important rate limiter in running (Clark and Whitall, 1989), it would appear that training interventions focusing on not just motor skill development but also on enhancing muscular strength will enable the young athlete to perform locomotive tasks more effectively and efficiently.

(ii) Stabilization skills

While balance training has been shown to be effective in significantly improving performance in children with hemiplegic cerebral palsy (Ledebt *et al.*, 2005), only a few studies have investigated the effects of selected balance exercise training in healthy children. Granacher *et al.* (2011) observed no effects of a specifically designed balance training programme on postural control, strength and jump performance of school children aged six to seven years old. Immaturity of the postural control system and deficits in intended foci during practice of balance exercises could be responsible for such results. Insufficient strength, muscular endurance and stability of the core may be specifically designed according to the level of performance, age and FSS of the individual (Myer *et al.*, 2011a). Thus, progressive trunk strengthening exercises should be included as part of an integrative neuromuscular training programme for all youths as a preventative measure to reduce the prevalence and severity of activity- and sports-related injuries to the spine. In children and adolescents the best strategy for improving balance and trunk control appears to be a combination of resistance-training exercises with or without displacement, combined with dynamic locomotive (jumps, hops, agility cuts) and manipulative (throws) tasks. Additionally, where appropriate, the inclusion of unstable surfaces to stress movement control may be specifically designed according the level of performance, age and FSS of the individual (Myer *et al.*, 2011a).

For children, the requirement to gain proficiency in postural control cannot be isolated, and consideration to both kinaesthetic and proprioceptive awareness is vital prior to the onset of puberty. Key to this development is the interaction of the young person with their learning environment and the people who are responsible for the creation of such an environment (Myer *et al.*, 2011a). Speculatively, if the ability to balance is not mastered during the early stages of athletic development, it can potentially reduce the efficiency of performing more complicated movement skills at later stages of development. Additionally, such deficiencies may increase the likelihood of a child sustaining an injury during these skills or during sports participation (Mickle *et al.*, 2011; Willems *et al.*, 2005).

(iii) Manipulation skills

Research has demonstrated that the integration of various exercise interventions can elicit improvements in key manipulative skills. Early work of Werner (1974) showed that an eight-week, twice-weekly FMS-driven training intervention during regular physical education classes was sufficient to enhance the throwing and kicking abilities of children aged three to five years of age. Similarly, 9–11-year-old children's ability to throw and catch was significantly improved following a six-month training intervention geared towards physical fitness and motor skill development (McKenzie *et al.*, 1998). More recently, Foweather and colleagues (2008) reported the effects of a nine-week multi-skills training programme on FMS proficiency in eight to nine-year-old children. Positive improvements were made by children who participated in the programme in their abilities to catch, throw and kick. While limited evidence exists into the effects of INT programmes on manipulative skill performance, it is reasonable to suggest that a combination of FMS and muscular strength training will transfer into increased muscular force production for all manipulative tasks. Additionally, from an injury prevention perspective, such training interventions should increase the active stability provided by the surrounding musculature of joints that are stressed during manipulative skills.

Practical applications

Motor skill training variables

Exercise selection

When planning training programmes to develop motor skill proficiency, it is imperative that the exercises selected are individualized, challenging, yet attainable for youths. For young children being introduced to INT programmes, a focus should be based on developing correct movement skills and improving muscular strength levels, within a fun-based environment. Over time, the level of exercise complexity can be increased in accordance with the training experience and motor skill ability of the individual. Stringent repetition and loading schemes that are successful with adults will typically be ineffective and potentially injurious for very young children. Therefore, the challenge for the strength and conditioning coach when working with young children is to design activities that are fun and interactive, yet contain key movement skills that will improve overall motor skill competency. Example exercises are provided in Figures 4.3 and 4.4. Figure 4.3 depicts a child moving across the floor in a 'spiderman' crawling position, where the child is unknowingly developing key athletic motor skills such as unilateral lower-body triple extension, hip mobilization, scapular stabilization, thoracic extension and core bracing. Figure 4.4 demonstrates a child performing a 'squat–throw–jump–catch', which involves moving from a semi-squat position, tossing a ball in the air, jumping to catch the ball, and landing in a universal athletic position (UAP). The exercise, while fun and challenging for the child, enables the development of skills such as upper-body vertical pushing (tossing the ball in the air), bilateral lower-limb concentric power (jumping to catch), manipulation (catching the ball) and bilateral lower-limb eccentric strength (landing in the UAP). The exercises selected within an age-appropriate INT programme are limited only by the imagination of the coach, however, it should be reiterated that at all times task complexity should not be increased at the expense of the quality or safety of movement.

While progression charts can be used to determine motor skill development and to assist the coach in the logical expectation process, and while many children will progress on the majority of occasions through the sequences in order, some children may skip elements of the developmental sequences and re-order them uniquely to their preferred learning style or stage of development. From a coaching standpoint, if coaches only possess a single method for development and adhere to the fact that each and every individual must do things a certain way, they are at risk of limiting the progression potential of children they are coaching. Fostering an environment in which children are encouraged to explore and create different movements is deemed important to enhance kinaesthetic awareness and global motor skill proficiency.

Session duration

Observations of children in recreational play activities reveal that brief periods of activity are intermittently mixed with periods of rest (Rowland, 1990). It has also been documented that children recover from high-intensity exercise more quickly than adults (Falk and Dotan, 2006). Therefore, it is recommended that the duration of INT sessions for very young children remain brief, with bouts of higher intensity exercise. Recent evidence has demonstrated that INT interventions of just 20 minutes at the start of a regular physical education lesson can make worthwhile improvements in a range of locomotor and stabilization motor skills (Faigenbaum *et al.*, 2011). While it is important to keep children interested by using a range of exercises and equipment, it is also vital that coaches have the opportunity to provide regular feedback of a positive nature to aid motor skill development.

FIGURE 4.3 A young child performing a 'Spiderman' crawling exercise

FIGURE 4.4 A young child performing a 'squat–throw–jump–catch' exercise

Volume and intensity

For young children embarking on an INT programme, the volume of exercises and repetitions will typically be higher than that prescribed for individuals with a greater training age, due to the relatively lower impact forces and joint loadings experienced during basic body-weight exercises, manipulation skills and stabilization tasks. In order to provide children with sufficient training exposure to aid motor control development, it is recommended that coaches prescribe approximately 2–4 sets of 6–12 repetitions (Lloyd *et al.*, 2012). However, for a child with some degree of training history who is being introduced to more complex movements, fewer repetitions with greater rest periods may be prescribed to enable time to provide real-time feedback (Lloyd *et al.*, 2012).

In comparison with traditional resistance training where intensity is commonly based on a percentage of one-repetition maximum (%1RM), motor skill training intensity is more challenging to determine, as children will typically only be working against gravitational forces in addition to their own body-weight. Therefore, training intensity could be based on the complexity of task for either locomotive, manipulative, stabilization or body-weight resistance exercises. For example, a static split squat position (unilateral lower-limb development) could be advanced by first asking the child to perform a number of walking lunges, which will stress dynamic stabilization in addition to locomotive competency. As a further progression, the child then performs the walking lunge while receiving a ball to catch, which will challenge all three of the FMS competencies. As with any training modality, should a child be unable to demonstrate continued technical competency, then the exercise should be stopped, corrective feedback provided and, should it be required, a regressive exercise administered instead.

Frequency

For general health and well-being, youths should participate in 60 minutes of MVPA per day (WHO, 2010). However, it is imperative that the higher intensity exercise typically experienced in formalized INT should be interspersed with at least 24 hours of rest (Faigenbaum *et al.*, 2009; Lloyd *et al.*, 2012). Previous research shows that performing an age-appropriate INT programme aimed at improving muscular strength and fundamental movement skills twice weekly is a sufficient training frequency to elicit positive training adaptations in locomotive and stabilizing motor tasks in pre-pubertal children (Faigenbaum *et al.*, 2011). Aside from the need to allow for recovery, it is also important to avoid young children becoming disinterested from overexposure to formalized training, therefore, in general it is recommended that children participate in structured INT sessions two or three days per week on non-consecutive days.

Repetition velocity

Certain exercises prescribed within a FMS development training programme will need to be performed slowly with control in order to sufficiently develop the correct movement patterns (Lloyd *et al.*, 2012). However, for the purposes of concentration retention, enjoyment and overall motor skill proficiency, coaches should also prescribe exercise that will require the child to move explosively. Such an approach will hopefully develop the child's ability to move correctly with appropriate form, but also enhance their neuromuscular coordination to produce movements with a high rate of force development. This will also help prepare the child for more advanced forms of training at a later stage of development.

Summary

An understanding of developmental processes and potential outcomes of well-developed and appropriately supervised INT programmes that incorporate opportunities to develop motor skills and muscular strength, will assist the strength and conditioning coach in the design of suitable training strategies to optimize positive adaptations in children's motor skill performance beyond a level achievable from growth and development alone. Moreover, INT is more likely to have optimal effects if qualified professionals who possess grounding in paediatric exercise science, and have previous experiences with the pedagogical intricacies of working with youth design, implement and coach the programmes. Regular participation in INT throughout childhood and into adolescence will likely improve movement mechanics, enhance force expression, minimize the risk of sports-related injury and promote positive long-term health outcomes in youths.

Key points

- Many of the locomotive, stabilization and manipulative skills should be mastered towards the end of childhood, however recent evidence would demonstrate that children are presenting with a lack of FMS proficiency.
- Due to the neural plasticity associated with childhood, this appears to be a vital time frame in which to develop motor skill performance through the use of INT programmes.
- Central to effective motor skill development is the combination of cognitive functioning, high-quality fundamental movement patterns and muscular strength.
- In addition to traditional FMS qualities (locomotion, stabilization and manipulation), children should also seek to develop generic athletic motor skill competencies to enable effective sports performance and advanced training strategies at a later stage of development.
- Numerous studies demonstrate that FMS can be enhanced through a variety of means, however INT may serve as a particularly effective method to develop motor skills, muscular strength and general fitness qualities.
- Within any motor skill development programme skills should be prescribed and coached from a basic to complex level. Training variables such as volume, intensity, frequency, duration and repetition velocity can easily be manipulated to integrate motor skill training into a long-term multifaceted programme.

References

Abernethy B., Baker, J. and Côté, J. (2005) 'Transfer of pattern recall skills may contribute to the development of sport expertise', *Applied Cognitive Psychology*, 19: 705–718.

Assaiante, C. (1998) 'Development of locomotor balance control in healthy children', *Neuroscience and Biobehavioral Review*, 22: 527–532.

Baker J., Côté, J. and Abernethy, B. (2003) 'Sport-specific practice and the development of expert decision-making in team ball sports', *Journal of Applied Psychology*, 15: 12–25.

Berhinger M., vom Heede, A., Matthews, M. and Mester, J. (2011) 'Effects of strength training on motor performance skills in children and adolescents: A meta-analysis', *Pediatric Exercise Science*, 23: 186–206.

Borms, J. (1986) 'The child and exercise: An overview', *Journal of Sports Sciences*, 4: 4–20.

Branta, C., Haubenstricker, J. and Seefeldt, V. (1984) 'Age changes in motor skills during childhood and adolescence'. In: R. J. Terjung (ed.) *Exercise and Sport Sciences Reviews*. Lexington, MA: Collamore.

Buchell, M., Mendez-Villanueva, A., Delhomel, G., Brughelli, M. and Ahmaidi, S. (2010) 'Improving sprint ability in young elite soccer players: Repeated shuttle sprints vs. explosive strength training', *Journal of Strength and Conditioning Research*, 24: 2715–2722.

Bunge, S. A., Dudukovic, N. M., Thomason, M. E., Vaidya, C. J. and Gabrieli, J. D. E. (2002) 'Immature frontal lobe contributions to cognitive control in children: Evidence from fMRI', *Neuron*, 33: 301–311.

Butterfield, S. A. and Michaelloovis, E. (1993) 'Influence of age, sex, balance, and sport participation on development of throwing by children in grades K-8', *Perceptual and Motor Skills*, 76: 459–464.

Casey, B. J., Tottenham, N., Liston, C. and Durston, S. (2005) 'Imaging the developing brain: What have we learned about cognitive development', *Trends in Cognitive Sciences*, 9: 104–110.

Christou, M., Smilios, I., Sotiropoulos, K., Volaklis, K., Pilianidis, T. and Tokmakidis, S. P. (2006) 'Effects of resistance training on the physical capacities of adolescent soccer players', *Journal of Strength and Conditioning Research*, 20: 783–791.

Clark, J. E. and Whittall, J. (1989) 'Changing patterns of locomotion: From walking to skipping'. In: M. H. Woolacott and A. Shumway-Cook (eds) *Development of posture and gait across the life span*. Columbia: University of South Carolina Press.

Cools, W., De Martelaer, K., Samaey, C. and Andries, C. (2009) 'Movement skill assessment of typically developing preschool children: A review of seven movement skill assessment tools', *Journal of Sports Science and Medicine*, 8: 154–168.

Cooper, R. M. and Zubek, J. P. (1958) 'Effects of enriched and restricted early environments on the learning ability of bright and dull rats', *Canadian Journal of Psychology*, 12: 159–164.

Cordova, M. L. and Armstrong, C. W. (1996) 'Reliability of ground reaction forces during a vertical jump: Implications for functional strength assessment', *Journal of Athletic Training*, 31: 342–345.

Davids, K. and Baker, J. (2007) 'Genes, environment and sport performance: Why the nature–nurture dualism is no longer relevant', *Sports Medicine*, 37: 961–980.

Faigenbaum, A. D. and Mediate, P. (2006) 'The effects of medicine ball training on physical fitness in high school physical education students', *The Physical Educator*, 63: 160–167.

Faigenbaum, A. D. and Myer, G. D. (2012) 'Exercise Deficit Disorder in youth: Play now or pay later', *Current Sports Medicine Reports*, 11: 196–200.

Faigenbaum, A. D., Farrell, A., Fabiano, M., Radler, T., Naclerio, F., Ratamess, N. A., Kang, J. and Myer, G. D. (2011) 'Effects of integrative neuromuscular training on fitness performance in children', *Pediatric Exercise Science*, 23: 573–584.

Faigenbaum, A. D., Kraemer, W. J., Blimkie, C. J., Jeffreys, I., Micheli, L. J., Nitka, M. and Rowland, T. W. (2009) 'Youth resistance training: Updated position statement paper from the National Strength and Conditioning Association', *Journal of Strength and Conditioning Research*, 23: S60–S79.

Faigenbaum, A. D., McFarland, J. E., Keiper, F. B., Tevlin, W., Ratamess, N. A., Kang, J. and Hoffman, J. R. (2007) 'Effects of a short-term plyometric and resistance training program on fitness in boys age 12 to 15 years', *Journal of Sports Science and Medicine*, 6: 519–525.

Falk, B. and Dotan, R. (2006) 'Child-adult differences in the recovery from high-intensity exercise', *Exercise and Sport Sciences Reviews*, 34: 107–112.

Foweather, L., McWhannel, N., Henaghan, J., Lees, A., Stratton, G. and Batterham, A. (2008) 'Effect of a 9–week after school multiskills club on fundamental movement skill proficiency in 8 to 9 year old children: An exploratory trial', *Perceptual and Motor Skills*, 106: 745–754.

Gogtay, N., Giedd, J. N., Lusk, L., Hayashi, K. M., Greenstein, D., Vaituzis, A. C., Hugent, T. F., Herman, D. H., Clasen, L. S., Toga, A. W., Rapoport, J. L. and Thompson, P. M. (2004) 'Dynamic mapping of human cortical development during childhood through early adulthood', *PNAS*, 101: 8174–8179.

Granacher, U., Muehlauer, T., Maestrini, L., Zahner, L. and Gollhofer, A. (2011) 'Can balance training promote balance and strength in pre-pubertal children?' *Journal of Strength and Conditioning Research*, 25: 1759–1766.

Halverson, L. E., Roberton, M. A. and Langendorfer, S. (1982) 'Development of the overarm throw: Movement and horizontal ball velocity changes by seventh grade', *Research Quarterly for Exercise and Sport*, 53: 198–205.

Haywood, K. M. and Getchell, N. (2009) *Life Span Motor Development*, Champaign, IL: Human Kinetics.

Jakovljevic, S. T., Karalejic, M. S., Pajic, Z. B., Macura, M. M. and Erculj, F. F. (in press) 'Speed and agility of 12 and 14 years old elite male basketball players', *Journal of Strength and Conditioning Research*.

Karlsson, A. A. and Frykberg, G. G. (2000) 'Correlations between force plate measures for assessment of balance', *Clinical Biomechanics*, 15: 365–369.

Ledebt, A., Becher, J., Kapper, J., Rozendaal, R. M., Bakker, R., Leenders, I. C. and Savelsbergh, G. J. P. (2005) 'Balance training with visual feedback in children with hemiplegic cerebral palsy: Effect on stance and gait', *Motor Control*, 9: 459–468.

Lephart, S. M., Abt, J. P., Ferris, C. M., Sell, C. T., Nagai, T., Meyers, J. B. and Irrgang, J. J. (2005) 'Neuromuscular and biomechanical characteristic changes in high school athletes: A plyometric versus basic resistance programme', *British Journal of Sports Medicine*, 39: 932–938.

Lloyd, R. S. and Oliver, J. L. (2012) 'The Youth Physical Development model: A new approach to long-term athletic development', *Strength and Conditioning Journal*, 34: 61–72.

Lloyd, R. S., Oliver, J. L., Hughes, M. G. and Williams, C. A. (2011) 'The influence of chronological age on periods of accelerated adaptation of stretch-shortening cycle performance in pre- and post-pubescent boys', *Journal of Strength and Conditioning Research*, 25: 1889–1897.

Lloyd, R. S., Oliver, J. L., Meyers, R. W., Moody, J. A. and Stone, M. H. (2012) 'Long-term athletic development and its application to youth weightlifting', *Strength and Conditioning Journal*, 34: 55–66.

Lubans, D. R., Morgan, P. J., Cliff, D. P., Barnett, L. M. and Okely, A. D. (2010) 'Fundamental movement skills in children and adolescents', *Sports Medicine*, 40: 1019–1035.

McKenzie, T. L., Alcaraz, J. E., Sallis, J. F. and Faucette, F. N. (1998) 'Effects of a physical education program on children's manipulative skills', *Journal of Teaching in Physical Education*, 17: 327–341.

Malina, R. (2008) 'Skill acquisition in childhood and adolescence'. In: H. Hebestreit and O. Bar-Or (eds) *The Young Athlete*. Oxford: Blackwell.

Malina, R. M., Bouchard, C. and Bar-Or, O. (2004) *Growth, Maturation, and Physical Activity*, Champaign, IL: Human Kinetics.

Mickle, K. J., Munro, B. J. and Steele, J. R. (2011) 'Gender and age affect balance performance in primary school-aged children', *Journal of Science and Medicine in Sport*, 14: 243–248.

Myer, G. D., Faigenbaum, A. D., Chu, D., Falkel, J., Ford, K. and Best, T. (2011a) 'Integrative training for children and adolescents: Techniques and practices for reducing sports-related injuries and enhancing athletic performance', *The Physician and Sportsmedicine*, 39: 74–84.

Myer, G. D., Faigenbaum, A. D., Ford, K. R., Best, T. M., Bergeron, M. F. and Hewett, T. E. (2011b) 'When to initiate integrative neuromuscular training to reduce sports-related injuries and enhance health in youth?' *Current Sports Medicine Reports*, 10: 157–166.

Myer, G. D., Ford, K. R., Palumbo, J. P. and Hewett, T. E. (2005) 'Neuromuscular training improves performance and lower-extremity biomechanics in female athletes', *Journal of Strength and Conditioning Research*, 19: 51–60.

Myer, G. D., Lloyd, R. S., Brent, J. L. and Faigenbaum, A. D. (in press) 'What "age" should kids start training', *ACSM Heath and Fitness Journal*.

Papaiakovou, G., Athanasios, G., Charalampos, M., Dimitrios, P., Bassa, E., Kalopsis, V., Anthrakidis, N. and Kotzamanidis, C. (2009) 'The effect of chronological age and gender on the development of sprint performance during childhood and puberty', *Journal of Strength and Conditioning Research*, 23: 2568–2673.

Pfeiffer, M., Kotz, R., Ledl, T., Hauser, G. and Sluga, M. (2006) 'Prevalence of flat foot in preschool-aged children', *Pediatrics*, 118: 634–639.

Rabinowickz, T. (1986) 'The differentiated maturation of the cerebral cortex'. In: F. Falkner and J. Tanner (eds) *Human Growth: A Comprehensive Treatise, Postnatal Growth: Neurobiology*, New York: Plenum.

Rosengren, K. S., Savelsbergh, G. J. P. and van der Kamp, J. (2003) 'Development and learning: A TASC-based perspective of the acquisition of perceptual-motor behaviors', *Infant Behavior and Development*, 26: 473–494.

Rowland, T. W. (1990) *Exercise and Children's Health*, Champaign, IL: Human Kinetics.

Schneiberg, S., Sveistrup, H., McFayden, B., McKinley, P. and Levin, M. F. (2002) 'The development of coordination for reach-to-grasp movements in children', *Experimental Brain Research*, 146: 142–154.

Sowell, E. R., Thompson, P. M. and Toga, A. W. (2001) 'Mapping continued brain growth and gray matter density reduction in dorsal frontal cortex: Inverse relationship during postadolescent brain maturation', *The Journal of Neuroscience*, 21: 8819–8829.

Stodden, D. F., Goodway, J. D., Langendorfer, S. J., Roberton, M. A., Rudisill, M. E., Garcia, C. and Garcia, L. E. (2008) 'A developmental perspective on the role of motor skill competence in physical activity: An emergent relationship', *Quest*, 60: 290–306.

Sugden, D. A. and Soucie, H. C. (2008) 'Motor development'. In: N. Armstrong and W. van Mechelen (eds) *Paediatric Exercise Medicine*. Oxford: Oxford University Press.

Sutherland, D. H., Olshen, R., Cooper, L. and Woo, S. L. (1980) 'The development of mature gait', *The Journal of Bone and Joint Surgery*, 62: 336–353.

Tsai, L. C., You, B., Mercer, V. S. and Gross, M. T. (2006) 'Comparison of different structural foot types for measures of standing postural control', *The Journal of Orthopaedic and Sports Physical Therapy*, 36: 942–953.

Thomas, J. R., Alderson, J. A., Thomas, K. T., Campbell, A. C. and Elliott, B. C. (2010) 'Developmental gender differences for overhand throwing in aboriginal Australian children', *Research Quarterly for Exercise and Sport*, 81: 432–441.

Thomas, K., French, D. and Hayes, P. R. (2009) 'The effect of plyometric training techniques on muscular power and agility in youth soccer players', *Journal of Strength and Conditioning Research*, 23: 332–335.

van Beurden, E., Zask, A., Barnett, L. M. and Dietrich, U. C. (2002) 'Fundamental movement skills: how do primary school children perform? The "Move it Groove it" program in rural Australia', *Journal of Science and Medicine in Sport*, 5: 244–252.

Viru, A., Loko, J., Harro, M., Volver, A., Laaneots, L. and Viru, M. (1999) 'Critical periods in the development of performance capacity during childhood and adolescence', *European Journal of Physical Education*, 4: 75–119.

Werner, P. (1974) 'Education of selected movement patterns of preschool children', *Perceptual and Motor Skills*, 39: 795–798.

Willems, T. M., Witvrouw, E., Delbaere, K., Mahieu, N., Bourdeaudhuij, L. and De Clercq, D. (2005) 'Intrinsic risk factors for inversion ankle sprains in male subjects: A prospective study', *American Journal of Sports Medicine*, 33: 415–423.

World Health Organization (WHO) (2010) *Global Recommendations on Physical Activity for Health*, Geneva, Switzerland: WHO Press.

5

STRENGTH DEVELOPMENT IN YOUTHS

Duncan N. French, Thomas Jones and William J. Kraemer

Introduction

Resistance training exercises that focus on the development of muscular strength and power have gained increasing popularity among children and youth populations. Growing numbers of adolescents now use resistance training as part of their preparation for sport performance and athletic events, while medical professionals are also recognizing the beneficial effects that resistance training can offer to healthy lifestyles and physical well-being. Historically, resistance training in children has been met with scepticism and controversy; largely as a consequence of misunderstandings about the objectives of resistance training and its potential dangers. Today, however, there is little doubt that, when performed correctly, resistance training and weightlifting can produce marked increases in strength and power among children and adolescents. Indeed, the benefits of a correctly prescribed resistance-training programme with competent supervision and correct coaching of exercise techniques now appear to far outweigh any potential risks (Faigenbaum *et al.*, 2009; Hamill, 1994). This chapter will explore how resistance training can be used safely and effectively to promote strength development in children and adolescent populations.

The development of muscular strength during childhood and adolescence

The natural development of muscular strength

The physiology of children and adolescents is complex, with natural growth and maturation resulting in increased muscle size, improved neural function and concomitant gains in muscular strength. Prior to puberty, anabolic hormone concentrations are low, which limits the potential for significant changes in muscle architecture (i.e.

muscle hypertrophy). Natural strength gains in pre-pubescent children are therefore likely regulated through neurological factors (Bernhardt *et al.*, 2001), with strength variations between individuals the consequence of different neural drive to the muscle, changes in motor unit synchronization or various inhibitory mechanisms. Following puberty, the internal anabolic hormonal milieu differs greatly between adolescents, inducing substantive differences in both muscle size and strength between children of the same age and training experience. Such differing endocrine profiles likely account for individual maturation responses, and thus explain the wide range of physical performance standards represented in post-pubescent populations. Interestingly, not all increases in strength development can be accounted for by changes in muscle architecture and/or neural adaptations alone. There remains evidence for an 'age effect' by which older children are simply stronger, relative to body mass, when compared to younger counterparts (Weir *et al.*, 1999).

The trainability of muscular strength

Effectively designed resistance-training programmes can enhance the muscular strength and power characteristics of children and adolescents beyond that produced by normal growth and development (Falk and Tenenbaum, 1996; Payne *et al.*, 1997). Beneficial strength gains have been demonstrated using a variety of resistance-training approaches; from single-set workouts with weight machines (Faigenbaum *et al.*, 2002, 2005), to multiple-set protocols using free weights (Benson *et al.*, 2007; Faigenbaum *et al.*, 2007), medicine balls (Faigenbaum and Mediate, 2006; Szymanski *et al.*, 2007), elastic bands (Annesi *et al.*, 2005) and body-weight exercises (Falk and Mor, 1996). Following short-term resistance training (8–20 weeks) in adolescents, gains in muscular strength of approximately 30 per cent can be expected; however, gains of up to 74 per cent have been observed in some previously untrained youths (Faigenbaum *et al.*, 1993, 2009). While all children respond favourably to appropriate resistance-training stimuli (e.g. 1–2 sets of 10–15 repetitions at 60–70 per cent), exaggerated individual variability should be expected in youth populations. This variability is likely the consequence of factors beyond the specifics of training programme design; including individual genetics, training experience and personal motivation (Faigenbaum, 2011). Furthermore, the acute hormonal increases observed in adults consequent to a single bout of resistance-type exercise are not seen in the same fashion with youth populations. Instead, overall exposure to anabolic pathways is significantly smaller (Fleck and Kraemer, 2004), and consequently the recruitment and up-regulation of neural signals continues to predominate in order to effectively manage the required force–output demands.

Health and fitness benefits of youth resistance training

Physical activity promotes natural growth and maturation and has wide-ranging health-related benefits that assist physical well-being and vitality in children (Falk and Tenenbaum, 1996). When habitual activity and informal play is complemented by age-appropriate resistance training, unique benefits can be observed in several indices of health and fitness, including musculoskeletal strength, body composition, cardiovascular risk factors, movement competency and psychosocial well-being (Faigenbaum *et al.*, 2009; Stodden *et al.*, 2009). Indeed, evidence indicates overall health is seen to improve, rather than be adversely affected, by regular participation in resistance training.

Bone health

A common and outdated misconception relating to youth strength training is that it is linked to attenuated bone growth and development. Historically, 'improper' resistance training was reported to cause damage to the epiphyseal plates (growth plates) at the ends of long bones in children and adolescents. Contrary to the majority of these misconceptions however, research indicates that childhood and adolescence is in fact the most opportune time for bones to respond to the compressive and tensile forces experienced during weight-bearing exercise (Falk and Eliakim, 2003; Turner and Robling, 2003; Vicente-Rodriguez, 2006). While peak bone mass is primarily influenced by genetic factors, regular participation in resistance training can significantly improve both bone mineral density (BMD) and total bone mass (TBM). Most methods of strength training elicit some form of skeletal adaptation; however exercise 'intensity' as opposed to 'duration' is the key determinant for improving bone health in adolescents.

Elite junior and adolescent weightlifters display above normative values of BMD and TBM compared to sedentary controls (Conroy *et al.*, 1993; Virvidakis *et al.*, 1990). Elsewhere, high-impact circuit training and plyometric jumps have been found to result in augmented BMD and TBM compared with age-matched controls not performing 'resistance training' (Linden *et al.*, 2006; McKay *et al.*, 2005; MacKelvie *et al.*, 2004). While the compressive and tensile forces experienced during load-bearing activities are directly beneficial to bone health, the associated increases in lean tissue mass and muscle strength also support aggregation of bone mass. With developing muscle capabilities it is possible to place more force on skeletal structures and thus augment osteogenic responses (Pietrobelli *et al.*, 2002). Eccentric strength training may be more beneficial to osteogenic adaptation than concentric training (Hawkins *et al.*, 1999), as eccentric contractions produce up to 25 per cent greater tensile force.

Body composition

In the past 20 years societal changes have resulted in decreased physical activity rates among adolescents. Limited exposure to physical exertion can lead to obesity and excessive weight gain, which in turn result in inhibited motor skills and lower self-confidence, further reducing the desire to participate in physical activity, sport and exercise (Ogden *et al.*, 2006). Recent research has demonstrated that strength training in youths can significantly improve lean mass and reduce body fat (Lillegard *et al.*, 1997; Watts *et al.*, 2004). Compared with typically prescribed forms of exercise for youth (e.g. light jogging, small-sided team games), resistance training is less aerobically taxing and enables overweight and obese adolescents to successfully participate in physical activity with a reduced risk of injury. Furthermore, due to increased muscular strength and functionality experienced as a result of resistance training, body-weight aerobic-type exercise may also be indirectly augmented (Watts *et al.*, 2005).

Cardiovascular risk factors

Hypertension and various cardiac risk factors are on the rise in young people due to increased inactivity (WHO, 2010). Resistance training represents an effective non-pharmacologic method of managing blood pressure. In hypertensive youths showing typical cardiovascular risk factors, resistance training was reported to lower blood pressure when included in a training programme that also involved aerobic exercise (Ewart *et al.*, 1998). Furthermore, cross-sectional data from youths who regularly participate in strength training indicates improved blood lipid profiles compared with their untrained age-matched counterparts (Shaibi *et al.*, 2006; Weltman *et al.*, 1987).

Psychosocial health

While social and psychological health improvements have rarely been associated with resistance training, this exercise modality may in fact have a positive impact on self-efficacy, confidence, self-esteem and body image (Tucker, 1987). Significantly improved self-efficacy and general self-esteem scores were found in female adolescents who completed a 12-week, school-based resistance-training programme (Tucker, 1987). This data indicates that engaging children in age-appropriate, strength-training programmes may have a beneficial impact on psychosocial perception and possibly defend against negativity and depressive states.

Practical applications

Hazards and safety considerations

The primary concern with resistance training and strength development in youth populations is safety. Several studies examining resistance training have, however, indicated a low risk of injury when age-appropriate training guidelines are followed (Falk and Tenenbaum, 1996). For example, with qualified instruction and step-wise progression, significant gains in muscular strength can be achieved without incidence of injury when weightlifting movements (i.e. snatch, clean and jerk, pulls and presses) are incorporated into youth resistance-training programmes. In comparison with traditional sporting activities such as gymnastics, basketball and soccer, weightlifting actually has lower reported injury rates among high school students (Faigenbaum and Myer, 2010; Hamill, 1994; Zaricznyj et al., 1980). Therefore, as a general rule, if a child or adolescent is ready to participate in organized sporting activities (generally aged 7 or 8 years), then it is likely they will be ready to partake in some form of organized strength training (Faigenbaum, 2011).

Programme design considerations

When considering resistance-training programme design, children and adolescents should begin with a basic training strategy that challenges all the major muscle groups of the body and around each joint (Fleck and Kraemer, 2004). At the earliest stage in the long-term development of a child, a 'general' approach to holistic physical conditioning and whole-body strengthening should be employed. No major distinction between boys and girls needs to be made regarding strength training. Instead, the successful performance of a particular exercise technique or movement skill depends on the strength and power of muscle groups used and not the gender of the participant.

The manner in which the acute training variables are manipulated over time ultimately determines the nature of the exercise stress and desired physiological adaptations. In youth populations, determining individual goals based on current performance standards, training history, and physical and psychological tolerance is critical. Table 5.1 gives an overview of the primary training variables that should be considered when designing strength development programmes for youths.

Training frequency

With any physical training programme designed for children and youths, it is critical that a holistic approach to developing all facets of motor performance is addressed, including cardiovascular fitness, speed, strength and power, flexibility, and balance and coordination. It is important, however, that the overall workload placed on youths (i.e. frequency of training) is appropriately managed and does not cause excessive physical exertion with inadequate amounts of rest. Ideally, strength- and power-specific training should be performed two to three times per week on non-consecutive days (Faigenbaum et al., 2009), alongside physical training for other biomotor qualities. Strength training one day per week is considered suboptimal and is only likely to maintain existing standards. By comparison, strength training twice or three times per week on non-consecutive days will allow children adequate recovery (48–72 hours) and would be effective for enhancing muscular strength and power capabilities (Faigenbaum et al., 2002). In planning training frequency, coaches and instructors should take caution trying to adopt similar periodization strategies as adults. Instead, variation in a youth resistance-training programme can be accomplished by following simple guidelines (Table 5.2).

TABLE 5.1 Acute training variable considerations

Variable	Specifics
Type of resistance	Body weight Medicine balls Elastic bands Fixed weight machines Free weights
Choice of exercise	Primary exercises Assistance exercises Multi-joint exercises Single-joint exercises Exercise equipment
Order of exercises	Primary exercises followed by assistance exercises Larger muscle groups followed by smaller muscle groups Lagging muscle groups trained first Straight sets for each exercise Super sets Complex training sets Cluster sets
Number of sets	Volume effect Single sets Multiple sets Number of sets per exercise Number of sets per muscle group Number of sets per workout session
Resistance (intensity)	Percentage of 1RM RM target zone Prescribed repetition range Incremental resistance Fixed resistance
Rest periods	Dependent on resistance used Dependent on muscle adaptation desired Dependent on metabolic pathway being trained Dependent on exercise technique

Notes: 1RM = one repetition maximum; RM = repetition maximum.

TABLE 5.2 Periodization model and concepts for youths

Training phase	Sets	Repetitions (RM range)
Base	3	10–15
Strength	3	6–10
Power	2–3	6–8
Peaking	1–2	5–8
Active rest	Unstructured physical activity (not resistance training)	

Source: adapted from Fleck and Kraemer (2004).

Note: RM = repetition maximum.

Exercise modality

The importance of selecting exercises that are appropriate for a child's body size, fitness level and technical competency is well established (Faigenbaum, 2011). From the outset, children should begin the process of strength development by engaging in exercises that develop their ability to manage body mass competently, and to perform gross whole-body movements in a controlled and coordinated fashion (e.g. body-weight squats, body-weight lunges, push-ups, body-weight pull-ups). The value of performing body-weight exercises with accuracy and technical proficiency should be promoted throughout, and children should initially be removed from the proprioceptively starved environment of fixed-weight machines, and instead be instructed on how to build foundational strength levels by controlling their own body mass in a variety of push, pull, squat and lunge movement patterns. Engaging with ground-based, whole-body, multiple-joint movements that rely on body-weight loads will allow young people to develop essential functional capabilities. This will serve to promote future strength gains at the point when additional external loading and resistance is introduced.

After progressing from ground-based body-weight exercises, elastic bands, medicine balls, manual-resistance, suspension training and, ultimately, free weights (both dumbbells and barbells) all represent suitable methods of progressive overload. As youths become stronger and more technically competent, then higher intensity exercises such as plyometrics and weightlifting movements (e.g clean and jerk, snatch) can be prioritised. However, regardless of the exercise modality of choice, performing a given motor task with proficiency and the correct technique is *always* the most appropriate way to make strength development advances at this stage.

Training intensity and volume

The design of strength-training programmes ultimately comes down to the management of resistance or load (i.e. intensity), and the number of sets and reps of an exercise performed at a given intensity (i.e. volume). The manner in which these variables are manipulated has a direct influence on: i) metabolic challenge; ii) fatigue levels; and iii) the extent to which the neuromuscular system is activated. Both intensity and volume should have a significant impact on the programming strategy for youth strength training, as they not only regulate the capacity to develop force expression characteristics, but can also offer the greatest risk of injury or overtraining to youths participating in resistance-type exercise.

Intensity is often considered the major factor affecting injury risk in youth strength-training programmes. Finding an appropriate balance between an intensity (i.e. load) that induces strength adaptations, while at the same time minimizing the risk of injury to epiphyseal growth plates and maturing tissues, is particularly challenging. As a general rule, lighter loads should initially be used in an effort to emphasize correct exercise techniques at the expense of any higher intensity loads. However, in a progressive fashion, intensity can be gradually increased over time. This may take weeks or even months, which underlines the importance of patience when coaching children and adolescents. Each time a new intensity is introduced to a training programme, emphasis of correct exercise techniques should be re-established and routinely monitored. Exercise technique should remain robust enough to handle the incremental loading at all times, and it is often this factor that will determine the rate at which progression can be made.

While training volume is determined by adjusting the number of sets and reps performed for a given exercise, there is no hard or fast rule that indicates all exercises should be performed for the same volume. In youth populations, 1–3 sets of the same exercise most likely provides sufficient training stimulus. Any more than this and too much demand may be placed on the child, or the individual might become disillusioned by the lack of variety, thus drawing focus away from performing an exercise accurately. Inter-set rest periods should allow sufficient neuromuscular and metabolic recovery in order to ensure that exercises can be performed with competence for ensuing sets. When fatigue significantly impacts exercise technique, then rest periods should be extended in order to support adequate recovery. This can largely be dependent upon the individual, but rest periods of 30–120s represent the norm.

The number of repetitions youth populations should perform for a given exercise can be anywhere between 5–20. Repetition number is largely a reflection of the external load, technical competence and the physical exertion required to perform a single repetition. When initially determining appropriate numbers of repetitions for a given exercise, establishing a 'repetition range' represents a suitable approach. Using this method, exercises are prescribed for a set number of repetitions (e.g. 15–20 reps). Beginning with a relatively light load to develop correct technique allows the maximum load that can be performed for the required number of repetitions to be determined by progressively increasing external resistance. As an individual improves and is able to lift heavier loads, then either the number of sets can be increased (e.g. from 1–2 sets) or a smaller repetition range (e.g. 6–8 reps) at a heavier load can be prescribed.

Example strength development programmes

This section highlights two example resistance-training programmes designed to develop the strength characteristics in children and adolescents. As an introductory strategy, training plans that focus on the use of body-weight exercises provide resistance. As a progression from body-weight training, the use of various pieces of resistance-training equipment can then further increase the neuromuscular demand.

Body-weight strength training

Body-weight strength training refers to workouts that stress most major muscle groups of the body while using the body mass of the individual to create resistance against which the muscle must produce force. This training strategy allows for large amounts of variety, thus meaning individual training bouts can be performed up to three times per week, for example on Monday, Wednesday and Friday, allowing for a day off between each session. Many experts believe frequency of training is important for gaining strength, and using a whole-body approach can be an effective means to do this in youth populations. As older adolescents often have a limited *training history*, the best way for youth of all ages to begin developing strength, irrespective of maturity status, is to use slightly higher repetitions of body-weight exercises which are performed more frequently, but at lower intensities.

Whole-body workouts usually include one exercise per major muscle group. Throughout a training week the order in which the exercises are performed should be changed. That way, each major exercise is trained at least once per week when the body is fresh. The programme can be performed as a circuit, moving from one exercise to the next, or in a set-repetition manner by which all sets of a given exercise are performed before moving onto the next. In certain circumstances, for example when an individual has developed a good tolerance to the desired number of repetitions, it may be that exercises are instead performed for a given work time (e.g. 30s), thus emphasizing *strength endurance* qualities. An example three-day body-weight training programme is shown in Table 5.3.

Free-weight strength training

Table 5.4 outlines a programme involving the use of free weights or resistance-training machines. At the start of this training programme the resistance used for each exercise should be such that the minimum number of repetitions can be performed. This load should be retained until the individual is able to perform the desired maximum number of repetitions for consecutive weeks; at which point a heavier load can be chosen and the minimum number of repetitions is once again performed.

TABLE 5.3 Body-weight strength training programme for youths

Workout 1: Monday		
Exercise	*Sets*	*Repetitions*
Parallel box squats	3	12–15
Inverted row	2	5–8
Hip bridge (feet on box)	2	8–10
Plank elbow to hand walks	3	8–10
Partner-resisted lateral arm raise	2	6–10
Front plank	3	30 s
Back foot elevated single leg squats	2	5–6 each
Bent knee windscreen wipers	3	8–10
Workout 2: Wednesday		
Push-ups	3	8–15
Walking lunges	3	8–12
45° chin-ups (feet on ground)	2	6–10
Swiss ball wall squats	2	8–12
Cat licks	2	5–8
Lying back extensions	3	8–12
Split-squat jump cycles	3	8–16
Side plank hip lifts	3	8–12 each
Workout 3: Friday		
Jump squats	3	5–8
Hand walk/crawl	3	10–20 m
High-knee step up	3	6–10 each
Tricep bench dips (feet raised)	2	8–12
Alternate lateral lunge	2	8–12
Decline push-ups (feet on low box)	2	6–10
Slow sit-ups (10 s)	3	3–5
Kneeling alternate arm/leg raise	3	8–12

An effective way to create variety in whole-body free-weight workouts for youth populations, yet maintaining structure in the training plan, is to adopt a 'push–pull' training split. This approach divides workouts into 'pushing' exercises one day, and 'pulling' exercises another. Push days should be separated from pull days by a rest day that does not include any form of resistance-training exercises. In doing so, it would likely mean that within one week there may be two push days and one pull, and the following there would be two pull days and one push.

TABLE 5.4 Free-weight strength training programme for youths

Exercise	Sets	Reps
Workout 1: 'Push' day		
Dumbbell loaded jump squats	3	5–6
Squat or leg press	3	6–10
Bench press	3	6–10
Dumbbell push press	3	5–8
Body-weight dips	2	6–12
Medicine ball walking lunges	2	8–12
Medicine ball toe touches	3	8–15
Workout 2: 'Pull' day		
Barbell high pull from the hang	3	5–8
Deadlift	3	6–10
Barbell or dumbbell bent over row	3	6–10
Stiff leg deadlift	2	6–10
Dumbbell lateral raises	3	8–10
Barbell curls	2	8–12
Barbell rollouts	2	5–8

Summary

Refuting many of the unfounded misconceptions and inaccuracies of the past, a large body of scientific evidence now supports the use of resistance training for the development of muscular strength and power in children and adolescents. Augmented strength levels can be considered advantageous to children and youth populations, as muscular strength supports the expression of many essential bio-motor qualities, including running, jumping, balance and coordination. When considering resistance-training programme design for children and adolescents, the value of performing exercises with accuracy and technical proficiency should be of utmost importance. However, if strength development programmes are well designed, allow for subtle progression over time, supervised by qualified and experienced coaches, and ensure correct exercise techniques are reinforced, then the benefits of resistance training and weightlifting techniques in the long-term adaptations of young athletes and children alike are unequivocal.

Key points

- Resistance training represents an effective exercise strategy for the development of muscular strength and power in children and youth populations.

- When designing a strength development programme, consideration should be given to the physical differences among children, their ability to tolerate exercise stress, their technical competency and their levels of mental maturity.
- Central to an effective strength development programme in youth populations is the need for direct supervision and instruction from certified strength and conditioning specialists.

References

Annesi, L., Westcott, W., Faigenbaum, A. D. and Unruh, J. (2005) 'Effects of a 12 week physical activity program delivered by YMCA after-school counselors (Youth Fit for Life) on fitness and self-efficacy changes in 5–12 year old boys and girls', *Research Quarterly for Exercise and Sport*, 76: 468–476.

Benson, A., Torade, M. and Fiataroni Singh, M. (2007) 'A rationale and method for high-intensity progressive resistance training with children and adolescents', *Contemporary Clinical Trials*, 28: 442–450.

Bernhardt, D. T., Gomez, J., Johnson, M. D., Martin, T. J., Rowland, T. W., Small, E., LeBlanc, C., Malina, R., Krein, C., Young, J. C., Reed, F. E., Anderson, S. J., Greisemer, B. A. and Bar-Or, O. (2001) 'Strength training by children and adolescents', *Pediatrics*, 107: 1470–1472.

Conroy, B., Kraemer, W. J., Maresh, C., Fleck, S., Stone, M. H., Fry, A. C., Miller, P. D. and Dalsky, G. P. (1993) 'Bone mineral density in elite junior Olympic weightlifters', *Medicine and Science in Sports and Exercise*, 5: 1103–1109.

Ewart, C., Young, D. and Hagberg, J. (1998) 'Effects of school-based aerobic exercise on blood pressure in adolescent girls at risk for hypertension', *American Journal of Public Health*, 88: 949–951.

Faigenbaum, A. D. (2011) 'Strength training for children and adolescents'. In: M. Cardinale, R. Newton and K. Nosaka (eds) *Strength and Conditioning: Biological Principles and Practical Applications*, Oxford: Wiley-Blackwell.

Faigenbaum, A. D., Kraemer, W. J., Blimkie, C. J. R., Jeffreys, I., Micheli, L. J., Nitka, M. and Rowland, T. W. (2009) 'Youth resistance training: Updated position statement paper from the National Strength and Conditioning Association', *Journal of Strength and Conditioning Research*, 23: S60–S79.

Faigenbaum, A. D., McFarland, J., Johnson, L., Kang, J., Bloom, J., Ratamess, N. A. and Hoffman, J. R. (2007) 'Preliminary evaluation of an after-school resistance training program', *Perceptual and Motor Skills*, 104: 407–415.

Faigenbaum, A. D. and Mediate, P. (2006) 'The effects of medicine ball training on physical fitness in high school physical education students', *The Physical Educator*, 63: 160–167.

Faigenbaum, A. D., Milliken, L., LaRosa Loud, R., Burak, B., Doherty, C. and Westcott, W. (2002) 'Comparison of 1 and 2 days per week of strength training in children', *Research Quarterly for Exercise and Sport*, 73: 416–424.

Faigenbaum, A. D., Milliken, L., Moulton, L. and Westcott, W. (2005) 'Early muscular fitness adaptationsin children in response to two different resistance training regimens', *Pediatric Exercise Science*, 17: 162–166.

Faigenbaum, A. D. and Myer, G. D. (2010) 'Resistance training among young athletes: Safety, efficacy and injury prevention effects', *British Journal of Sports Medicine*, 44: 56–63.

Faigenbaum, A. D., Zaichkowsky, L., Westcott, W., Micheli, L. J. and Fehlandt, A. (1993) 'The effects of a twice per week strength training program on children', *Pediatric Exercise Science*, 5: 339–346.

Falk, B. and Eliakim, A. (2003) 'Resistance training, skeletal muscle and growth', *Pediatric Endocrinology Reviews*, 1: 120–127.

Falk, B. and Mor, G. (1996) 'The effects of resistance and martial arts training in 6- to 8-year old boys', *Pediatric Exercise Science*, 8: 48–56.

Falk, B. and Tenenbaum, G. (1996) 'The effectiveness of resistance training in children: A meta-analysis', *Sports Medicine*, 22: 176–186.

Fleck, S. and Kraemer, W. J. (2004) *Designing Resistance Training Programmes*, Champaign, IL: Human Kinetics.

Hamill, B. P. (1994) 'Relative safety of weightlifting and weight training', *Journal of Strength and Conditioning Research*, 8: 53–57.

Hawkins, S. A., Schroeder, T. E., Wiswell, R. A., Jaque, V. S., Marcell, T. J. and Costa, K. (1999) 'Eccentric muscle action increases sitespecific osteogenic response', *Medicine and Science in Sports and Exercise*, 31: 1287–1292.

Lillegard, W. A., Brown, E. W., Wilson, D. J., Henderson, R. and Lewis, E. (1997) 'Efficacy of strength training in pre-pubescent to early postpubescent males and females: Effects of gender and maturity', *Pediatric Rehabilitation*, 1: 147–157.

Linden, C., Ahlborg, H., Besjakov, J., Gardsell, P. and Karlsson, M. K. (2006) 'A school curriculum-based exercise program increases bone mineral accrual and bone size in pre-pubertal girls: Two-year data from the pediatric osteoporosis prevention (POP) study', *Journal of Bone and Mineral Research*, 21: 829–835.

McKay, H. A., MacClean, L., Petit, M. A., MacKelvie-O'brien, K. J., Janssen, P., Beck, T. J. and Khan, K. M. (2005) '"Bounce at the Bell": A novel program of short bouts of exercise improves proximal femur bone mass in early pubertal children', *British Journal of Sports Medicine*, 39: 521–526.

MacKelvie, K. J., Petit, M. A., Khan, K. M., Beck, T. J. and McKay, H. A. (2004) 'Bone mass and structure and enhanced following a 2–year randomized controlled trial of exercise in pre-pubertal boys', *Bone*, 34: 755–764.

Ogden, C. L., Carroll, M. D., Curtin, L. R., McDowell, M. A., Tabak, C. J. and Flegal, K. M. (2006) 'Prevalence of overweight and obesity in the United States, 1999–2004', *Journal of the American Medical Association*, 295: 1549–1555.

Payne, V., Morrow, J., Johnson, L. and Dalton, S. (1997) 'Resistance training in children and youth: A meta-analysis', *Research Quarterly for Exercise and Sport*, 68: 80–88.

Pietrobelli, A., Faith, M. S., Wang, J., Brambilla, P., Chiumello, G. and Heymsfield, S. B. (2002) 'Association of lean tissue and fat mass with bone mineral content in children and adolescents', *Obesity Research*, 10: 771–775.

Shaibi, G., Cruz, M., Ball, G., Weigensberg, M., Salem, G., Crespo, N. and Goran, M. (2006) 'Effects of resistance training on insulin sensitivity in overweight Latino adolescent males', *Medicine and Science in Sports and Exercise*, 38: 1208–1215.

Stodden, D., Langendorfer, S. and Roberton, M. (2009) 'The association between motor skill competence and physical fitness in young adults', *Research Quarterly for Exercise and Sport*, 80: 223–229.

Szymanski, D., Szymanski, J., Bradford, J., Schade, R. and Pascoe, D. (2007) 'Effects of twelve weeks of medicine ball training on high school baseball players', *Journal of Strength and Conditioning Research*, 21: 894–901.

Tucker, L. (1987) 'Effect of weight training on body attitudes: Who benefits most?' *Journal of Sports Medicine*, 27: 70–78.

Turner, C. and Robling, A. (2003) 'Designing exercise regimens to increase bone strength', *Exercise and Sport Sciences Reviews*, 31: 45–50.

Vicente-Rodriguez, G. (2006) 'How does exercise affect bone development during growth?' *Sports Medicine*, 36: 561–569.

Virvidakis, K., Georgiou, E., Korkotsidis, A., Ntalles, K. and Proukakis, C. (1990) 'Bone mineral content of junior competitive weightlifters', *International Journal of Sports Medicine*, 11: 244–246.

Watts, K., Beye, P., Siafarikas, A., Davis, E., Jones, T., O'Driscoll, G. and Green, D. (2004) 'Exercise training normalizes vascular dysfunction and improves central adiposity in obese adolescents', *Journal of the American College of Cardiology*, 43: 1823–1827.

Watts, K., Jones, T. W., Davis, E. A. and Green, D. (2005) 'Exercise training in obese children and adolescents', *Sports Medicine*, 35: 375–392.

Weir, J. P., Housh, T. J., Johnson, G. O., Housh, D. J. and Ebersole, K. T. (1999) 'Allometric scaling of isokinetic peak torque: The Nebraska Wrestling study', *European Journal of Applied Physiology*, 80: 240–248.

Weltman, A., Janney, C., Rians, C. B., Strand, K. and Katch, F. I. (1987) 'The effects of hydraulic-resistance strength training on serum lipid levels in pre-pubertal boys', *American Journal of Diseases of Children*, 141: 777–780.

World Health Organization (2010) *Global recommendations on physical activity for health*, Geneva: WHO Press.

Zaricznyj, B., Shattuck, L., Mast, T., Robertson, R. and D'Elia, G. (1980) 'Sports-related injuries in school-aged children', *American Journal of Sports Medicine*, 8: 318–324.

6

SPEED DEVELOPMENT IN YOUTHS

Jon L. Oliver and Michael C. Rumpf

Introduction

Speed is a desirable characteristic that has been associated with successful sports performance in children (Reilly *et al.*, 2000). A failure to fully develop sprint speed during childhood may also restrict opportunities in adulthood, as speed is often reported to distinguish between adults of differing competitive standards (Pyne *et al.*, 2005). Both the ability to accelerate and to attain maximal velocity are components of speed and should be considered in the development of speed during childhood. For the purpose of this chapter, speed will be considered with regards to overground running as this is the most common application of speed in competition and training. The term speed will be used as a generic term that ignores the phase of sprinting.

It is clear that all aspects of speed develop through childhood and, as with other components of fitness, improvements have been reported to follow a non-linear process (Borms, 1986; Viru *et al.*, 1999). The development of speed throughout childhood is influenced by increases in muscle cross-sectional area and limb length, biological and metabolic changes, morphological alterations to the muscle and tendon, neural and motor development as well as biomechanical and coordination factors (Ford *et al.*, 2011). Given the interaction of so many variables, identifying a single primary mechanism responsible for improvements in speed at different stages of growth and maturation is difficult. However, biomechanical analyses can provide useful information regarding the development of speed, which, in its simplest form, is a function of stride frequency and stride length. Stride frequency at maximal speed changes very little through childhood into adulthood, with gains in maximal speed attributable to gains in stride length (Schepens *et al.*, 1998). Therefore, considering factors that contribute to increased stride length in childhood seems a useful strategy.

The developmental changes that underpin natural gains in speed may help to identify the types of training regimes that can be most successful at different stages of growth and development (Balyi and Hamilton, 2004; Viru *et al.*, 1999). The interaction of different training regimes, different phases of sprinting, different mechanistic adaptations and growth and maturation effects make this a potentially complex topic. This chapter will consider the theory and evidence of the development and trainability of speed during childhood, whether any interaction effects exist with growth and maturation and how different types of training influence chronic adaptations.

Basic theoretical concepts

Natural development of speed during childhood

Developmental trends

Improvements in speed during childhood follow a non-linear process. During the first decade of life both boys and girls have similar sprint speeds (Borms, 1986; Malina *et al.*, 2004). A period of accelerated adaptation is suggested to occur between the ages of 5 and 9 years in both boys and girls and is thought to primarily reflect development of the central nervous system and improved coordination (Borms, 1986; Viru *et al.*, 1999). The central nervous system undergoes rapid growth in the first seven years of life (Malina *et al.*, 2004) and coordination patterns and locomotor skills reach adult levels by this time (Whithall, 2003), although the process is not complete until sexual maturation or adulthood (Fields, 2005). Consequently, improvements in whole-body, inter-muscular and intra-muscular recruitment and coordination may underpin speed gains in younger children.

A second period of accelerated adaptation has been termed the adolescent spurt (Viru *et al.*, 1999) and has been observed to occur somewhere between 11 and 14 years old in girls and 12 and 16 years old in boys (Balyi and Hamilton, 2004; Borms *et al.*, 1986; Viru *et al.*, 1999). During this time improvements in speed become divergent across the genders with boys able to make greater gains than their female counterparts. Speed development will typically cease without involvement in sport during the latter part of this stage for girls (Papaiakovou *et al.*, 2009; Szczesny and Coudert, 1993). Although a maturational effect is inferred by the term 'adolescent spurt', whether this period of accelerated adaptation is determined by maturation is debatable (Ford *et al.*, 2011). In the popular Long-Term Athlete Development model proposed by Balyi and Hamilton (2004), this secondary window of rapid improvement in speed is aligned to chronological age. This chronological perspective is most likely attributable to continued growth and development of the central nervous system (Borms, 1986). Supporting a maturational role, gains in strength, power output and speed during this period have all been attributed to the rise of hormone levels associated with puberty (Viru *et al.*, 1999).

Some authors have suggested that speed development is directly linked to the timing of puberty and subsequent growth. Philippaerts *et al.* (2006) suggest speed gains peak around the time of peak height velocity (PHV), while Yagüe and de la Fuente (1998) suggested that gains peak approximately one year prior to and one year post-PHV. However, identifying a cause and effect relationship to explain improved speed is difficult, although Gravina *et al.* (2008) reported a significant but only moderate correlation ($r = 0.4$) between changes in testosterone levels and sprint speed in male youth soccer players. While only weak relationships have been found between growth rates of stature or body mass with sprint performance in children (Butterfield *et al.*, 2004; Williams *et al.*, 2011), collectively these findings suggest that speed will be at least partly determined by factors independent of maturation. For instance, it is likely that neural development also continues to facilitate improved sprint speed in older children. In reality, both chronological and maturational factors are likely to influence the natural development of speed during the pre- to mid-teenage years.

Biomechanical factors in the development of acceleration and maximal velocity sprinting

Developmental trends of speed are predominantly based on sprint performances of distances between 25–50 m (e.g. Viru *et al.*, 1999), which will combine elements of both acceleration and maximal speed. However, acceleration and maximal velocity sprinting will represent the slow and fast stretch-shortening cycle (SSC), respectively. Slow and fast SSCs are known to follow different developmental trends during childhood (Lloyd *et al.*, 2011b). Acceleration is associated with longer periods of ground contact, providing the opportunity to generate a large net impulse (Salo *et al.*, 2005), while maximal velocity sprinting is associated with shorter periods of ground contact and a rapid rate of force development (Weyand *et al.*, 2000). Supporting the specificity of acceleration and maximal speed, Chelly and Denis (2001) reported a common variance of only 21 per cent between these two variables in 16-year-old children. The authors reported that acceleration was dependent on relative power, whereas a greater absolute power and increased leg stiffness were required for maximal speed. The ability to rapidly generate power to achieve maximal sprint speed has been suggested to be dependent on the elastic components of the lower-limb musculature (Chelly and Denis 2001; Kubo *et al.*, 2000). These elastic properties are known to develop throughout childhood (Kubo *et al.*, 2001) and are likely to facilitate improved maximal sprint speed. Development of the intrinsic properties of the muscle-tendon complex may also drive positive adaptations that are observed in the neural system during childhood, shifting from a more inhibitory to a more excitatory response (Lloyd *et al.*, 2012; Oliver and Smith, 2010). These developmental changes result in a ten-fold increase in muscle-tendon stiffness in the first two decades of life (Lin *et al.*, 1997).

A study on a group of 33 adult participants showed that even though maximal sprint speed spanned a range of 6.2–11.1 m/s, stride frequency did not impact top running speed (Weyand *et al.*, 2000). Instead, the ability to generate large ground reaction forces (relative to body weight) over shorter ground contact periods allowed a longer stride length and increased maximal sprint speed. Similarly, in a study where maximal sprint speed increased three-fold from infancy to adulthood stride frequency at maximal speed remained unchanged, with increases in velocity attributed to proportional increases in stride length (Schepens *et al.*, 1998). Collectively these findings support a primary role of stride length in developing maximal velocity, which is dependent on the ability to generate high relative ground reaction forces in a short ground contact period. An influence of leg length on maximal running speed is appealing given the concomitant increases in leg length and maximal running velocity throughout childhood (Schepens *et al.*, 1998), however, a cause and effect relationship is not clear. Increased leg length will increase contact length (the distance covered when in contact with the ground) but the aerial phase will contribute more to stride length than the ground contact phase. Leg length does not differentiate between senior professional 100m sprinters of differing ability, whereas the morphological characteristics of the muscle do help to explain performance differences (Kumagai *et al.*, 2000). Increases in leg length in childhood will be occurring simultaneously to other developmental changes, such as increased muscle mass, changes to muscle-tendon morphology and changes in neural control.

Adolescent awkwardness

Adolescent awkwardness can be defined as a temporary disruption to motor coordination arising from rapid growth of the limbs, which has been suggested to affect approximately 25 per cent of adolescents (Beunen and Malina, 1988). During a growth spurt a child will need to adjust to their rapidly changing body dimensions and this can temporarily impair coordination and performance of motor tasks. In a longitudinal study of 30m sprint times in youth soccer players, Philippaerts *et al.* (2006) reported impairments in performance in the 12 months prior to PHV, which may coincide with a growth spurt of the lower limbs, followed by peak improvements in performance around the time of PHV. These findings support the existence of a potential period of adolescent awkwardness in the development of speed. It is also interesting to note that the impairments in the 30m sprint time 12 months pre-PHV (0.6s/year) were greater than the gains made around PHV (0.4s/year). The peak gains reported around PHV may simply reflect a correction period in this population, and, in athletes who do not experience adolescent awkwardness, smaller but consistent gains in sprint performance may be observed throughout the growth spurt. This supports the need for a long-term monitoring programme to allow the coach to make informed judgements regarding any potential confounding factors influencing decrements or improvements in sprint speed.

Trainability of speed during childhood

A primary concern for the strength and conditioning coach should be whether or not they can influence gains in sprint speed with training over and above gains achieved through natural development. An additional consideration is whether responsiveness to training is influenced by the age and/or maturation of child athletes. Sensitivity to training is inferred by the concepts of 'windows of opportunity'

(Balyi and Hamilton, 2004), which suggests that periods of naturally occurring accelerated adaptation represent a period when a system will have a heightened response to additional stimuli (such as training). Unfortunately, limited empirical studies exist to specifically answer this question. However, examination of a collection of discrete studies can begin to provide some insight.

Recently Rumpf et al. (2012) reviewed the effectiveness of different training programmes on speed development in boys. A total of 15 studies satisfied their inclusion criteria, giving a total sample of 503 children with an average age of 13.3 years. Examining the effect of different types of training regimes, the authors reported average gains in sprint performance of 3.5 per cent following sprint training, 1.1 per cent following strength training, 2.7 per cent following plyometric training and 2.7 per cent following combined training programmes (strength combined with other types of training). Given the strong reliability and sensitivity inherent to sprint indices in child populations (Drinkwater et al., 2007; Rumpf et al., 2011) these findings demonstrate that a number of different training regimes can have a meaningful impact on sprint performance in children.

Examining the interaction of maturation and training responsiveness, Rumpf et al. (2012) concluded that: children pre-PHV benefitted most from plyometric and then sprint training; children circum-PHV benefitted most from plyometric and then strength training; and children post-PHV benefitted most from combined training methods and then strength training. A broad conclusion from this review is that children who are pre-PHV benefit most from training that has a primarily neural basis, whereas children post-PHV will benefit from training that aims to strengthen the muscles and adapt morphological characteristics. This provides some support for the concept of windows of opportunity, with training adaptations appearing to align to mechanisms thought to underpin natural development during different stages of childhood. However, the review also highlights limitations of current research. No studies on the effects of strength training on speed gains in children who were pre-PHV were included, only two studies examined the effectiveness of sprint training programmes (and these were confined to pre-PHV children), while no research was identified for resisted or assisted sprint training programmes in children. This is surprising given the benefits that resisted sprint training is believed to offer in terms of power production for acceleration (Harrison and Bourke, 2009) and that assisted sprint training offers for increasing stride frequency to aid maximal velocity (Paradisis et al. 2006).

Mechanisms that underpin training-related gains in sprint speed are often inferred from the type of training performed, rather than by any direct measurement of underlying neuromuscular adaptations. For instance, the fact that high-speed coordination training has been shown to improve sprint speed as much as linear sprint training in pre-adolescents suggests that an adaptive response related to neural improvements exists in this group (Venturelli et al., 2008). Coordination training may be seen as a preferential option in pre-adolescents as this type of training also allowed for improvements in a skill-related activity, which was not observed with linear sprint training alone (Venturelli et al., 2008).

Some studies have been able to identify physiological adaptations that occur with sprint training in children and these may be able to inform the type of training that can stimulate improvements. Sprint training can cause metabolic adaptations in pre- and post-adolescent boys, which increased substrate and enzyme concentrations associated with anaerobic metabolism (Cadefau et al., 1990; Eriksson, 1980; Fournier et al., 1982). However, the magnitude of the training-induced change is reported to be below that of adults, and any adaptation is lost following a detraining period (Fournier et al., 1982). Sprint training has also been shown to have a limited effect on catecholaminergic response to sprint exercises in adolescent girls, with any adaptation lost with detraining (Botcazou et al., 2006). These limited studies highlight the rapid potential for detraining in some aspects of developmental physiology, suggesting a need for children to continue accumulating training. It is most likely that improvements in either acceleration or maximal sprint speed following a period of training is the result of the interaction of a number of adaptive processes. Different mechanisms may predominate the adaptive response at different stages of growth or maturation, however, this is a mostly speculative suggestion. What is clear from the limited amount of research available is that children of all ages and maturation are able to make some training-induced gains in sprint speed.

Practical applications

Training prescription

Providing a variety of training stimuli and methods should help to maintain the interest of child athletes (Oliver et al., 2011) and this should be well suited to the development of speed during childhood. Training to develop the various aspects of speed throughout childhood should incorporate a combination of sprint-specific training supplemented with fundamental/locomotor movement skills, strength and plyometric training. Consequently, training for speed should be considered within the overall context of developing a range of interrelated physical abilities. Based on evidence presented above and below, Table 6.1 provides an overview of the types of sprint and complementary training that should be encouraged at different stages during childhood, with the aim to maximize speed development. A greater depth of detail on training to improve physical literacy, strength and plyometric abilities during childhood is available elsewhere within this book.

As this section is concerned with improving sprint speed (and not repeated sprint ability), the intention is that all exercises are performed with a focus on quality, technically sound execution of drills, and with full or near-full recovery between sets, unless otherwise stated. On the latter point, the younger/more immature the child the quicker they are likely to recover, similarly, the shorter the exercise duration the more rapid the recovery (Ratel et al., 2004). Specifically, maximal force generating capacity will recover more rapidly than the ability to sustain forceful contractions, meaning acceleration will recover more rapidly than maximal velocity sprint speed. This means the younger the child and the shorter

TABLE 6.1 Overview of programme design to maximize speed development throughout childhood

	Early childhood	Pre-pubertal (pre-PHV)	Pubertal (circum-PHV)	Adolescent (post-PHV)
Suggested age ranges	0–7 years	Girls: 8–11 years Boys: 8–12 years	Girls: 11–15 years Boys: 12–16 years	Girls 15+ years Boys 16+ years
Sprint training focus	Locomotor movement skills	Technical development	Technical development Maximal sprints	Maximal sprints
Complementary training	Physical literacy development	Plyometric coordination/ movement skills	Plyometric Strength Hypertrophy (latter part of this stage) Coordination (during growth spurts)	Hypertrophy Strength Complex training
Primary training adaptations	Neural	Neural	Neural and morphological	Morphological and neural

the exercise duration or sprint distance the less time is required for recovery. This is important as, although recovery will be required to maintain technical performance and maximal motor unit recovery, children may become disinterested if they are not kept active during training.

Early childhood (0–7 years old in both boys and girls)

The primary goal with the young child is to engage them in physical activity and develop movement skills that will aid with this goal. Therefore, the aim of this phase is centered around technical development with any physical conditioning a by-product of this training, rather than a target of the training. While even very young children will quickly develop the ability to run, the primary focus at this stage is not to focus on sprinting as a form of training. Consequently, different phases of sprinting are not really considered at this stage. Up to the age of seven the central nervous system is experiencing rapid growth and by this age adult gait will be established (Whithall, 2003). Therefore, training should capitalize on this natural development by trying to promote central nervous system growth and programming (i.e. coordination patterns) and establishing technically sound movement patterns. To achieve this, tasks should be introduced with various instructions or conditions used to promote different aspects associated with good locomotor and sprint technique. It is expected that children at this age should be habitually active and as such should be practising and refining movement skills on a daily basis, most likely during relative brief bouts of exercise repeated throughout the day and week. However, an experienced coach (or well-informed teacher or parent) is needed to provide appropriate instruction and feedback to help promote learning of desirable movement patterns.

Pre-peak height velocity (8–11 in girls, 8–12 in boys)

During the pre-PHV phase there should be a transition to a focus on greater technical development of sprint mechanics needed in the different phases of sprinting, including acceleration and maximal sprint speed. As well as more specific technical development of sprint mechanics, physical training should also be introduced at this time. Sprint, plyometric and high-speed coordination training have all been shown to be effective training modalities at this stage of development (Rumpf *et al.*, 2012). This suggests a window for training adaptations that have a neural basis during this age range. Consequently, there should be an integration of technical training and physical conditioning.

Technical training should predominate the training volume but physical training can also be dual purpose and aid technical development. Conditioning drills should be specific to mimic the technical elements of the different phases of sprinting and to promote neural adaptations in terms of motor unit recruitment and coordination. This will also be the case in all future phases of training where physical conditioning is primarily attempting to improve factors that will assist in the rapid production of forces against the ground. Movement patterns with greater joint displacements, more loading and longer times to generate forces will stimulate maximal motor unit recruitment, generate greater impulse and mirror the demands of the acceleration phase. Movement patterns with smaller joint displacements and rapid force generation will stimulate reflex muscle activity and reflect the demands of maximal velocity sprinting. Both types of movement patterns are likely to facilitate a longer stride length throughout the different phases of sprinting.

Essentially this phase can be considered a technical and broad physical training phase, with development still focused around neural adaptations and motor learning. Consequently, training can be progressed by starting with simple drills and progressing these to more complex movements once proficient execution has been consistently exhibited. Extensive resisted and assisted sprinting should be avoided in this phase, allowing the technical components of the different phases of sprinting to be fully developed. However, additional sprint-specific horizontal power training, such as resisted sprinting, may be included as a preparatory strategy to facilitate more focused strength training in latter stages of development. This broad physical training perspective allows the coach plenty of variety in the choice of training drills, which should enable the training programme to contain an element of variation to keep young athletes motivated to train. Sprint distances of 15–30 m at this age are likely to represent a sufficient sprint distance to train all phases of sprinting and avoid fatigue and deceleration, while shorter sprint distances can be used to focus more specifically on first step quickness and acceleration.

Circum-peak height velocity (11–15 years in girls, 12–16 years in boys)

Generally the circum–PHV phase should mark a transition to focus more on physical training to support sprint performance but with continued technical training of sprint mechanics. Given the possibility of a period of adolescent awkwardness, fundamental and sprint-specific skills that have been developed in earlier phases should be reinforced to maintain technical proficiency. Physical training should continue to utilize only drills that can be performed in a technically sound manner. Strength training, and specifically exercises favouring horizontal force production, can be incorporated into the training programme. Once strength-based exercises have been learnt with lower loads and volumes to maximize technical competency, training may progress to manipulate some muscular hypertrophy. This seems favourable in the mid to latter stages of this phase, with Viru et al. (1999) suggesting that gains in sprint performance around adolescence are due to selective hypertrophy of fast twitch fibres.

Gains in muscle size and strength should be continued to be translated to expressing force at speed, primarily with the use of plyometric exercises and sprint training. The neural conditioning programme implemented in the previous phase can be extended in this phase with the introduction of more complex and physically demanding drills, for instance introducing greater eccentric loads during plyometric exercises (Lloyd et al., 2011a). Such a progression in plyometric training may also help to stimulate growth of the tendon cross-sectional area and intrinsic properties of the muscle and tendon during this period of maturation. This is supported by suggestions that plyometric training adaptations in adults may not be solely neural in origin but may also include changes to muscle cross-sectional area (Vissing et al., 2008). Resisted and assisted sprinting may be introduced as a sprint-specific conditioning tool. Resisted sprints should begin with additional minimal loading and sensible upper limits should be set at an additional 7.5 per cent of body mass pre-PHV and 10 per cent of body mass around and post-PHV. Practitioners should take caution when utilizing resisted and assisted sprint training, as paediatric research is limited in this area and suggestions are based on one currently unpublished study. The purpose of resisted and assisted sprints is to overload different aspects of force and power generating capabilities of the muscle to aid with acceleration and maximal sprint speed. Resisted sprints can provide additional overload to help develop power and impulse to translate to the acceleration phase. Assisted sprints are known to increase speed and stride length (Weyand et al., 2000), which, if translated to free running, will improve maximal velocity sprinting.

Post-peak height velocity (15+ years in girls, 16+ years in boys)

In the post-PHV phase the majority of time will be spent on physical training and less time in technical training of sprint mechanics (providing these have been satisfactorily learnt previously). However, physical training should still continue to demand technical quality in movement patterns. Both strength and combined training have been reported to be most successful at manipulating improvements in all aspects of sprint performance at this stage of development (Rumpf *et al.*, 2012). Strength training should move from a focus on hypertrophy to increasing maximal force production and relative strength. Increases in training volume at this time should also allow for the continued development of explosive qualities via continued plyometric and sprint training, the latter of which may have extended to longer sprint distances (e.g. >60 m). With the accumulation of training history and establishment of well-developed training skills, a greater emphasis can now also be placed on complex training, combining different training methods (e.g. specific and non-specific) and/or different training forms (resisted and assisted sprinting) in a single drill (e.g. a combination of a back squat followed by a sprint) to account for different training purposes (e.g. horizontal versus vertical force production). This will stimulate further development and aid in efficient use of training time. Performers should continue to use resisted and assisted sprints as a training tool either in isolation or as part of a combined training session.

Frequency, duration, volume and intensity of training

The intention is that all physical training drills are completed at maximal intensity and in a technically sound manner. Movement skills and sprint-specific skills should be completed at an intensity where proper technique can be practised and repeated for the entire session. As previously stated, the intention is to allow for full recovery to enable the maintenance of maximal efforts and correct technique. Monitoring performance times will provide an indication of whether sufficient recovery is being provided between sprint efforts. Table 6.2 provides a summary of guidelines relating to programme design for sprint training sessions at different stages of childhood. Early childhood is not included in this table as it is anticipated that at this stage of development training will primarily focus on enhancing physical literacy, which will provide long-term speed benefits.

The suggested sprint training guidelines shown in Table 6.2 should be considered within the context of a comprehensive training programme that incorporates additional training complementary to speed development (Table 6.1), together with other desirable training goals such as strength, power and agility development. Consequently, the frequency of sessions partly reflects the need for children to be engaging in other forms of training in addition to speed training. It is also possible that sprint sessions could be incorporated within larger sessions, providing technical competency and maximal performance can be maintained.

There should be a gradual progression in training volume with increasing development. However, the overall training volume and frequency of sessions is going to be largely dependent on the training history of the child, individual rate of progression and the goals of any training programme. The majority of child training studies have reported training frequencies of 1–3 sessions per week (Rumpf *et al.*, 2012), with a training volume of 240–480 m per session, consisting of 8–15 sprints over

TABLE 6.2 Suggested guidelines for sprint-specific training prescription throughout childhood

Training variable	Pre-pubertal (pre-PHV)	Pubertal (circum-PHV)	Adolescent (post-PHV)
Suggested age ranges (years)	Males: 8–12 Females: 8–11	Males: 12–16 Females: 11–15	Males: 16+ Females: 15+
Volume (m)[a]	100–250	250–450	up to 600
Total number of exercises per session[b]	3–4	2–3	1–2
Training focus	Sprint technique, movement patterns	Sprint technique, sport-specific sprints	Sport-specific sprints
Intensity (execution speed)[c]	Submax-maximal	Submax-maximal	Maximal
Sprint distance (m)	0–30	0–50	0–60+
Between-sprint recovery[d]	Full to near full (10–20 s per 10 m)	Full (20–30 s per 10 m)	Full (30 s per 10 m)
Frequency (sessions per week)	1–2	2–3	3–4
Between-session recovery (hrs)	72	72–48	48–24

Notes

a Total distance per main part of the training session.

b These values do not necessarily equate to designated sprint exercises, but rather broad-ranging exercises to develop physical literacy.

c Some sub-maximal drills may be needed to allow for technical competency.

d These values represent the minimum amount of recovery time provided between sprint efforts.

10–30 m. However, with accumulated training history and potentially diminishing returns it is likely that a long-term programme would have to progress to a greater volume per session and number of sessions. This should be achievable given the multifaceted nature of sprint training, which combines a variety of training modalities. Training duration is likely to be limited by practical factors as the need for full recovery between efforts will lead to a relatively low training volume in individual sessions. Training volume can be increased by increasing the frequency of training, the duration of training or by introducing combined training as the developing athlete demonstrates the capability to progress through the phases of training.

Key points

- The natural development of speed in childhood is non-linear, with periods of more rapid improvements observed in a pre-adolescent spurt and then again in an adolescent spurt. Neural development is thought to underpin gains in the pre-adolescent phase, whereas both chronological and maturational related development will interact during the adolescent spurt.

- Both acceleration and maximal velocity sprinting appear to be trainable at all stages of maturation, although it is likely that different mechanisms underpin training adaptations. Limited training studies support the belief that trainability is associated with natural development; neural-based training is most successful before the growth spurt, whereas strength and more complex training is most successful after the growth spurt.

- Training prescription should follow a continuum from focusing on movement and technical skills with limited direct physical training at a young age, to focusing predominantly on physical training with some technical training at older ages. The aim is to progressively develop sound technical movement patterns for each phase of sprinting and improve the ability to rapidly generate large forces and power against the ground.

- The coach can utilize many different training modalities during physical training to develop the speed of child athletes. This opportunity should allow the coach to provide long-term training programmes that contain a high degree of variation, but yet remain specific at all times.

References

Balyi, I. and Hamilton, A. (2004) *Long-Term Athlete Development: Trainability in Childhood and Adolescence. Windows of Opportunity, Optimal Trainability*, Victoria: National Coaching Institute British Columbia and Advanced Training and Performance Ltd.

Beunen, G. and Malina, R. M. (1988) 'Growth and physical performance relative to the timing of the adolescent spurt', *Exercise and Sport Sciences Reviews*, 16: 503–540.

Borms, J. (1986) 'The child and exercise: an overview', *Journal of Sports Sciences*, 4: 3–20.

Botcazou, M., Zouhal, H., Jacob, C., Gratas-Delamarche, A., Berthon, P. M., Bentue-Ferrer, D. and Delamarche, P. (2006) 'Effect of training and detraining on catecholamine responses to sprint exercise in adolescent girls', *European Journal of Applied Physiology*, 97: 68–75.

Butterfield, S. A., Lehnhard, R., Lee, J. and Coladarci, T. (2004) 'Growth rates in running speed and vertical jumping by boys and girls ages 11–13', *Perceptual and Motor Skills*, 99: 225–234.

Cadefau, J., Casademont, J., Grau, J. M., Fernandez, J., Balaguer, A., Vernet, M., Cusso, R. and Urbano-Marquez, A. (1990) 'Biochemical and histochemical adaptation to sprint training in young athletes', *Acta Physiologica Scandinavica*, 140: 341–351.

Chelly, S. M. and Denis, C. (2001) 'Leg power and hopping stiffness: relationship with sprint running performance', *Medicine and Science in Sports and Exercise*, 33: 326–333.

Drinkwater, E. J., Hopkins, W. G., McKenna, M. J., Hunt, P. H. and Pyne, D. B. (2007) 'Modelling age and secular differences in fitness between basketball players', *Journal of Sports Sciences*, 25: 869–878.

Eriksson, B. O. (1980) 'Muscle metabolism in children: a review', *Acta Paediatrica Scandinavica Supplement*, 283: 20–28.

Fields, R. D. (2005) 'Myelination: an overlooked mechanism of synaptic plasticity?' *Neuroscientist*, 11: 528–531.

Ford, P., De Ste Croix, M., Lloyd, R., Meyers, R., Moosavi, M., Oliver, J., Till, K. and Williams, C. (2011) 'The long-term athlete development model: physiological evidence and application', *Journal of Sports Sciences*, 29: 389–402.

Fournier, M., Ricci, J., Taylor, A. W., Ferguson, R. J., Montpetit, R. R. and Chaitman, B. R. (1982) 'Skeletal muscle adaptation in adolescent boys: sprint and endurance training and detraining', *Medicine and Science in Sports and Exercise*, 14: 453–456.

Gravina, L., Gil, S. M., Ruiz, F., Zubero, J., Gil, J. and Irazusta, J. (2008) 'Anthropometric and physiological differences between first team and reserve soccer players aged 10–14 years at the beginning and end of the season', *Journal of Strength and Conditioning Research*, 22: 1308–1314.

Harrison, A. J. and Bourke, G. (2009) 'The effect of resisted sprint training on speed and strength performance in male rugby players', *Journal of Strength and Conditioning Research*, 23: 275–283.

Kubo, K., Kanehisa, H., Kawakami, Y. and Fukunaga, T. (2000) 'Elasticity of tendon structures of the lower limbs in sprinters', *Acta Physiologica Scandinavica*, 168: 327–335.

Kubo, K., Kanehisa, H., Kawakami, Y. and Fukunaga, T. (2001) 'Growth changes in the elastic properties of human tendon structures', *International Journal of Sports Medicine*, 22: 138–143.

Kumagai, K., Abe, T., Brechue, W. F., Ryushi, T., Takano, S. and Mizuno, M. (2000) 'Sprint performance is related to muscle fascicle length in male 100-m sprinters', *Journal of Applied Physiology*, 88: 811–816.

Lin, J. P., Brown, J. K. and Walsh, E. G. (1997) 'Soleus muscle length, stretch reflex excitability, and the contractile properties of muscle in children and adults: a study of the functional joint angle', *Developmental Medicine and Child Neurology*, 39: 469–480.

Lloyd, R. S., Meyers, R. W. and Oliver, J. L. (2011a) 'The natural development and trainability of plyometric ability during childhood', *Strength and Conditioning Journal*, 33: 23–32.

Lloyd, R. S., Oliver, J. L., Hughes, M. G. and Williams, C. A. (2011b) 'The influence of chronological age on periods of accelerated adaptation of stretch-shortening cycle performance in pre and postpubescent boys', *Journal of Strength and Conditioning Research*, 25: 1889–1897.

Lloyd, R. S., Oliver, J. L., Hughes, M. G. and Williams, C. A. (2012) 'Age-related differences in the neural regulation of stretch-shortening cycle activities in male youths during maximal and sub-maximal hopping', *Journal of Electromyography and Kinesiology*, 22: 37–43.

Malina, R. M., Bouchard, C. and Bar-Or, O. (2004) *Growth, Maturation and Physical Activity*, Champaign, IL: Human Kinetics.

Oliver, J. L. and Smith, P. M. (2010) 'Neural control of leg stiffness during hopping in boys and men', *Journal of Electromyography and Kinesiology*, 20: 973–979.

Oliver, J. L., Lloyd, R. S. and Meyers, R. W. (2011) 'Training elite child athletes: welfare and well-being', *Strength and Conditioning Journal*, 33: 73–79.

Papaiakovou, G., Giannakos, A., Michailidis, C., Patikas, D., Bassa, E., Kalopisis, V., Anthrakidis, N. and Kotzamanidis, C. (2009) 'The effect of chronological age and gender on the development of sprint performance during childhood and puberty', *Journal of Strength and Conditioning Research*, 23: 2568–2573.

Paradisis, G. P. and Cooke, C. B. (2006) 'The effects of sprint running training on sloping surfaces', *Journal of Strength and Conditioning Research*, 20: 767–777.

Philippaerts, R. M., Vaeyens, R., Janssens, M., Van Renterghem, B., Matthys, D., Craen, R., Bourgois, J., Vrijens, J., Beunen, G. and Malina, R. M. (2006) 'The relationship between peak height velocity and physical performance in youth soccer players', *Journal of Sports Sciences*, 24: 221–230.

Pyne, D. B., Gardner, A. S., Sheehan, K. and Hopkins, W. G. (2005) 'Fitness testing and career progression in AFL football', *Journal of Science and Medicine in Sport*, 8: 321–332.

Ratel, S., Williams, C. A., Oliver, J. L. and Armstrong, N. (2004) 'Effects of age and mode of exercise on power output profiles during repeated sprints', *European Journal of Applied Physiology*, 92: 204–210.

Reilly, T., Williams, A. M., Nevill, A. and Franks, A. (2000) 'A multidisciplinary approach to talent identification in soccer', *Journal of Sports Sciences*, 18: 695–702.

Rumpf, M. C., Cronin, J. B., Oliver, J. L. and Hughes, M. G. (2011) 'Assessing youth sprint ability: methodological issues, reliability and performance data', *Pediatric Exercise Science*, 23: 442–467.

Rumpf, M. C., Cronin, J. B., Oliver, J. L. and Hughes, M. G. (2012) 'Effect of different training methods on running sprint times in male youth', *Pediatric Exercise Science*, 24: 170–186.

Salo, A. I. T., Keranen, T. and Vitasalo, J. T. (2005) 'Force production in the first four steps of sprint running'. In: Q. Wang (ed.) *Proceedings of the XIII Internartional Symposium on Biomechanics in Sports* (pp. 313–317). Beijing: The China Institute of Sport Science.

Schepens, B., Willems, P. A. and Cavagna, G. A. (1998) 'The mechanics of running in children', *Journal of Physiology*, 509: 927–940.

Szczesny, S. and Coudert, J. (1993) 'Changes in running speed and endurance among girls during puberty'. In: J. A. P. Day and J. W. Duguet (eds) *Kinanthropometry IV* (pp. 268–284). London: Routledge.

Venturelli, M., Bishop, D. and Pettene, L. (2008) 'Sprint training in pre-adolescent soccer players', *International Journal of Sports Physiology and Performance*, 3: 558–562.

Viru, A., Loko, J., Harrow, M., Volver, A., Laaneots, L. and Viru, M. (1999) 'Critical periods in the development of performance capacity during childhood and adolescence', *Europeam Journal of Physical Education*, 4: 75–119.

Vissing, K., Brink, M., Lonbro, S., Sorensen, H., Overgaard, K., Danborg, K., Mortensen, J., Elstrom, O., Rosenhoj, N., Ringgaard, S., Andersen, J. L. and Aagaard, P. (2008) 'Muscle adaptations to plyometric vs. resistance training in untrained young men', *Journal of Strength and Conditioning Research*, 22: 1799–1810.

Weyand, P. G., Sternlight, D. B., Bellizzi, M. J. and Wright, S. (2000) 'Faster top running speeds are achieved with greater ground forces not more rapid leg movements', *Journal of Applied Physiology*, 89: 1991–1999.

Whithall, J. (2003) 'Development of locomotor coordination and control in children'. In: G. J. P. Savelsberg, K. Davids and J. Van Der Kamp (eds) *Development of Movement Coordination in Children* (pp. 251–270). London: Routledge.

Williams, C. A., Oliver, J. L. and Faulkner, J. (2011) 'Seasonal monitoring of sprint and jump performance in a soccer youth academy', *International Journal of Sports Physiology and Performance*, 6: 264–275.

Yagüe, P. H. and Fuente, D. L. (1998) 'Changes in height and motor performance relative to peak height velocity: a mixed-longitudinal study of Spanish boys and girls', *American Journal of Human Biology*, 10: 647–660.

7

PLYOMETRIC DEVELOPMENT IN YOUTHS

Rhodri S. Lloyd and John B. Cronin

Introduction

In it simplest form, muscular power is defined as the product of force and velocity (Komi, 2003). It has previously been acknowledged that the ability to generate high levels of power is essential for sporting success (Young, 2006), with the ability to produce high velocity at release or impact being the end goal of a given athletic movement sequence (Newton and Kraemer, 1994). The ability to produce high levels of muscular power is salient upon the type of muscular action involved (Cormie *et al.*, 2011), and previous research has demonstrated that when a muscle is stretched prior to shortening, it can produce an enhanced power output as compared to a concentric contraction in isolation (Komi, 2000). This muscular phenomenon is referred to as the stretch–shortening cycle (SSC), and for optimal SSC enhancement, eccentric and concentric contractions need to be rapid, and the transition between the eccentric and concentric contractions (coupling time) minimal. The SSC has been correlated to various measures of human performance, including acceleration (Bret *et al.*, 2002), maximal running velocity (Chelly and Denis, 2001) and running economy (Kerdok *et al.*, 2002; Kram, 2000), and it is the muscle action that is central to successful plyometric performance. Due to its strong association with performance, the development of plyometric ability throughout childhood and adolescence has been a topic of recent interest (Korff *et al.*, 2009; Lloyd *et al.*, 2011b; Oliver and Smith, 2010).

Prior to discussing the literature surrounding the potential benefits and concerns associated with youth plyometric training, it is pertinent to define key terminologies used throughout the chapter:

- *Stretch–shortening cycle (SSC).* Where pre-activated muscle is first stretched (eccentric) and immediately followed by a shortening (concentric) action (Komi, 2000; Nicol *et al.*, 2006).

- *Fast SSC.* Represents a form of SSC action during vertical jump or rebounding tasks that utilizes short ground contact times, minimal displacement of centre of mass and small angular displacements at the hip, knee and ankle. An example of fast SSC mechanics would be during maximum velocity sprinting where the ground contact times are approximately 70–100 ms.
- *Slow SSC.* SSC function during vertical jump or rebounding tasks characterized by long ground contact times, large displacements of centre of mass and large angular displacements at the hip, knee and ankle joints. The countermovement jump is an example of slow SSC mechanics where prolonged ground contacts of >300 ms are routinely used.

Measuring plyometric ability

Plyometric ability can be measured in a variety of ways, ranging from expensive, laboratory-based equipment, to cheaper, field-based methods. Laboratory-based testing might use force plates, accelerometers, linear position transducers, or combinations of these, to directly measure power during a range of movements. However, owing to cost implications, the ease of use and non-invasive nature of field-based testing, plyometric ability in children and adolescents have most commonly been measured indirectly using some form of vertical jump protocol. Recent developments in testing equipment have led to the design of mobile contact mats that can assess various aspects of SSC performance (Figure 7.1), and such measures now available to coaches include:

- *Jump height/distance (cm).* Assessed during basic vertical or horizontal jump tests (squat, counter-movement, drop or broad jumps). The protocols result in large ranges of motion at the joints of the lower limbs, and rely predominantly on the reutilization of stored elastic energy (Bobbert et al., 1996).
- *Reactive strength index (mm/ms).* The measure is a function of jump height and ground contact time, and is derived during rebound-based protocols. Researchers have suggested that the measure is reliant on contributions from parallel and series elastic components, and reflex potentiation (Lloyd et al., 2011c).
- *Leg stiffness (kN/m^{-1}).* This variable is calculated as the ratio between peak ground reaction force and peak centre of mass displacement (McMahon and Cheng, 1990). This measure is most representative of spring–mass model behaviour, is typically displayed in fast SSC actions and is heavily reliant on stretch reflex properties (Komi and Gollhofer, 1997).

The development of plyometric ability during childhood and adolescence

The natural development of muscular power

Despite its omission from popular long-term athletic development models (Balyi and Hamilton, 2004), muscular power has been tested for many years in youth

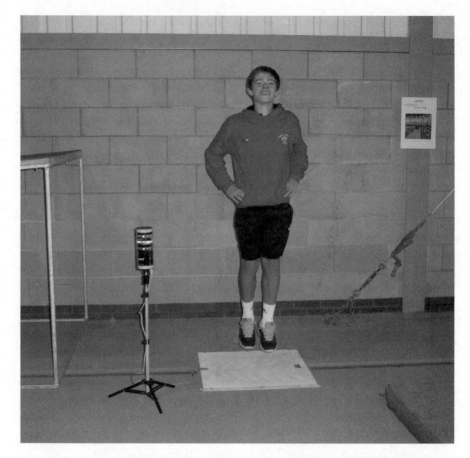

FIGURE 7.1 Example of a portable contact mat being used to collect various forms of SSC function

populations (Branta *et al.*, 1984). Early developmental literature has used basic vertical jump tests to quantify maximal muscular power, often looking at both squat and counter-movement jump tests (Harrison and Gaffney, 2001; Isaacs, 1998). Using such testing protocols, previous research has indicated that there exist periods of rapid development in muscular power between the ages of 5 and 10 years (Branta *et al.*, 1984). There appear to be no sex-related differences during this window due to it occurring prior to the pubertal spurt. Consequently, any improvements in muscular power during this time frame are likely to be due to age-related neuromuscular coordination. A secondary spurt in muscular power has been established between the ages of 9 and 12 years in girls, and between 12 and 14 in boys (Beunen, 1997). This developmental phase occurs in accordance with the onset of puberty (Ford *et al.*, 2011), and owing to the differential maturation rates between males and females, clear sex differences exist. When the velocity curve of lower-limb muscular power is aligned with peak height velocity (PHV), it appears that the adolescent spurt in muscular power is initiated approximately 1.5 years pre-PHV, and peaks 0.5–1.0 year post-PHV (Beunen and Malina, 1988). Therefore, while improvements in maximal muscular power occur circa-PHV, it would appear that peak gains coincide more readily with peak weight velocity (PWV). Potential morphological mechanical adaptations during the PWV period that are associated with the rapid secondary spurt in maximal muscular power include increases in muscle cross-sectional area, alterations in fascicle length and changes in pennation angle.

The natural development of plyometric ability

Given the significance of the SSC in human movement, it is important that this muscular action is measured in a manner specific to the event of interest. Previously, researchers have suggested that basic vertical jump tests (squat and counter-movement jumps) are not able to elicit the stretch reflex, which is fundamental to successful SSC performance (Komi and Gollhofer, 1997). Conversely, it has been established that movement patterns during cyclical hopping protocols activate stretch reflexes, and typically represent spring-mass model behaviour (Hobara et al., 2008). Consequently, more recent research has examined the development of SSC ability in male youths during rebounding test protocols (Lloyd et al., 2011b). The research suggested that, with 75–99 per cent certainty, periods of accelerated adaptation existed between the ages of 10–11 years (pre-pubertal) and between 14–15 years (post-pubertal) for both reactive strength index (RSI) and leg stiffness, respectively (Lloyd et al., 2011b). Both RSI and leg stiffness are measures of SSC ability that require some form of rebounding with the ground, and therefore more closely reflect the prerequisites of true SSC function (Komi, 2000). While the concept of long-term athlete development (LTAD) models has been discussed in depth in Chapter 3, it should be noted that the current LTAD model proposed by Balyi and Hamilton (2004) provided no indication of a 'window of opportunity' for muscular power development. Researchers have suggested that this may be due to the fact that, as the product of velocity of movement (speed) and force production (strength), the component 'windows' have already been included within the model (Ford et al., 2011). However, owing to recent research (Lloyd et al., 2011b) it would appear that distinct windows of opportunity should be included on the model for plyometric development, and that these windows should differ for varying expressions of SSC function.

It is postulated that SSC performance is governed by effective neuromuscular function, requiring an efficient combination of both neural and muscular systems (Komi, 2000; Nicol et al., 2006). Both morphological and neural factors develop naturally from childhood to adulthood, which enable more effective neuromuscular regulation of human locomotion (Malina et al., 2004). Musculotendon size and architecture, tendon stiffness (the resistance of the tendon to deformation in length), fascicle length and joint stiffness (the ratio of the joint torque to angular displacement) are all morphological variables that are likely to change as a result of natural growth and development alone. Neural mechanisms that underpin the natural development of SSC function include: motor unit recruitment and synchronization; firing frequency; synergistic contribution; muscle activity prior to ground contact (preactivation); reflex activity immediately after ground contact; and co-contraction (simultaneous contraction of agonist and antagonist muscles crossing the same joint). In contrast to adults, young children display more inhibitory mechanisms to protect the musculotendon unit, such as increased co-contraction (Lambertz et al., 2003), greater antagonist activation (Croce et al., 2004), reduced preactivation and lower stretch reflex utilization (Grosset et al., 2007; Oliver and Smith, 2010). Recent research has indicated that some of these neuromuscular qualities adapt throughout childhood, thus enabling a more efficient neural regulation of SSC function (Lloyd et al., 2012a; Oliver and Smith, 2010).

The trainability of plyometric ability

Researchers have reported that plyometric training can lead to positive adaptations for children in rebound jump height (Meylan and Malatesta, 2009), maximal running velocity (Kotzamanidis, 2006), agility performance (Thomas et al., 2009), vertical jump ability (Faigenbaum et al., 2007), rate-of-force development (Matavulj et al., 2001) and leg stiffness (Lloyd et al., 2012b). The aforementioned studies have utilized plyometric training programmes that have varied in duration, ranging from four weeks (Lloyd et al., 2012b) up to 10 weeks (Kotzamanidis, 2006), which highlights the effectiveness of the training mode. Previous researchers have suggested a range of potential mechanisms to explain the performance adaptations following exposure to plyometric training, including: improvements in motor unit recruitment patterns and firing frequencies (Thomas et al., 2009); increased muscle force and rate of force development within the leg extensors (Matavulj et al., 2001); greater joint stiffness and elastic energy recoil (Kubo et al., 2007); earlier and increased activation of the stretch reflexes (Bosco et al., 1982); and desensitization of the Golgi Tendon Organs, enabling a greater stretch of the elastic component of the muscle (Hutton and Atwater, 1992).

In accordance with the literature that suggests there exists key periods of heightened sensitivity to training adaptation during childhood (Viru et al., 1999), recent research has attempted to determine whether the training response to power training is related to age (Lloyd et al., 2012b). The researchers collected a range of SSC measurements from 9-, 12- and 15-year-old boys, and reported that, following exposure to a four-week training programme, both 12 and 15 year olds made significant improvements in leg stiffness, with the 12 year olds also making significant improvements in RSI. The corresponding control groups did not make any significant improvements. Additionally, both the 9-year-old-training and control groups failed to make significant improvements in either leg stiffness or RSI. The authors speculated that improvements in RSI and leg stiffness were therefore age-dependent, however, given the absence of any detrimental effects, pre-pubescent children should still engage in plyometric training with a primary focus on developing fundamental plyometric movement competency (Lloyd et al., 2012b).

Practical applications

Plyometric training variables

When planning and designing training programmes for any fitness component, it is essential for strength and conditioning coaches to consider the variables of volume, intensity, frequency, repetition velocity and recovery in a bid to maximize training adaptation, avoid excessive fatigue and reduce injury risk. Table 7.1 provides an overview of maturity-related plyometric training prescription inclusive of these variables. With respect to the overall design of youth-based plyometric training programmes, it should be stressed that any long-term athletic development model must be flexible to accommodate for individual differences in physiological maturation rates and training history, and shoud not be limited by an athlete's chronological age. Such an individualized approach should minimize the risk of late-maturing or inexperienced youths being exposed to excessive eccentric loading, but also avoid early-maturing and experienced youths being restricted to a low-level training stimulus.

TABLE 7.1 Suggested guidelines for plyometric training prescription related to maturational status

Training variable	Pre-pubertal	Pubertal	Adolescent
Training history and techinical competency	Low	Moderate	High
Suggested age ranges (years)	Males: 6–12 Females: 6–11	Males: 12–16 Females: 11–15	Males: 16+ Females: 15+
Volume (total repetitions per exercise)[a]	6–10	18–30	12–30
Total number of exercises per session	6–10[b]	3–6	2–6
Intensity (eccentric load)	Minimal-low	Moderate	Moderate-high
Repetition velocity (speed of movement)	Moderate-fast	Moderate-maximal	Fast-maximal
Frequency (sessions per week)	1–2	1–2	2–4
Recovery (inter-session hours)	72	72–48	48–24

a The total number of repetitions can be divided between different configurations of sets and repetitions based on the goal of the training session, and phase of the periodized plan.

b These values do not necessarily equate to designated plyometric exercises, but rather broad-ranging exercises to develop physical literacy.

Pre-exercise screening

As with any mode of training, a young athlete should undergo a movement screening protocol prior to starting a structured plyometric-based training programme in order to determine initial technical competency. The concepts of fundamental movement skills and physical literacy have previously been discussed in Chapter 4, however, it should be noted that a strength and conditioning coach should be aware of the movement and strength competencies required to effectively perform plyometric exercises. Furthermore, it should be stressed, that in the event of an individual failing to display appropriate competencies (e.g. landing mechanics), then they should regress to an earlier developmental stage. Conversely, should the athlete demonstrate efficient and effective technique, more progressive exercises can be prescribed.

Volume and intensity

The relationship between volume and intensity to ensure effective periodization has long been a source of debate in strength and power development, and has received considerable attention in the literature (Bompa and Haff, 2009). In the case of plyometrics, *volume* typically refers to the total number of foot contacts performed during a single session (Gambetta, 2007), while *intensity* relates to the amount of eccentric strain (e.g. drop height) placed on the musculotendon unit during a given exercise (Potach and Chu, 2008). Due to the high neural demands placed on the neuromuscular system during plyometric actions, it is imperative that children are gradually introduced to this training mode. Additionally, a gradual progressive approach will likely ensure that the training emphasis remains on movement quality (e.g. alignment, stability) and thereafter short ground-contact times, recruitment of a large number of motor units, stimulation of high rate of force development (RFD) and utilization of the stretch reflex.

It is important to acknowledge that plyometrics should not be viewed as a single training entity, but instead as a contribution to the overall strength and conditioning provision for a youth athlete. Therefore, while youths might experience a large number of ground contacts during free play or sport-specific training sessions, strength and conditioning coaches should refrain from unnecessarily overloading youths with excessive ground contacts. For example, while a racket-sports player might experience hundreds of ground contacts during match play, it is not advised that coaches simply match this volume in actual plyometric training sessions, due to differences in loading patterns and impulses between free-play activity and formalized plyometric training. This notion is underlined by research that reported how excessive plyometric loading (>250 repeated squat jumps) can lead to exertional rhabdomyolysis in children (Clarkson, 2006). Therefore, to enhance performance and prevent injury, *under*prescribing as opposed to *over*prescribing plyometric provision would be more advantageous to the athletic development of any young athlete.

The total volume of a plyometric session will be largely dependent on the intensity of the exercises selected (based on eccentric loading). For pre-pubescent children it is recommended that a moderate volume (6–10 exercises) of low-intensity exercises is prescribed, using a breadth of different exercises to expose the child to a range of movement stimuli to help condition them for later technical specificity. Additionally, through a fun-based environment, one of the key aims of the strength and conditioning coach should be to develop effective landing mechanics in pre-pubescent children (Lloyd et al., 2011a). Such mechanics would include: a heel–toe landing, supporting triple-flexion at the ankle, knee and hip ('soft knees'), neutral lumbothoracic spine position, and coordination of upper and lower limbs (Lloyd et al., 2011a). These qualities should be developed within a fun environment to maintain interest and enthusiasm, and it is largely down to the skill and imagination of the strength and conditioning coach to develop such competencies within an overall fundamental movement skill development programme (Lloyd et al., 2012c). As children enhance technical competency and experience the onset of puberty and enter post-pubescence, they can generally be exposed to increased intensity within the training programme with a concomitant decrease in training volume. Previously, authors have suggested that in terms of volume prescription, children should start with a single set of 6–10 repetitions, and progress to multiple sets of 6–10 repetitions (Faigenbaum and Chu, 2001).

However, while total number of foot contacts can be used as an indicator of training volume, alternatively training thresholds can be used to ensure volume of training is not completed at the expense of quality of training (Lloyd et al., 2011a). Previous research has shown that SSC function is negatively affected by fatigue, leading to a greater reliance on feedback processes during ground contact as opposed to feed-forward neural regulation prior to ground contact (Padua et al., 2006). In addition to visual observations by the coach, portable contact mats can be used to monitor training thresholds for performance variables such as contact time, jump height or RSI, and real-time feedback can be used to determine the end of a given set as opposed to relying on a predetermined number of repetitions. When performance deteriorates below that threshold (for example an increase in contact time, or a decrease in jump height or RSI), the child is told to stop. If using RSI as the performance indicator, it is important to stress that coaches should monitor both ground contact time and jump height because, while RSI may remain constant, values for the component parts can fluctuate as a result of neural fatigue. Using performance thresholds can account for both inter- and intra-individual variation, and provides a more specific and individualized approach to plyometric training.

Frequency

Training frequency like volume and intensity will be affected by the training status and sport involvement of the youth athlete. For example, the young gymnast can train up to 15–25 hours a week with much of the time spent in high-intensity plyometric activity each day of the week. However, for the untrained athlete it is suggested that a twice-weekly training frequency is appropriate for children, owing to the eccentric loading and potential for muscle damage and the need for sufficient recovery (Faigenbaum, 2006; Faigenbaum and Chu, 2001). A twice-weekly training frequency has also proven to be a sufficient training stimulus to produce positive training adaptations for RSI and leg stiffness in pre-pubescent children and adolescents (Lloyd et al., 2012b). It is expected that, as a child develops from pre-pubescence and enters adolescence, he or she will be able to be exposed to a gradual increase in training frequency, however, due to the neural demands placed on the neuromuscular system, it would be unlikely for adolescents to complete more than 3–4 sessions in a given microcycle.

For a more objective and individualized prescription of plyometric training frequency, the strength and conditioning coach could assess the child for neuromuscular readiness. Previous research has demonstrated that, even when exercise intensity is controlled, children experience less muscle damage than adults, which is likely to be attributable to a more pliable musculotendon unit (Eston et al., 2003). Consequently, using muscle soreness as a neuromuscular monitoring criterion is deemed unsuitable. Alternatively, in addition to visual observation and coach intuition, the use of performance measures, such as the monitoring of RSI during rebounding activities (e.g. drop jump), could provide an insight of neuromuscular fatigue in the child (Lloyd et al., 2011a).

Repetition velocity

Secondary to technical execution, and perhaps the most important training variable to consider when prescribing plyometric exercise, is repetition velocity. Research has demonstrated that the training or testing protocol used determines the category of SSC required (Lloyd et al., 2011c; Schmidtbleicher, 1992). Considering this fact, it is essential that the exercise(s) selected allow the child to perform to the desired repetition velocity. The concept of 'children are not miniature adults' is particularly relevant in this instance, and strength and conditioning coaches should not superimpose those exercises prescribed for adults onto children who may be unable to tolerate high-impact landings. The use of real-time feedback on performance measures (e.g. RSI) and intermittent feedback from the strength and conditioning coach can help educate the athlete, increase motivation and enhance performance outcomes (Flanagan and Comyns, 2008). It is expected that children will naturally develop their repetition velocity of a given plyometric exercise as a consequence of growth and maturational factors. However, when prescribing plyometric programmes, strength and conditioning coaches should at all times emphasize the importance of a fast and powerful interaction with the surface, and consequently there are no maturity-specific guidelines for repetition velocity.

Plyometric exercise progressions

Previous researchers have proposed different progression schemes, however, it is generally accepted that pre-pubescent children with minimal training history should commence with a low-level structure approach to training, inclusive of landing-mechanics exercises, minimal to low eccentric-loading plyometrics and fundamental movement skill development. As children enhance technical competency and enter the pubertal period, both the level of structure and intensity of plyometric exercise can increase. During this phase of development, children can be introduced to greater loadings during exercises such as multiple hops, jumps onto boxes and repeated jumps over mini hurdles. Adolescents and young adults can engage in a much more structured approach to training, and, for this population, training programmes can consist of higher intensity exercises, such as bounding, multiple box jumps and drop jumping from various heights (Lloyd *et al.*, 2011a). As a caveat to this approach, and as with any training prescription, consideration must be given to the training history and technical competency of the individual, and therefore a flexible approach to youth plyometric training prescription should be encouraged (Lloyd and Oliver, 2012).

Summary

Existing research has highlighted that, as a consequence of natural gains in muscular power, plyometric ability increases during childhood and adolescence. One of the key physiological mechanisms underpinning efficient movement is the utilization of the SSC. Researchers have demonstrated that the neural regulation of this specific muscle action improves during the developmental years with a transient shift from protective, long-latency reflexes to preactive, short-latency reflex recruitment. However, in addition to the mechanistic developmental literature, there is a growing body of evidence that demonstrates youths of all ages can make significant performance adaptations by following a well-structured and developmentally appropriate plyometric training programme.

Key points

- Researchers suggest the potential existence of pre-pubertal and adolescent 'windows of opportunity' for different forms of SSC function.
- Improvements in SSC function and a range of other performance measures have been reported in youths following plyometric training programmes ranging in duration from 4 to 10 weeks.
- It is thought that neural mechanisms are largely responsible for both natural and training-induced developments in SSC function, in particular in pre-pubescent children.
- Strength and conditioning coaches must first introduce pre-pubescents to a range of low-intensity plyometrics ensuring that technical competency is mastered prior to loading with any great intensity, volume and/or frequency.

- With an increase in training history, technical competency and maturational status, plyometric training focus can then move towards moderate and higher-intensity plyometrics.
- In order to maximize training adaptations and minimize injury risk, all plyometric training programmes must be individualized, to accommodate for individual variations in maturation rates, training history and sport involvement.

References

Balyi, I. and Hamilton, A. (2004) *Long-Term Athlete Development: Trainability in Children and Adolescents. Windows of Opportunity, Optimal Trainability*, Victoria: National Coaching Institute British Colombia and Advanced Training and Performance Ltd.

Beunen, G. P. (1997) 'Muscular strength development in children and adolescents'. In: K. Froberg, O. Lammert, H. S. Hansen and C. J. R. Blimkie (eds) *Children and Exercise XVIII. Exercise and Fitness: Benefits and Risks*. Odense: Odense University Press, pp. 193–207.

Beunen, G. and Malina, R. M. (1988) 'Growth and physical performance relative to the timing of the adolescent spurt', *Exercise and Sport Sciences Reviews*, 16: 503–540.

Bobbert, M. F., Gerritsen, K. G., Litjens, M. C. and Van Soest, A. J. (1996) 'Why is counter-movement jump height greater than squat jump height?' *Medicine and Science in Sports and Exercise*, 28: 1402–1412.

Bompa, T. O. and Haff, G. G. (2009) *Periodization: Theory and Methodology of Training*, Champaign, IL: Human Kinetics.

Bosco, C., Vitasalo, J. T., Komi, P. V. and Luhtanen, P. (1982) 'Potentiation during stretch-shortening cycle exercise', *Acta Physiologica Scandinavica*, 114: 557–565.

Branta, C., Haubenstricker, J. and Seefeldt, V. (1984) 'Age changes in motor skills during childhood and adolescence', *Exercise and Sport Sciences Reviews*, 12: 467–520.

Bret, C., Rahmani, A., Dufour, A. B., Messonnier, L. and Lacour, J. R. (2002) 'Leg strength and stiffness as ability factors in 100m sprint running', *Journal of Sports Medicine and Physical Fitness*, 274: 274–281.

Chelly, S. M. and Denis, C. (2001) 'Leg power and hopping stiffness: relationship with sprint running performance', *Medicine and Science in Sports and Exercise*, 33: 326–333.

Clarkson, P. M. (2006) 'Case report of exertional rhabdomyolysis in a 12–year old boy', *Medicine and Science in Sports and Exercise*, 38: 197–200.

Cormie, P., McGuigan, M. R. and Newton, R. U. (2011) 'Developing maximal neuromuscular power: Part 1 – biological basis of maximal power production', *Sports Medicine*, 41: 17–38.

Croce, R. V., Russell, P. J., Swartz, E. E. and Decoster, L. C. (2004) 'Knee muscular response strategies differ by developmental level but not gender during jump landing', *Electromyography and Clinical Neurophysiology*, 44: 339–348.

Eston, R., Byrne, C. and Twist, C. (2003) 'Muscle function after exercise-induced muscle damage: considerations for athletic performance in children and adults', *Journal of Exercise Science and Fitness*, 1: 85–96.

Faigenbaum, A. D. (2006) 'Plyometrics for kids: facts and fallacies', *Performance Training Journal*, 5: 13–16.

Faigenbaum, A. D. and Chu, D. A. (2001) 'Plyometric training for children and adolescents', ACSM Current Comment.

Faigenbaum, A. D., McFarland, J. E., Keiper, F. B., Tevlin, W., Ratamess, N. A., Kang, J. and Hoffman, J. R. (2007) 'Effects of a short-term plyometric and resistance training program on fitness in boys age 12 to 15 years', *Journal of Sports Science and Medicine*, 6: 519–525.

Flanagan, E. P. and Comyns, T. M. (2008) 'The use of contact time and the reactive strength index to optimize fast stretch-shortening cycle training', *Strength and Conditioning Journal*, 30: 32–38.

Ford, P., De Ste Croix, M., Lloyd, R., Meyers, R., Moosavi, M. and Oliver, J. (2011) The Long-Term Athlete Development model: physiological evidence and application', *Journal of Sports Sciences*, 29: 389–402.

Gambetta, V. (2007) *Athletic Development*, Champaign, IL: Human Kinetics.

Grosset, J. F., Mora, I., Lambertz, D. and Perot, C. (2007) 'Changes in stretch reflexes and muscle stiffness with age in pre-pubescent children', *Journal of Applied Physiology*, 102: 2352–2360.

Harrison, A. J. and Gaffney, S. (2001) 'Motor development and gender effects on stretch-shortening cycle performance', *Journal of Science and Medicine in Sport*, 4: 406–415.

Hobara, H., Kimura, K., Omuro, K., Gomi, K., Muraoka, T., Iso, S. and Kanouse, K. (2008) 'Determinants of difference in leg stiffness between endurance- and power-trained athletes', *Journal of Biomechanics*, 41: 506–514.

Hutton, R. S. and Atwater, S. W. (1992) 'Acute and chronic adaptations of muscle proprioceptors in response to increased use', *Sports Medicine*, 14: 406–421.

Isaacs, L. D. (1998) 'Comparison of the Vertec and Just Jump systems for measuring height of vertical jump by young children', *Perceptual and Motor Skills*, 86: 659–663.

Kerdok, A. E., Biewener, A. A., McMahon, T. A., Weyand, P. G. and Herr, H. M. (2002) 'Energetics and mechanics of human running on surfaces of different stiffnesses', *Journal of Applied Physiology*, 92: 469–478.

Kram, R. (2000) 'Muscular force or work: what determines the metabolic energy cost of running?' *Exercise and Sport Sciences Reviews*, 28: 138–143.

Komi, P. V. (2000) 'Stretch-shortening cycle: a powerful model to study normal and fatigued muscle', *Journal of Biomechanics*, 33: 1197–1206.

Komi, P. V. (2003) 'Units of measurement and terminology'. In: P.V. Komi (ed.) *Strength and Power in Sport*, Oxford: Blackwell Science.

Komi, P. V. and Gollhofer, A. (1997) 'Stretch reflex can have an important role in force enhancement during SSC-exercise', *Journal of Applied Biomechanics*, 33: 1197–1206.

Korff, T., Horne, S. L., Cullen, S. J. and Blazevich, A. J. (2009) 'Development of lower limb stiffness and its contribution to maximum jumping power during adolescences', *Journal of Experimental Biology*, 212: 3737–3742.

Kotzamanidis, C. (2006) 'Effect of plyometric training on running performance and vertical jumping in pre-pubertal boys', *Journal of Strength and Conditioning Research*, 20: 441–445.

Kubo, K., Morimoto, M., Komuro, T., Tsunoda, N., Kanehisa, H. and Fukunaga, T. (2007) 'Influences of tendon stiffness, joint stiffness, and electromyographic activity on jump performances using single joint', *European Journal of Applied Physiology*, 99: 235–243.

Lambertz, D., Mora, I., Grosset, J. F. and Perot, C. (2003) 'Evaluation of musculotendinous stiffness in pre-pubertal children and adults, taking into account muscle activity', *Journal of Applied Physiology*, 95: 64–72.

Lloyd, R. S. and Oliver, J. L. (2012) 'The Youth Physical Development model: a new approach to long-term athletic development', *Strength and Conditioning Journal*, 34: 61–72.

Lloyd, R. S., Oliver, J. L., Hughes, M. G. and Williams, C. A. (2012a) 'Age-related differences in the neural regulation of stretch-shortening cycle activities in male youths during maximal and sub-maximal hopping', *Journal of Electromyography and Kinesiology*, 22: 37–43.

Lloyd, R. S., Oliver, J. L., Hughes, M. G. and Williams, C. A. (2012b) 'Effects of 4-week plyometric training on reactive strength index and leg stiffness in male youths', *Journal of Strength and Conditioning Research*, 26: 2812–2819.

Lloyd, R. S., Oliver, J. L., Meyers, R. W., Moody, J. and Stone, M. H. (2012c) 'Long-term athletic development and its application to youth weightlifting', *Strength and Conditioning Journal*, 34: 55–66.

Lloyd, R. S., Oliver, J. L. and Meyers, R. W. (2011a) 'The natural development and trainability of plyometric ability during childhood', *Strength and Conditioning Journal*, 33: 23–32.

Lloyd, R. S., Oliver, J. L., Hughes, M. G. and Williams, C. A. (2011b) 'The influence of chronological age on periods of accelerated adaptation of stretch-shortening cycle performance in pre- and post-pubescent boys', *Journal of Strength and Conditioning Research*, 25; 1889–1897.

Lloyd, R. S., Oliver, J. L., Hughes, M. G. and Williams, C. A. (2011c) 'Specificity of test selection for the appropriate assessment of different measures of stretch-shortening cycle function in children', *Journal of Sports Medicine and Physical Fitness*, 51: 595–602.

McMahon, T. A. and Cheng, G. C. (1990) 'The mechanics of running: how does stiffness couple with speed?', *Journal of Biomechanics*, 23: 65–78.

Malina, R. M., Bouchard, C. and Bar-Or, O. (2004) *Growth, Maturation, and Physical Activity*, Champaign, IL: Human Kinetics.

Matavulj, D., Kukolj, M., Ugarkovic, D., Tihanyi, J. and Jaric, S. (2001) 'Effects of plyometric training on jumping performance in junior basketball players', *Journal of Sports Medicine and Physical Fitness*, 41: 159–164.

Meylan, C. and Malatesta, D. (2009) 'Effects of in-season plyometric training within soccer practice on explosive actions of young players', *Journal of Strength and Conditioning Research*, 23: 2605–2613.

Newton, R. U. and Kraemer, W. J. (1994) 'Developing explosive muscular power: implications for a mixed method training strategy', *Strength and Conditioning Journal*, 16: 20–31.

Nicol, C., Avela, J. and Komi, P. V. (2006) 'The stretch–shortening cycle: a model to study naturally occurring neuromuscular fatigue', *Sports Medicine*, 36: 977–999.

Oliver, J. L. and Smith, P. M. (2010) 'Neural control of leg stiffness during hopping in boys and men', *Journal of Electromyography and Kinesiology*, 20: 973–979.

Padua, D. A., Arnold, B. L., Perrin, D. H., Gansneders, B. M., Carcia, C. R. and Granata, K. P. (2006) 'Fatigue, vertical leg stiffness, and stiffness control strategies in males and females', *Journal of Athletic Training*, 41: 294–304.

Potach, D. H. and Chu, D. A. (2008) 'Plyometric training'. In: T. R. Baechle and R. W. Earle (eds) *Essentials of Strength Training and Conditioning*, Champaign, IL: Human Kinetics.

Schmidtbleicher, D. (1992) 'Training for power events'. In: P. V. Komi (eds) *Strength and Power in Sport*, Oxford: Blackwell Scientific Publications, pp. 381–395.

Thomas, K., French, D. and Hayes, P. R. (2009) 'The effect of plyometric training techniques on muscular power and agility in youth soccer players', *Journal of Strength and Conditioning Research*, 23: 332–335.

Viru, A., Loko, J., Harro, M., Volver, A., Laaneots, L. and Viru, M. (1999) 'Critical periods in the development of performance capacity during childhood and adolescence', *European Journal of Physical Education*, 4: 75–119.

Young, W. B. (2006) 'Transfer of strength and power training to sports performance', *International Journal of Sports Performance and Physiology*, 1: 74–83.

8

AGILITY DEVELOPMENT IN YOUTHS

Ian Jeffreys

Introduction

Chapter 4 outlined the importance of developing physical literacy in youth athletes, as the basis of both sporting excellence and physical activity for health. Physical literacy is itself composed of fundamental movement skills together with fundamental sport skills (Higgs *et al.*, 2008). One key element of fitness closely linked to fundamental movement capacity is the concept of agility, and the development of high levels of agility should be a key part of any long-term physical development programme for a youth athlete.

What is agility?

While agility is generally regarded as a key component of athletic performance and long-term athlete development models (Balyi and Hamilton, 2000), the term 'agility' is perhaps the most difficult of all fitness components to define. Ultimately, agility expression will be dictated by the sporting context in which it is expressed, and will differ between sports. Given its importance to the majority of field- and team-based sports, this chapter will focus on the development of locomotive agility in youths, and the term agility from here on in will refer to locomotive agility. However, even definitions of locomotive agility vary considerably, and significantly impact upon how agility is measured and developed. Classic definitions have defined agility in terms of its constituent movement components, with particular emphasis on change of direction ability (Vescovi, 2006). However, it is important to remember that agility will ultimately be applied in a sports situation with the young athlete attempting to utilise effective movement in the completion of sport-related tasks. Therefore, many definitions are limited by the fact that they do not take account of a context for the application of agility, and therefore fail to address the wide range of movements that the young athlete will need to carry out in the playing of their sport. While the aforementioned movements are important, they cannot totally explain an athlete's agility capabilities, as sports where pre-planned changes of movement direction or velocity occur are rare, and most sports involve decision-making with subsequent movement dependent upon these cognitive processes (Jeffreys, 2011). When agility becomes contextualised, it becomes evident that agility is a complex parameter and involves far more than the performance of certain movements (Young *et al.*, 2002). Therefore, agility can be viewed as game speed being context-specific movement where an athlete maximises their sports performance via the application of sport-specific movement of optimal velocity, precision, efficiency and control in anticipation of, and in response to, the key perceptual stimuli, and skill requirements of the game (Jeffreys, 2010). This definition provides a context for agility and requires that a coach carefully study the agility requirements for sports, and then develops these appropriately in the young athlete to maximise transfer from training to performance.

The importance of agility to youth sports performance

High levels of agility have the ability to enhance the levels of performance of youth athletes in a large number of sports, as agility is an important bridge between technical training and actual performance. Often, the quality of a youth performer's skills will be closely linked to their ability to react and move into optimal positions to perform these skills. Agility may therefore be considered as a fundamental skill required for effective performance in a range of sports, with competency in underpinning movement abilities providing a base upon which successful sports performance can be built. This is supported by the fact that children can often perform new skills effectively because of general underlying motor abilities (Schmidt and Lee, 2005). The development of effective movement capabilities should therefore be an integral part of all youth athlete development programmes. This is especially important as youth athletes are often likely to participate in a range of sports, and underpinning athleticism and movement capacity are likely to enhance performance across all of these sports.

Factors affecting agility

Prior to examining the trainability of agility in the youth population it is important to examine the key factors underpinning effective agility. This requires that agility is first viewed from the perspective of its ultimate application, and then analysed against the key factors involved in its optimal development in youth athletes. Essentially, effective agility in a game context involves a perception–action cycle that seeks information from the external environment and processes this to elicit the appropriate movement response (Jeffreys, 2011).

When the limits to the expression of effective agility are examined, three main constraints can be identified: organismic, task and environmental (Jeffreys, 2011).

Organismic constraints refer to the specific qualities of the individual in relation to the entire perception–action cycle. Task-based constraints involve the unique characteristics of the task itself – essentially the rules under which the athlete will have to perform – while environmental constraints refer to the unique characteristics of the environment in which the task is being undertaken (Jeffreys, 2011). Many of these constraints will become of increasing importance as the level of specific sports performance increases, and as the youth athlete progresses through the development pyramid (Figure 8.1). However, given that, in the main, the focus on youth sport is on development, and that youth athletes often take part in more than one sport, the focus here will be upon the organismic constraints affecting the young athlete.

As agility involves a perception–action cycle, the organismic constraints on agility will therefore affect each part of the cycle. The organismic constraints affecting agility can be classified as perceptual, cognitive, physical and motor control (Jeffreys, 2011). Physical constraints are those typically associated with the strength and conditioning coach. Factors will be diverse, such as the athlete's force production capacities, their stretch-shortening cycle (SSC) capabilities and their mobility. While important, these alone cannot determine the quality of agility performance. Effective movement requires the development of high-quality motor programmes (motor control constraints), and, as with all skills, these need to be developed over a long period of time. This requires the development of key agility-based movement patterns and their subsequent application in sport settings.

Agility is ultimately expressed during sports performance, and this requires the ability to move effectively in response to the evolving game. Perceptive constraints to agility performance refer to the ability to pay attention to, and detect, key

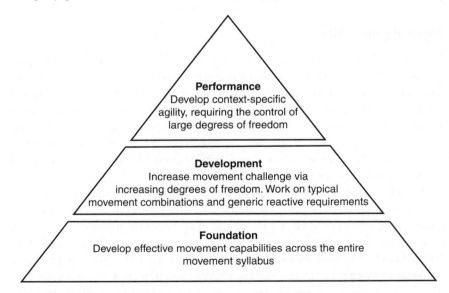

FIGURE 8.1 The agility development pyramid

Source: adapted from Jeffreys, 2010.

elements of the external environment. Similarly, performance will be affected by cognitive constraints, which relate to the ability to process this information and make appropriate movement choices. Optimal agility development requires that youth athletes develop the appropriate mind–body links to ensure that the entire perception–action cycle is addressed and optimally developed.

The development of agility during childhood and adolescence

The application of agility will ultimately require the learned ability to deploy movements with consistency, efficiency and effectiveness in a sport-specific context. Quite clearly, agility is a skill, and, as with most skills, needs to be developed in accordance with optimal models of learning and development. It is important, therefore, to examine the natural development of agility in youth athletes and how this can be optimised through an appropriate training programme. A challenge to the development of an optimal model for agility development in youth athletes is that agility remains one of the most under-researched aspects of paediatric performance. This makes it difficult to ascertain the effects of age and maturation on agility performance, and also makes any recommendations as to the optimal trainability of agility largely speculative. To offset this limitation, it is useful to categorise agility performance via the organismic constraints outlined in Figure 8.2. Examining agility under the banners of physical, perceptual, cognitive and motor control constraints allows research in other domains of paediatric physical development to be examined and the results extrapolated to agility performance.

Physical constraints

In terms of physical constraints, two key factors closely associated with agility performance are linear running speed and the athlete's force-producing capacities. In terms of force-producing capacities, it can be expected that healthy children will demonstrate noticeable gains in muscle strength during the developmental years as a result of natural maturation (Rowland, 2005). Adolescents make greater absolute gains than children. Given that agility expression requires the application of force, then an associated increase in force-producing capacity should result in a natural increase in agility performance.

A key factor is whether this force-producing capacity can be augmented through training. A compelling body of evidence indicates that, with an appropriate resistance-training programme, children and adolescents can significantly increase their strength over and above that resulting from growth and maturation alone (Faigenbaum et al., 2009). During and after puberty, strength gains are associated with hypertrophic factors as well as neural factors, while in children it appears that strength gains elicited from a training programme are predominantly related to neural mechanisms (Faigenbaum et al., 2008). Neural adaptations include increased motor unit activation, and changes in motor unit coordination, recruitment and firing (Ramsey et al.,

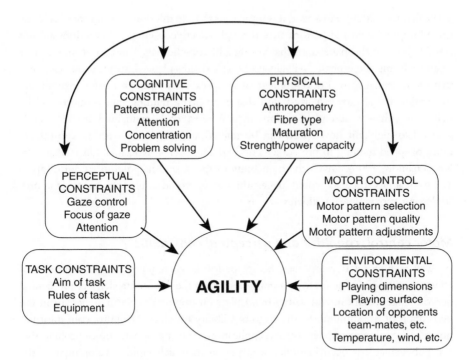

FIGURE 8.2 Agility constraints

Source: adapted from Jeffreys, 2011.

1990; Ozmun *et al.*, 1994), and an associated increase in motor skill performance (Ramsey *et al.*, 1990). Improvements have been recorded in a number of motor performance skills following resistance training, including standing long jump, vertical jump, sprint speed and medicine ball toss (Faigenbaum *et al.*, 2008). While no data currently exists as to whether agility can be improved via enhancing a youth athlete's force-producing capacity, these potential neural adaptations, and their subsequent affect on motor performance would suggest the potential to increase agility performance via an enhancement of force-producing capacity, and that this would exist for both children and adolescents.

In terms of linear speed development, Papalakovou *et al.* (2009) found that age uniformly affected running speed during each 10 m section of a 30 m sprint. They found that there was a significant development of speed evident every 2–3 years, indicating a growth and maturation effect to speed. While boys performed on average better than girls, this differential increased after the age of 15. Additionally, speed increases appear to reach a plateau, which occurred after the age of 15 for boys and between 12 and 13 for girls. In relation to strength development, speed is improved earlier than strength and with approximately 75 per cent of the performance achieved at age 18 visible at age 12, whereas strength is typically 40–50 per cent (Bassa *et al.*, 2001). This supports the assertions that scores in motor performance, in the absence of training interventions, appear to plateau at the end of the peak height velocity (PHV) phase (Phillipaerts *et al.*,

2006; Gamble, 2008). However, it is important to note this does not indicate that continued improvements in performance through effective training interventions are not possible beyond this plateau, or that young athletes who have missed out on effective training during these phases will always be at a disadvantage. Instead, it only suggests that the maximal natural development of speed capacity through natural growth and maturation has already occurred, and that appropriate training interventions will be needed to enhance subsequent performance. In terms of the trainability of speed, studies to date highlight how speed can be trained and improved with an appropriate input of speed training in pre-adolescents and adolescents (Kotzamanidis *et al.*, 2005; Kotzamanidis, 2006). Given the trainability of speed, and its potential relationship to aspects of agility, the data would suggest that agility would similarly be trainable in pre-adolescent and adolescent athletes.

Motor control, cognitive and perceptual constraints

As well as physical development, agility performance requires the development of effective and consistent motor programmes. Movement is controlled via the central nervous system (CNS), and so the brain plays an important role in agility, from the perception of the stimulus, to the cognitive ability to select the appropriate information and the subsequent selection and application of an appropriate motor programme. Pre-pubescence has been identified as a period in which rapid development of the neuromuscular system occurs (Borms, 1986), and pre-adolescents have considerable potential for motor learning with a prime window of opportunity prior to puberty (Gamble, 2008). This would fit in with the fact that around the ages of 11–12 pre-adolescents go through a growth spurt in synaptic elaboration (Howard, 2006).

This process starts in the rear of the brain, moving progressively to the middle and finally to the pre-frontal cortex (Howard, 2006). This sequence has important implications for agility learning. The rear part of the brain is responsible for processing sensory information, and is involved in dealing with the perceptive information required for effective agility performance. The middle section of the brain is the part that coordinates movement, and is thus responsible for the development of effective motor programmes. The pre-frontal cortex is responsible for governing decision-making and planning, and is ultimately responsible for making effective movement-based decisions in sports contexts. While there is little direct data to support the concept of a prime window of opportunity, it would seem logical that agility development should play an important role in the training of an athlete through this pre-pubescent period, developing the motor programmes, along with the perceptive and cognitive capacities that will underpin performance in subsequent phases of training. This should also maximise the natural development of the brain by involving sensory information from the start and progressively developing efficient and effective motor programmes and effective task-based, decision-making capabilities.

Studies of the way a brain functions can also give an insight into the value of open drills to agility development, for both novice and advanced youth athletes.

To perform well in sports, the brain has to develop optimal synaptic linkages that directly connect the areas responsible for the decision-making processes with those involved in optimising the physical responses (Vickers, 2007). When cognitively challenging tasks are presented, both areas of the brain are active, effectively developing these synaptic linkages. In the early stages of development these linkages need to be encouraged, but due to the delayed development of the pre-frontal cortex, decision-making capacities will be limited. Therefore, exercises need to be used that initially limit the amount of information to be taken in and also limit the subsequent movement decisions and options required. As the young athlete develops, increasing information can be provided, and an increase in the number of movement options given to progressively develop key synaptic linkages. If exercises are not progressed, or remain predominantly closed in nature, the athlete will only be able to perform these with less and less cognitive involvement. This has potential downsides to learning and performance as, once automation is achieved, the higher centres are not stimulated, and the centres for automacy take over. The centres for automacy are able to perform well in predictable environments, but are unable to detect new cues and adapt to unpredictable environments (Draganski *et al.*, 2004). This makes movement patterns developed in closed environments at risk of breaking down when unusual or stressful conditions are encountered (Winstein and Schmidt, 1990). Therefore, as a young athlete progresses, there needs to be an increased cognitive challenge, to ensure that learning continues and is ultimately maximised.

Practical applications

Effective skill development is based upon an appropriate sequence of development, as individuals learn skills in progression (Schmidt and Lee, 2005). Therefore, just as in an educational setting, a sequential syllabus can be developed by which movement abilities can be sequentially developed as to ultimately maximise game performance. Figure 8.1 outlines such a sequential agility pyramid, whereby movement patterns are introduced and then sequentially progressed through stages until the athlete is capable of applying the movements in the sport-specific setting.

Children begin to develop locomotor skills at an early age, although activity at this stage is relatively unstructured. Formal development of agility through the foundation phase can be introduced between the ages of 9 and 12 years, where a window of opportunity for skill development is thought to exist (Gamble, 2008). In these early stages of development, analogous to the cognitive stage of skill development (Schmidt and Lee, 2005), the complexity of movements needs to be largely controlled. Here, the aim should be to develop the full range of movement capacities, and also to introduce the perceptive skills required for optimal performance. At this stage, movement competency is likely to be relatively low, and the use of closed, relatively simple drills, utilising a behavioural approach to learning, can be of use at this stage. These can be especially effective where a degree of variation and randomness are introduced to the drills and where they are supplemented by effective questioning. A key aim here is to draw the young athlete's attention to the key rules of movement and to aid in the development of some of the cognitive skills required of advanced performance. However, the inexperience of the athlete also presents a challenge to the use of drills at this stage. Young athletes often need a context in which to effectively learn skills, and where drills are performed in isolation, young athletes can often be unaware of how they relate to performance (Vickers, 2007). In order to contextualise the movement patterns, and to start to link perceptive and cognitive elements together with movements, a small range of more open drills can be utilised within each session. Providing a contextual activity prior to the use of a drill can help young athletes understand the context of the subsequent drill, and can also help develop an external focus of attention (Jeffreys, 2011). The relative weighting of closed to open drills will depend upon the training age and the ability of the individual athlete. At this stage the quality of the movement patterns should take precedence over the speed of the pattern.

The development phase will occur predominantly between the ages of 12 and 15. At these times young athletes who have successfully completed the previous stage are likely to enter the associative stage of learning and here, the aim is to master the general movement patterns and develop these in relation to key movement combinations and general sporting tasks. The movement combinations involve the deployment of a series of movement patterns, similar to those typically seen in sport. While closed drills will still be used in the earlier stages of this phase, there is a far greater emphasis on open drills, whereby the athlete is required to respond to increasing movement challenges and movement tasks that become increasingly sport specific as the stage progresses. This increases the cognitive effort required and helps develop and reinforce the synaptic linkages required for optimal performance in the random environment experienced in the majority of sports. Exercise can still be generic at the start of this stage, and a dynamic systems approach to learning is especially useful at this time (Holcomb, 2009). Towards the end of this stage, athletes are likely to start specialising in one or two sports, and so exercises can become more specific and more task-based challenges can be introduced (Jeffreys, 2011).

An important note here is that this stage will normally include the onset of PHV. At these times the athlete's coordination will be significantly challenged as they learn to cope with their rapid increase in body dimensions. Thus, progress in this stage is non-linear, and the coach might occasionally need to regress drill complexity to enable an appropriate level of stimulus to the athlete undergoing the growth spurt.

In the performance phase, the athlete will have undertaken a significant degree of training, and their movement patterns should show an appropriate level of consistency and effectiveness. During this stage the athlete may reach the autonomous level of skill development. Here, their movement patterns will become highly automated, and a greater degree of challenge is needed in order to provide sufficient stimulus and cognitive challenge to ensure further gains in agility performance. The athlete at this stage is likely to be specialising in a given sport, and the use of context-specific tasks utilising a high degree of context specificity and a high number of degrees of freedom, are ideal (Jeffreys, 2011).

What movements need to be developed? Breaking down agility into component parts

The development pathway in Figure 8.1 outlines how agility can be sequentially developed in young athletes, from basic movement skills to context specific movement. However, agility involves a wide range of movement patterns that are closely linked to sports performance. A key aspect of typical skill development programmes is that skills are first broken down into component parts and then progressively pieced together into a whole form that matches performance requirements. While this can be relatively simple to do with some sports, it can be a daunting task for agility, given the range of movements deployed in any sport. However, the target classifications of agility (Jeffreys, 2006) allow coaches to break down movements into clearly identifiable component parts. These then allow an agility syllabus to be developed that can be applied across a wide range of sports.

The first element in this classification is the 'target function', which looks at movement in terms of what the athlete is trying to achieve. Essentially, all movements can be broken down into three classifications: initiation movements, transition movements and actualisation movements (Figure 8.3). Initiation movements refer to times where an athlete is trying to start movement or change the direction of movement. They look predominantly at the processes by which an athlete attempts to initiate these movements, essentially looking at the quality of the first step in this process. Once the initiation takes place, it is often followed by actualisation movements, which refer to the full expression of performance, and involve elements such as acceleration and high-speed running. Actualisation movements have traditionally been the focus of speed and agility training. However,

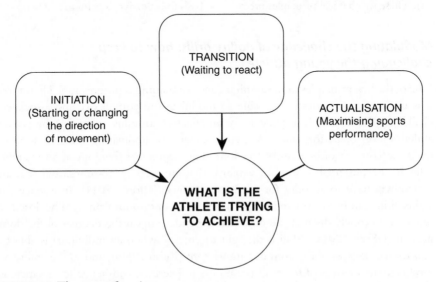

FIGURE 8.3 The target functions

close inspection of most sports shows that athletes spend a relatively small amount of time in initiation and actualisation movements and instead spend a large amount of time waiting to react to a given stimulus, and at this time undertake transition movements. The key determinant of performance in transition movements is seldom speed alone, but rather the maintenance of a position of control from where to react and make a subsequent initiation movement.

The agility syllabus: the target movements and target mechanics

Within these target functions, a number of key movements can be identified. In this way each target function will include a number of movements that an athlete may be required to perform. These form the basis of the target movements that the athlete will have to learn to make in order to effectively perform in the sport. In general the following movements can be identified for the vast majority of sports (Table 8.1). These can be viewed as a movement syllabus, and athletes who have developed high capabilities in each of these movements will be able to perform effectively in the vast majority of sports situations.

It must always be remembered that the performance of an exercise is not guaranteed to develop that ability unless it is performed correctly. A vital prerequisite for effective coaching is that the coach must have a firm understanding of the movement patterns to be developed, and how they are deployed in sport. Similarly, they must possess the ability to identify and correct errors in movement, and ensure athletes deploy optimal technique at all times to ensure the development of effective motor programmes. Using mechanical principles, these target movements can be further broken down into the preferred techniques with which to perform these movements (the target mechanics). These mechanical principles provide the basis for effective coaching.

Modulating the challenge of agility drills: how to keep challenging the young athlete

One of the key principles underpinning effective training is progression. Therefore, it is important that coaches are able to modulate the complexity and associated challenge of agility drills to provide for an effective stimulus, whatever the young athlete's level of performance. A useful concept in modulating agility complexity is the concept of degrees of freedom. The degrees of freedom of an exercise refer to the potential sources of variance that an exercise possesses, and that an athlete will have to account for when performing (Jeffreys, 2011). In essence, all agility drills can be considered as appearing on a continuum from totally closed at one end, to totally open at the other, all dependent upon the degrees of freedom present (Jeffreys, 2011). Skill is thought to emerge when an individual is able to control the degrees of freedom of a movement (Kelso, 1995), and so the ability to modulate the degrees of freedom present in an exercise, and hence its variance, is an extremely useful tool in the development of agility skills.

TABLE 8.1 Target movements and target mechanics

Initiation

Target function	Target movement	Target movement patterns
Starting	Starting to the front	Acceleration pattern
	Starting to the side	Hip turn
	Starting to the rear	Drop step
Changing direction	Changing direction laterally	Cut step
	Changing direction from front to back and vice versa	Plant step

Transition

Target function	Target movement	Target movement patterns
Static wait to react	Static wait	Athletic position
In motion	In place	Jockeying
	To the front	Controlled run
	Laterally	Side shuffle
	Diagonally	Cross-step run
	To the rear	Backpedal/backtrack
Decelerating	Linear	Plant/chop to athletic position
	Lateral	Cut step

Actualisation

Target function	Target movement	Target movement patterns
Acceleration	Acceleration	Acceleration pattern
Maximal speed	Linear	Maximum speed pattern
	Curvilinear	Curved run

Source: adapted from Jeffreys, 2010.

Variance itself can come via two forms: spatial and temporal. Spatial variance refers to variations in elements such as distance and direction, while temporal variation refers to changes in the timing of a stimulus (Jeffreys, 2011). In typical closed drills there are no degrees of freedom, as movement is totally pre-planned for a predetermined distance using predetermined movements and in a predetermined direction and where the timing of the movement is totally dependent upon the athlete. The addition of a temporal variant, or a spatial variant, adds to the degrees of freedom the athlete will have to cope with, and provides a further challenge to the drill, as the athlete cannot pre-plan their movements. This will add complexity to the exercise, and thus require a greater cognitive effort and provides a method of progression of any agility exercise. Progression should be based upon the demonstration of competency in the previous exercise and, once competency is shown, degrees of freedom can be added to provide subsequent challenge.

Key points

Agility is ultimately a highly context-specific capability and underpins the performance of many sport skills. In constructing an effective agility development programme the following key points should be kept in mind:

- Agility is a key performance in many sports, and needs to be a vital component in the training of all young athletes.
- Agility performance will be affected by organismic, task and environmental constraints.
- Agility development is optimised via a sequential model of development that is based upon the physiological and cognitive development of the young athlete.
- The target classifications allow the component parts of effective agility to be identified, and then sequentially developed to enable young athletes to ultimately perform in sport-specific contexts.
- The use of degrees of freedom allows agility challenges to be progressively enhanced to increase the cognitive challenge to the young athlete.

References

Balyi, I. and Hamilton, A. (2000) 'A key to success: Long term athlete development', *Sport Coach*, 23: 10–32.

Bassa, E., Kotzamanidis, C., Patikas, D. and Paraschos, I. (2001) 'The effect of age on isokinetic concentric and eccentric moment of knee extensors', *Isokinetics and Exercise Science*, 9: 155–161.

Borms, J. (1986) 'The child and exercise: An overview', *Journal of Sports Sciences*, 4: 3–20.

Draganski, B., Gaser, C., Busch, V., Schuierer, T., Bogdahn, U. and May, A. (2004) 'Neuroplasticity: Changes in grey matter induced by training', *Nature*, 427: 311–312.

Faigenbaum, A. D., Kraemer, W. J., Blimkie, C. J., Jeffreys, I., Micheli, L. J., Nitka, M. and Rowland, T. W. (2009) 'Youth resistance training: Updated position statement paper from the National Strength and Conditioning Association', *Journal of Strength and Conditioning Research*, 23: S60–S79.

Gamble, P. (2008) 'Approaching physical preparation for youth team sport players', *Strength and Conditioning Journal*, 30: 29–42.

Higgs, C., Balyi, I., Way, R., Cardinal, C., Norris, S. and Bluechardt, M. (2008) *Developing Physical Literacy: A Guide for Parents of Children Aged 0–12*, Vancouver: Canadian Sports Centres.

Holcomb, P.M. (2009) 'Agility training for experienced athletes: A dynamical systems approach', *Strength and Conditioning Journal*, 31: 73–78.

Howard, P.J. (2006) *The Owner's Manual of the Brain*, Austin, TX: Bard Press.

Jeffreys, I. (2006) 'Motor learning: Applications for agility, Part 1', *Strength and Conditioning Journal*, 28: 72–76.

Jeffreys, I. (2010) *Gamespeed: Movement Training for Superior Sports Performance*, Monterey, CA: Coaches Choice.

Jeffreys, I. (2011) 'A task based approach to developing reactive agility', *Strength and Conditioning Journal*, 33: 52–59.

Kelso, J.A.S. (1995) *Dynamic Patterns: The Self Organization of Brain and Behaviour*, Boston, MA: MIT Press.

Kotzamanidis, C. (2006) 'The effect of plyometric training on running performance and vertical jump in pre-adolescent boys', *Journal of Strength and Conditioning Research*, 44: 225–240.

Kotzamanidis, C., Chatzopoulos, D., Michailidis, C., Papaiakovou, G. and Patikas, D. (2005) 'The effect of a combined high-intensity strength and speed training program on the running and jumping ability of soccer players', *Journal of Strength and Conditioning Research*, 19: 369–375.

Ozmun, J., Mikesky, A. and Surburg, P. (1994) 'Neuromuscular adaptations following pre-pubescent strength training', *Medicine and Science in Sports and Exercise*, 26: 510–514.

Papaiakovou, G., Giannakos, A., Michailidis, C., Patikas, D., Bassa, E., Kalopisis, V., Anthrakidis, N. and Kotzamanidis, C. (2009) 'The effect of chronological age and gender on the development of sprint performance during childhood and puberty', *Journal of Strength and Conditioning Research*, 23: 2568–2573.

Philippaerts, R.M., Vaeyens, R., Janssens, M., Van Renterghem, B., Matthys, D., Craen, R., Bourgois, J., Vrijens, J., Beunen, G. and Malina, R. M. (2006) 'The relationship between peak height velocity and physical performance in youth soccer players', *Journal of Sports Sciences*, 24: 221–230.

Ramsay, J., Blimkie, C., Smith, K., Garner, S., Macdougall, J. and Sale, D. (1990) 'Strength training effects in pre-pubescent boys', *Medicine and Science in Sports and Exercise*, 22: 605–614.

Rowland, T. (2005) *Children's Exercise Physiology*, Champaign, IL: Human Kinetics.

Schmidt, R.A. and Lee, T.D. (2005) *Motor Control and Learning: A Behavioural Emphasis*, Champaign, IL: Human Kinetics.

Vescovi, J. D. (2006) 'Agility', *NSCA Hot Topics*.

Vickers, J.N. (2007) *Perception, Cognition and Decision Training: The Quiet Eye in Action*, Champaign, IL: Human Kinetics.

Winstein, C.J. and Schmidt, R.A. (1990) 'Reduced frequency of knowledge of results enhances motor skill learning', *Journal of Experimental Psychology: Learning, Memory and Cognition*, 16: 677–691.

Young, W.B., James, R. and Montgomery, I. (2002) 'Is muscle power related to running speed with changes of direction?' *Journal of Sports Medicine and Physical Fitness*, 42: 282–288.

9

METABOLIC CONDITIONING DEVELOPMENT IN YOUTHS

Paul Gamble

Introduction

The natural process of growth and maturation encompasses a host of physiological and hormonal changes. This in turn has a profound influence on the young athlete's capacity for aerobic and anaerobic metabolism, as well as impacting upon neuromuscular coordination factors, which alter efficiency and economy of locomotion (Boisseau and Delamarche, 2000). In addition to influencing the young athlete's capacity for different forms of training, the phase of growth and maturation of the athlete will also dictate the mechanisms through which training effects occur (Stratton *et al.*, 2004).

As with other forms of training, what constitutes appropriate metabolic conditioning for a young athlete will be determined to a large degree by their age and stage of physical development (Gamble, 2009b). With respect to metabolic conditioning, this pertains to both the energy systems involved and also what form metabolic conditioning takes, in terms of the mode and format of training employed. Popular long-term athlete development models advocate that the nature of endurance training should differ markedly for young athletes at the different stages of development (Balyi and Hamilton, 2004). The rationale for this approach will be critically examined in this chapter.

The development of metabolic conditioning during childhood and adolescence

The natural development of metabolic conditioning

It has been identified that the metabolic responses of a young athlete to an acute bout of endurance exercise differ according to their age and stage of biological maturation (McManus and Armstrong, 2008). The adenosine triphosphate (ATP) and phosphocreatine (PCr) content of the muscles of young athletes of varying ages is reported to be comparable to that of adults (Boisseau and Delamarche, 2000). However, prior to adolescence, the glycolytic metabolic system is less well developed. This is reflected in their metabolic response to exercise, with oxidative metabolism dominating (Boisseau and Delamarche, 2000).

The reduced capacity for glycolytic metabolism may, in part, be a consequence of the difference in muscle fibre profiles between pre-pubescent and adolescent athletes. Prior to puberty, a greater proportion of type-I fibres is evident in the lower-limb muscles relative to untrained adults, whereas this difference is not observed with adolescent athletes (Boisseau and Delamarche, 2000). Similarly, energy metabolism in pre-pubescent athletes is fuelled to a greater extent by lipid oxidation than is the case for adults. This is reflected in both higher concentrations of free fatty acids and glycerol in the blood during exercise and the lower respiratory exchange ratio observed with these young athletes (Boisseau and Delamarche, 2000).

These observations have led authors to conclude that, in view of the apparently limited capacity for anaerobic exercise, this form of endurance training should be avoided during these early stages of growth and maturation (Boisseau and Delamarche, 2000; Naughton *et al.*, 2000). Accordingly, long-term athlete development models in popular use commonly advocate that metabolic conditioning during these stages of development is characterized by various forms of aerobic exercise. While this rationale would appear sound in theory, more recent data examining training responses of pre-pubescent athletes to anaerobic training challenges this assertion (Baquet *et al.*, 2002, 2010; McManus *et al.*, 2005), as will be discussed in the following section.

The trainability of metabolic conditioning

Aerobic metabolic conditioning

The equivocal findings of some earlier studies investigating endurance conditioning with children have previously led to suggestions that pre-pubescents are relatively less responsive to metabolic conditioning (Baquet *et al.*, 2002). From this arose concepts such as the 'trigger hypothesis' that suggested there might be a threshold age prior to which training responsiveness is limited; and that after this 'trigger point' follows a window of opportunity for gains in endurance (McManus and Armstrong, 2008). Such theories underpin long-term athlete development models that feature in the coaching literature for various sports, which commonly stipulate that different forms of conditioning are necessary at different stages of growth and maturation (Ford *et al.*, 2011).

However, it appears that the equivocal findings of these earlier studies may be attributed to flaws in experimental design, and specifically the efficacy of the metabolic conditioning employed in the study. Data from a number of more recent studies indicate that a variety of endurance training protocols produce significant improvements in aerobic fitness with children at different stages of growth and maturation (Baquet *et al.*, 2002, 2010; McManus *et al.*, 2005). As a result, some authorities in the field now question that the data in the literature supports the idea that growth and maturation affects trainability with respect to aerobic fitness (McManus and Armstrong, 2008).

The contemporary consensus, therefore, is that children and adolescents exhibit comparable gains in cardio-respiratory fitness with aerobic training (Naughton *et al.*, 2000). Overall gains in aerobic fitness (e.g. VO_2peak) reported in response to metabolic conditioning with young athletes are, however, suggested to be less than those observed with adults (Matos and Winsely, 2007). Prior to puberty, both boys and girls are typically reported to be similarly responsive to endurance training interventions, indicating no effect of gender at this stage of development (Baquet *et al.*, 2002). Significant natural gains in aerobic endurance are observed during puberty in young athletes as they reach peak height velocity (PHV) (around age 14 in boys, 12 in girls). This trend is attributed to maturation-related changes to the musculoskeletal and cardio-respiratory systems (Philippaerts *et al.*, 2006).

A continuing emphasis on appropriate metabolic conditioning during and post-puberty would appear to be vital for female athletes particularly in order to counter the decline in aerobic endurance that is otherwise observed in females after the onset of puberty (Naughton *et al.*, 2000). Furthermore, due to its high metabolic demand, aerobic training is likely to be beneficial in order to offset the unfavourable changes in body composition (increase in body mass and fat mass specifically) that are characteristically observed in females during this stage of development.

During the developmental stages around and following puberty there may be a need to train at a higher intensity in order to produce continued gains in endurance with trained young athletes. For example, a study of pubertal (14-year-old) male elite junior soccer players reported that a continuous sub-maximal training protocol (10–30 minutes at an average intensity of 50–70 per cent HRmax) failed to produce gains within the five-week study period (Sperlich *et al.*, 2011). Conversely, a long aerobic interval protocol employing repeated bouts of 1–4 minutes at 90–95 per cent HRmax did produce significant gains in VO_2max (Sperlich *et al.*, 2011).

Anaerobic metabolic conditioning

Prior to puberty the young athlete's propensity for high-intensity anaerobic conditioning is believed to be limited (Naughton *et al.*, 2000). As discussed previously, this contention is based upon the finding that pre-pubescent athletes have a less well-developed capacity for glycolytic metabolism, however, this view is becoming increasingly challenged. Anecdotally, during both competition and free play, young athletes often engage in exertion that would be characterized as repeated sprint activity. This is perhaps unsurprising in view of the fact that that the high energy phosphagen (ATP and PCr) system is similarly well developed in children as it is in adults (Boisseau and Delamarche, 2000). Similarly, the fact that pre-pubescent athletes encounter greatly reduced levels of acidosis as a consequence of the lower glycolytic enzyme activity in fact serves to allow them to recover more rapidly between bouts of exertion.

Recent data raises further questions about the previous assumption that pre-pubescent athletes are limited in their capacity for, and responsiveness to, anaerobic conditioning. For example, a recent study reported that pre-pubescent swimmers responded very positively to high-intensity interval training (Sperlich *et al.*, 2010). The improvements in time trial and competitive performance reported in this study were also reflected in positive changes in lactate accumulation parameters. Significant improvements in endurance performance following high-intensity, interval-based anaerobic training interventions have likewise been reported by a number of other studies that have employed cycling-based (McManus *et al.*, 2005) and running-based (Baquet *et al.*, 2002, 2010) conditioning protocols.

It has therefore been concluded that pre-pubescent athletes do in fact respond to anaerobic interval conditioning (Matos and Winsley, 2007). What is also clear is that physiological changes during puberty enhance young athletes' capacity for anaerobic training (Naughton *et al.*, 2000). The rate of maturation-related improvements in anaerobic capacity during puberty peaks around the time that the young athlete's growth curve attains PHV, but 'natural' gains can also occur following this period (Philippaerts *et al.*, 2006). During and following puberty, young athletes are reported to become progressively better adapted to anaerobic exercise with respect to their capacity for glycolytic metabolism (Naughton *et al.*, 2000).

Economy of locomotion and movement efficiency

Although less widely recognized, running economy or efficiency of locomotion is identified as a key parameter of endurance performance (Jones and Carter, 2000). Natural growth and maturation-related improvements in different measures of neuromuscular performance are observed with increases in chronological age, and, in the case of young male athletes, these improvements continue at an accelerated rate during the period during and immediately following puberty (Quatman *et al.*, 2006). These include measures of anaerobic power, such as vertical jump ability (Philippaerts *et al.*, 2006), as well as development of active stiffness and performance during stretch–shortening cycle activities (Ford *et al.*, 2010) and sprint performance (Papaiakovou *et al.*, 2009). However, even in late adolescence, physiological and neuromuscular performance capacities differ markedly to those of mature adults (Naughton *et al.*, 2000).

It follows that, when undertaking metabolic conditioning, the opportunity to instruct and reinforce key technical aspects of efficient locomotion and sound movement mechanics should not be overlooked. Refining technique and developing the neuromuscular coordination aspects involved has the potential to improve the young athlete's efficiency of locomotion and thereby their endurance performance independently of any metabolic changes.

Mechanisms for improvements in endurance at different stages of development

There is a lack of data from young athletes, in part due to ethical reasons, which preclude invasive methods of assessment being undertaken with children. In particular, it is not yet clear to what extent central cardio-respiratory adaptations or peripheral adaptations are responsible for the improvements in endurance seen in pre-pubescent, pubertal and adolescent athletes in response to different training interventions (Baquet *et al.*, 2010). It has been speculated by Baquet and colleagues (2010) that the relative contribution of central versus peripheral adaptations might differ according to the mode, format and intensity of conditioning employed.

It is also likely that different mechanisms may be attributed to the training responses observed following high-intensity anaerobic conditioning with pre-pubescent versus adolescent athletes. For example, the limited capacity of pre-pubescent athletes for glycolytic metabolism results in reduced levels of lactate production during this form of exercise. Lower muscle lactate concentrations are reported with pre-pubescent athletes, and the drop in muscle pH is correspondingly less due to the reduced levels of H^+ ions released with lactate production via glycolysis (Boisseau and Delamarche, 2000). It follows that this is likely to limit specific training adaptations associated with buffering H^+ ions and clearing lactate that are seen following puberty in response to anaerobic training.

Practical applications

Designing metabolic conditioning at different stages of development

Intensity and volume

Although recent data indicates that prior to puberty young athletes are responsive to anaerobic metabolic conditioning, it would appear prudent to modify the design of high-intensity, anaerobic-type metabolic conditioning for pre-pubescent athletes. For example, a training format that allows the young athlete to self-limit the intensity of 'work' bouts offers a practical means to safeguard pre-pubescent athletes when undertaking metabolic conditioning (Gamble, 2009b).

Other necessary modifications will include the training volume parameters employed. Particularly during early stages of development the young athlete will have smaller glycogen stores relative to adults (Boisseau and Delamarche, 2000). To some extent this may be offset by the apparent greater relative use of lipids as a fuel source for aerobic metabolism by pre-pubescent athletes, which is likely to spare muscle glycogen stores. However, some reduction in overall training volume would appear necessary for pre-pubescent athletes particularly, in order to avoid training to exhaustion and non-functional overreaching and ultimately prevent potential harm to the health of the immature athlete (McManus and Armstrong, 2008).

In the phases that follow puberty, the intensity and volume of metabolic conditioning prescribed for young athletes will begin to increasingly resemble what is employed with adult athletes. Based upon data from trained pubertal and adolescent athletes it appears that higher-intensity conditioning may be necessary to produce continued gains in endurance measures with these young athletes (Sperlich *et al.*, 2011), in much the same way as is observed with adult athletes (Midgeley *et al.*, 2006).

Training format

Both continuous and interval protocols have proven to be effective in producing improvements in endurance performance in young athletes (Baquet *et al.*, 2003). The efficacy of a high-intensity training protocol on a cycle ergometer that employed 30 s sprints was shown in pre-pubescent boys (McManus *et al.*, 2005). The high-intensity interval training produced comparable gains in peak oxygen uptake with another group that performed continuous sub-maximal training (bouts of cycling for 20 minutes at 75–85 per cent HRmax). Similar findings have been reported with running-based conditioning protocols (Baquet *et al.*, 2002, 2010). For example, significant gains in maximal shuttle-run performance were demonstrated with an interval training intervention that featured 10–20 s bouts of running at 100–130 per cent maximum aerobic speed (MAS), interspersed with recovery intervals of 10–20 s (Baquet *et al.*, 2002). There is also some suggestion that the shorter work bouts that feature in interval training protocols are better tolerated by young athletes and for such reasons the intermittent conditioning format might be more conducive to metabolic conditioning for younger athletes (Oliver *et al.*, 2011).

Baquet *et al.* (2010) investigated the training responses of pre-pubertal children (8–11 years of age) by employing a high-intensity interval training protocol featuring short intervals of 5–30 s of running at or above MAS, interspersed with rest periods of 10–30 s (Baquet *et al.*, 2010). The significant gains in endurance performance reported were similar to those elicited by a continuous protocol consisting of repeated sets of moderate-high intensity (80–85 per cent MAS) running exercise ranging from 6–12 minutes duration and single continuous bouts of 15–20 minutes running during the latter part of the 21-week intervention.

The findings of such studies underline two important points. The first is that even prior to puberty young athletes respond positively to high-intensity 'anaerobic' interval training protocols. However, equally important is the observation that a range of different formats for conditioning exercise are effective in producing significant gains in endurance with pre-pubescent athletes. Therefore a 'mixed approach' featuring a range of training formats may be employed with young athletes, including continuous bouts, long aerobic intervals, high-intensity anaerobic intervals and repeated sprint protocols. While high-intensity interval training protocols are shown to produce positive results with pre-pubescent athletes, the relative durations of work and rest bouts may require some modification for these young athletes. In view of the differences in the relative capacities of different metabolic systems it has been advocated that prior to puberty the duration of work bouts should be limited to a maximum of 15 s when performing high-intensity interval exercise (Boisseau and Delamarche, 2000). It is also suggested that pre-pubescent athletes may require less-extensive rest periods between work bouts.

Selection of training modes

With respect to training modes, a greater variety of activities are advocated for young athletes than is typically recommended for those competing at senior level (Gamble, 2009b). There are two major reasons for this. The first is to expose the young athlete to a broader range of activities and thereby provide a more varied training stimulus to encourage more extensive improvements in neuromuscular coordination. The second reason is to try to reduce the likelihood of overuse injuries commonly seen with young athletes, which are associated with high volumes of repetitious training and technical practices (Valovich-McLeod et al., 2011).

Although cross-training modes might have less direct transfer to the young athlete's sport in the short term, the greater use of such 'non-specific' metabolic conditioning modes is reflective of a longer-term perspective to the young athletes' physical development. It is nonetheless important that some proportion of the metabolic conditioning undertaken by young athletes comprises the mode of locomotion that features in the sport. This is important in terms of facilitating transfer of conditioning gains to sports performance and also from the point of view of developing the economy and efficiency component of endurance in the sport.

In the case of team sports and racket sports, for example, in addition to traditional running-based conditioning, more skill-based conditioning activities might also be employed. One such approach that has been successfully implemented in these sports involves adapting sport skill-based drills for the purpose of metabolic conditioning. Similarly, another approach is to employ skill-based conditioning games, which can be designed and modified in order to achieve the desired metabolic response (Hill-Haas et al., 2010).

Both of these approaches have been reported to elicit physiological responses in the upper ranges that are required to produce improvements in endurance for trained athletes (Hoff et al., 2002; Little and Williams, 2006). Accordingly, significant improvements in endurance parameters have been reported for elite professional youth soccer players with this approach (McMillan et al., 2005). In addition, other advantages have been identified with these skill-based approaches to conditioning. Specifically, skill-based conditioning offers concurrent development of technical and tactical aspects and thus develops sport-specific metabolic conditioning, and is also suggested to facilitate enhanced motivation and compliance (Gamble, 2009a).

By definition, skill-based conditioning modes are less structured, which makes it necessary to monitor the work rate of each player to ensure they maintain the desired intensity for the duration of each session (Gamble, 2009a). On the other hand, when this form of conditioning is implemented for pre-pubescent athletes, for example, the fact that the player is able to self-regulate work intensity can be viewed as favourable from the point of view of safeguarding these younger athletes.

The tables below provide summaries of training prescription guidelines for young athletes of different maturational stages, notably pre-pubertal (Table 9.1), circum-pubertal (Table 9.2) and post-pubertal (Table 9.3). While these guidelines can be applied to any young athlete, as a caveat, metabolic conditioning prescription should at all times be individually prescribed, and be consistent with the needs, goals and abilities of younger populations.

TABLE 9.1 Pre-pubertal athletes

Training modes (in rank order)	Training format	Intensity	Volume, frequency
Cross-training Running-based conditioning (or locomotion-specific for non-running sports) Conditioning games	Long aerobic intervals (ranging from 90 s to 4 min work bouts) Short aerobic intervals (10–30 s work bouts)	Self-regulated intensity Self-selected recovery between bouts	4 per week (mixed sessions) Moderate volume – consider alternating short and longer overall durations for sessions on consecutive days

TABLE 9.2 Circum-pubertal athletes

Training modes (in rank order)	Training formats	Intensity	Volume, frequency
Running-based conditioning (locomotion-specific for non-running sports)	Long aerobic intervals (90 s to 6 min work bouts)	Moderate-high intensity	4 per week (blend of sessions) Moderate volume/ duration each session
Conditioning games	Short aerobic intervals (10–30 s work bouts)	$\approx VO_2$max intensity	
Cross-training	Aerobic–anaerobic intervals (e.g. 20 s work bouts, 20 s rest)	Supra-(above) VO_2max intensity	

TABLE 9.3 Post-pubertal athletes

Training modes (in rank order)	Training formats	Intensity	Volume, frequency
Conditioning games	Long aerobic intervals (90 s to 6 min work bouts)	High intensity, moderate recovery ($\approx$2 minutes)	4–5 per week (blend of sessions)
			Moderate-high volume/duration – alternating moderate and longer session duration on consecutive days
Skill-based conditioning drills	Short aerobic intervals (10–30 s work bouts)	$\approx$VO$_2$max intensity, brief recovery	
Running-based conditioning	Aerobic–anaerobic intervals (e.g. 20 s work, 10 s rest)	'Supramaximal' intensity (above VO$_2$max)	
Cross-training	Anaerobic repeated sprint intervals (5–30 s sprints)	Maximal, all out efforts, extensive recovery (1–4 min, depending on work bout duration)	

Summary and conclusions

The accumulating evidence pertaining to the responsiveness of young athletes, and particularly pre-pubescent athletes, to metabolic conditioning would, to some extent, seem to refute the more dogmatic models of long-term athlete development. As has been identified by other authors, to date the evidence does not support the contention that there is a threshold age prior to which children are limited in their capacity for either aerobic or anaerobic training interventions (McManus and Armstrong, 2008). While the mechanisms for training adaptations may vary, the data does not currently exist to say that the dose-response to endurance training is markedly influenced by age or stage of growth and maturation. The frequency and intensity of metabolic conditioning required to elicit improvements in endurance performance in fact appears to be broadly similar between phases of development and is comparable to what is reported for adults.

Nevertheless, it is likely that there is a need for the strength and conditioning coach to adapt their approach to metabolic conditioning during the respective development stages until the athlete reaches early adulthood. The modifications required would, however, seem to be more subtle than has typically been advocated, and in the main will concern the overall volume of endurance training as well as the training modes and activities employed. For instance, consecutive days of high volumes of repetitive endurance training should be avoided, particularly during sensitive periods such as growth spurts, in order to avert the cumulative stresses that can ultimately lead to overuse injury. The dangers of early specialization in terms of sport participation and the training employed with young athletes have likewise been highlighted with regards to training maladaptation, athlete burn-out and overuse injury (Malina, 2010). This underlines the importance of incorporating a range of different training modes and activities when designing metabolic conditioning with young athletes, with a much greater use of cross-training year-round than is the case for mature athletes (Gamble, 2009b). The emotional and psychological maturity of the individual is a further factor to be considered when designing and implementing training, particularly for pre-pubescent athletes (Kraemer and Fleck, 2005; Stratton *et al.*, 2004). While a young athlete might have the propensity for a particular type of training, the strength and conditioning specialist will need to give consideration to their emotional and psychological maturity when deciding what training modes might be employed to achieve the greatest athlete motivation and compliance.

To conclude, while there may be flaws in some of the long-term athlete development models in popular use, it remains critical that those who are responsible for training young athletes retain a long-term perspective in the design of metabolic conditioning and when implementing the overall training plan. The temptation to allow early specialization to permeate into the design of the young athlete's physical preparation must be avoided (McManus and Armstrong, 2008). Likewise, the delivery of training should be undertaken in a highly responsive manner, with the young athlete being closely monitored, and the coach being prepared to modify their sessions as required.

Key points

- While the physiological make-up and metabolic responses of young athletes may differ, they still show a broadly similar dose-response to metabolic conditioning to adults, in terms of frequency and intensity required to elicit a training response.
- The evidence does not support the contention that a particular form of metabolic conditioning, such as high-intensity interval training, is contraindicated at any given stage of growth and maturation.
- A long-term perspective is required when approaching metabolic conditioning for young athletes. In general, cross-training modes should be employed to a greater degree, particularly for pre-pubescent athletes and during early puberty, in order to help guard against overuse injury.

- The selection of training modes and emphasis on particular forms of training employed should reflect both the phase of growth and maturation, and the emotional and psychological maturity of the athlete.
- The way in which different forms of metabolic conditioning is delivered should also reflect age and stage of development. In particular, with respect to rest intervals employed and overall training volume, training sessions should be conducted in a highly responsive manner in order to be sensitive to short-term fluctuations in performance capacities during critical phases of development.

References

Balyi, I. and Hamilton, A. (2004) *Long-Term Athlete Development: Trainability in Children and Adolescents. Windows of Opportunity, Optimal Trainability*, Victoria: National Coaching Institute British Colombia and Advanced Training and Performance Ltd.

Baquet, G., Berthoin, S., Dupont, G., Blondel, N., Fabre, C. and Van Praagh, E. (2002) 'Effects of high intensity intermittent training on peak VO_2 in pre-pubertal children', *International Journal of Sports Medicine*, 23: 439–444.

Baquet, G., Van Praagh, E. and Berthoin, S. (2003) 'Endurance training and aerobic fitness in young people', *Sports Medicine*, 33: 1127–1143.

Baquet, G., Gamelin, F. X., Mucci, P., Thevenet, D., Van Praagh, E. and Berthoin, S. (2010) 'Continuous vs. interval aerobic training in 8- to 11-year-old children', *Journal of Strength and Conditioning Research*, 24: 1381–1388.

Boisseau, N. and Delamarche, P. (2000) 'Metabolic and hormonal responses to exercise in children and adolescents', *Sports Medicine*, 30: 405–422.

Ford, K.R., Myer, G.D. and Hewett, T.E. (2010) 'Longitudinal effects of maturation on lower extremity joint stiffness in adolescent athletes', *American Journal of Sports Medicine*, 38: 1829–1837.

Ford, P., De Ste Croix, M., Lloyd, R., Meyers, R., Moosavi, M., Oliver, J., Till, K. and Williams, C.A. (2011) 'The long-term athlete development model: Physiological evidence and application', *Journal of Sports Sciences*, 29: 389–402.

Gamble, P. (2009a) 'Metabolic conditioning for team sports'. In: P. Gamble (ed.) *Strength and Conditioning for Team Sports: Sport-Specific Physical Preparation for High Performance*, London: Routledge.

Gamble, P. (2009b) 'Physical preparation for youth sports'. In: P. Gamble (ed.) *Strength and Conditioning for Team Sports: Sport-Specific Physical Preparation for High Performance*, London: Routledge.

Hill-Haas, S.V., Coutts, A.J., Dawson, B.T. and Rowsell, G.J. (2010) 'Time–motion characteristics and physiological responses of small-sided games in elite youth players: The influence of player number and rule changes', *Journal of Strength and Conditioning Research*, 24: 2149–2156.

Hoff, J., Wisloff, U., Engen, L.C., Kemi, O.J. and Helgerud, J. (2002) 'Soccer specific aerobic endurance training', *British Journal of Sports Medicine*, 36: 218–221.

Jones, A.M. and Carter, H. (2000) 'The effect of endurance training on parameters of aerobic fitness', *Sports Medicine*, 29: 373–386.

Kraemer, W.J. and Fleck, S.J. (2005) *Strength Training for Young Athletes*, Champaign, IL: Human Kinetics.

Little, T. and Williams, A.G. (2006) 'Suitability of soccer training drills for endurance training', *Journal of Strength and Conditioning Research*, 20: 316–319.

McManus, A.M. and Armstrong, N. (2008) 'The elite young athlete'. In: N. Armstrong and M.V. Mechelen (eds) *Paediatric Exercise Science and Medicine*, Oxford: Oxford University Press.

McManus, A.M., Cheng, C.H., Leung, M.P., Yung, T.C. and Macfarlane, D.J. (2005) 'Improving aerobic power in primary school boys: A comparison of continuous and interval training', *International Journal of Sports Medicine*, 26: 781–786.

McMillan, K., Helgerud, J., Macdonald, R. and Hoff, J. (2005) 'Physiological adaptations to soccer specific endurance training in professional youth soccer players', *British Journal of Sports Medicine*, 39: 273–277.

Malina, R.M. (2010) 'Early sport specialization: Roots, effectiveness, risks', *Current Sports Medicine Reports*, 9: 364–371.

Matos, N. and Winsley, R.J. (2007) 'Trainability of young athletes and overtraining', *Journal of Sports Science and Medicine*, 6: 353–367.

Midgley, A.W., McNaughton, L.R. and Wilkinson, M. (2006) 'Is there an optimal training intensity for enhancing the maximal oxygen uptake of distance runners? Empirical research findings, current opinions, physiological rationale and practical recommendations', *Sports Medicine*, 36: 117–132.

Naughton, G., Farpour-Lambert, N.J., Carlson, J., Bradley, M. and Van Praagh, E. (2000) 'Physiological issues surrounding the performance of adolescent athletes', *Sports Medicine*, 30: 309–325.

Oliver, J.L., Lloyd, R.S. and Meyers, R.W. (2011) 'Training elite child athletes: Promoting welfare and well-being', *Strength and Conditioning Journal*, 33: 73–79.

Papaiakovou, G., Giannakos, A., Michailidis, C., Patikas, D., Bassa, E., Kalopisis, V., Anthrakidis, N. and Kotzamanidis, C. (2009) 'The effect of chronological age and gender on the development of sprint performance during childhood and puberty', *Journal of Strength and Conditioning Research*, 23: 2568–2573.

Philippaerts, R.M., Vaeyans, R., Janssens, M., Van Renterghem, B., Matthys, D., Craen, R., Bourgois, J., Vrijens, J., Beunen, G. and Malina, R.M. (2006) 'The relationship between peak height velocity and physical performance in youth soccer players', *Journal of Sports Sciences*, 24: 221–230.

Quatman, C.E., Ford, K.R., Myer, G.D. and Hewett, T.E. (2006) 'Maturation leads to gender differences in landing force and vertical jump performance', *American Journal of Sports Medicine*, 34: 806–813.

Sperlich, W., Zinner, C., Heilemann, I., Kjendlie, P.L., Holmberg, H.C. and Mester, J. (2010) 'High-intensity interval training improves VO_2max, maximal lactate accumulation, time trial and competition performance in 9–11-year-old swimmers', *European Journal of Applied Physiology*, 110: 1029–1036.

Sperlich, W., De Marées, M., Koehler, K., Linville, J., Holmberg, H.C. and Mester, J. (2011) 'Effect of 5 weeks' high-intensity interval training vs. volume training in 14-year-old soccer players', *Journal of Strength and Conditioning Research*, 25: 1–8.

Stratton, G., Jones, M., Fox, K.R., Tolfrey, K., Harrris, J., Maffulli, N., Lee, M. and Frostick, S.P. (2004) 'BASES position statement on guidelines for resistance training in young people', *Journal of Sports Sciences*, 22: 383–390.

Valovich-McLeod, T.C., Decoster, L.C., Loud, K.J., Micheli, L.J., Parker, J.T., Sandrey, M.A. and White, C. (2011) 'National Athletic Trainers' Association Position Statement: Prevention of pediatric overuse injuries', *Journal of Athletic Training*, 46: 206–220.

10

MOBILITY DEVELOPMENT AND FLEXIBILITY IN YOUTHS

William Sands and Jeni McNeal

Introduction

Flexibility has long been recognized as an essential physical ability to be developed in both youths and adults. The perceived importance of flexibility by health and fitness professionals as well as coaches is reflected in the presence of flexibility tests in many fitness batteries, including those conducted on young athletes (Mirkov *et al.*, 2010; Rost and Schon, 1997). The term 'flexibility' has been defined from a structural perspective as 'the range of motion in a joint or a related series of joints' (McNeal and Sands, 2006: p.142), and from a functional viewpoint as 'the ability to move joints fluidly through a full range of motion' (Heyward, 1984: p.5). According to the *Cambridge English Dictionary*, the idea of mobility expands the concept of flexibility in that it encompasses the ability 'to move freely or be easily moved'. In the case of an athlete, whether young or mature, the ability to move freely and effectively through an optimal range of motion is an important performance goal (Figure 10.1). The idea of free and fluid motion has also been described by others (McNeal and Sands, 2006; Miletic *et al.*, 2004). Thus, mobility is not simply determined by flexibility in terms of structure, but also incorporates strength, power and motor control to effectively move a joint or series of joints at the desired speed, in the proper sequence, at a specific time and in a given direction for a particular movement. Unfortunately, the term flexibility is most often used when mobility or fluidity is more likely the appropriate term. The relative importance of flexibility as fluid mobility in the young athlete varies depending on the nature of the sport and specific skills, as well as athlete maturity. For example, most acrobatic sports are scored, at least partially, on demonstrations of skills that specifically display extreme body positions (McNeal and Sands, 2006; Yamamura *et al.*, 1999), while other sports utilize movements in which a large range of motion enhances the mechanical effectiveness of a task, such as in throwing (Stodden *et al.*, 2001) and striking sports (Marey *et al.*, 1991; Schmidt-Wiethoff, 2003).

FIGURE 10.1 A team warm-up incorporating static and dynamic stretching exercises

It has been suggested that childhood is an especially 'sensitive period' for the development of flexibility. 'Sensitive' or 'critical' periods for training various physical and motor abilities have been described in numerous models of long-term athlete development (Burgess and Naughton, 2010; Norris, 2010; Smith, 2003). Moreover, specific sensitive periods for flexibility development have been identified, particularly for appearance sports (Drabik, 1996; Malina, 2007; Sands, 2002). Such models describe the sensitive period for flexibility development as occurring between the ages of around 6–11 years. The physiological constitution of the young child at these ages may allow for a better return on the training time investment for flexibility. Conversely, it is observed that flexibility tends to plateau or decline with the onset of the growth spurt and/or the onset of puberty, even in those sports where there is a premium placed on flexibility (Beunen and Malina, 1996; Brodie and Royce, 1998; Malina, 2007). Males show greater and more rapid declines in flexibility compared with females at all ages from eight years old to early adulthood. Obtaining the requisite flexibility and mobility for a given sport is paramount in the pre-pubescent athlete, while maintaining optimal levels is the goal for adolescents.

Flexibility is thought to be a morphological characteristic more than a health- or performance-related fitness property (Bouchard et al., 1997). Bouchard and colleagues describe a paucity of investigations on the heritability of flexibility, citing Eastern European literature with ratios of 0.69 for lower-back flexibility in 11–15-year-old males, and in male and female twins of 12–17 years, 0.84 for the trunk, 0.70 for hip and 0.91 for shoulder. Heritability is the proportion of phenotypic variation in a population that is due to genetic variation between individuals. Bouchard et al. (1997) concluded that genetics have a more powerful influence on flexibility than on strength. The relative contribution of genetic predisposition to flexibility remains to be fully determined and further research in this area is warranted.

Flexibility training methods have been applied to adults and children with little age-related variation. These methods range from classic static stretching methods to more novel approaches such as vibration (McNeal and Sands, 2006). Unfortunately, relatively few studies have directly compared stretching methods in children or made comparisons of children and adults. As with many of the training methods often incorporated into children's exercise and sports programmes, most prescriptions for enhancing range of motion are derived from research and experience with adult subjects. Further investigation is required that specifically targets youth populations to clearly establish the benefits and importance of flexibility for performance enhancement, to determine optimal methods for specific needs (active versus passive flexibility for example) and to further elucidate basic underlying physiological mechanisms and their possible relationship to developmental stages.

Basic theoretical concepts

Flexibility is not a generalized fitness quality, and is known to be training-, joint- and motion-specific (Chandler *et al.*, 1990; Marshall *et al.*, 1980). That is, being flexible about one joint in a particular plane of motion has no bearing on the range of motion about another joint, or even about a different plane about the same joint. Flexibility is determined by a number of factors subject to intra- and inter- individual characteristics, including the nature of the anatomical features of the articulating bones, ligament and joint capsule arrangement and stiffness, collagen types, and degree of cross-linking and musculotendinous stiffness (Cribb and Scott, 1995). Musculotendinous stiffness is considered to be the element most modified through regular flexibility training, primarily through the use of various stretching modalities. Musculotendinous stiffness has both active and passive components. The passive components refer to the material properties of the contractile (actin- myosin filaments and cross-bridges) and connective tissues (parallel and series elastic components) (Gajdosik, 2001). Active musculotendinous stiffness is regulated by nervous system input, both reflex and voluntary (Magnusson *et al.*, 1997). The relative contribution of the passive elements in determining range of motion about a joint *in vivo* in adults is known for some joints, while the contribution of muscle relaxation factors, previous tension levels and types of tension appear to contribute in different ways that are less well understood (Nordez *et al.*, 2010).

Virtually all information regarding active and passive stiffness regulating range of motion has been determined from studies on adult subjects. The effect of growth and maturation on stiffness has largely been investigated using animal models. From these studies it is generally concluded that passive stiffness is lower in young than adult animals. Musculotendinous stiffness has been related to increased restriction of titin filaments (Ochi *et al.*, 2008), collagen filaments and collagen cross-linking, all of which have been shown to increase with growth and/or maturation (Feit *et al.*, 1989; McCormick, 2003; McCormick and Thomas, 1998).

Comparable information on human subjects during growth and maturation is scarce. It is known that neonates exhibit characteristic passive ranges of motion associated with gestational position. For example, it is not unusual for the foot to contact the tibia in passive dorsiflexion in the newborn, while, in contrast, knee extension limitations exist due to gestation in a knee-flexed position (Waugh *et al.*, 1983; Wong *et al.*, 1998). Passive ankle dorsiflexion approaches adult values by the age of seven years (Sutherland *et al.*, 1988), however, the time-course of other joints and motions is not known. Lambertz and colleagues (2003) compared musculotendinous stiffness of the ankle plantarflexors in pre-pubertal children and adults using quick-release movements. They determined that there was an increase in the stiffness of the musculotendinous unit from 7–10 years of age, and that this stiffness was less than that of adults. Grosset *et al.* (2005, 2007) later expanded on this result, concluding that the lower stiffness in children compared with adults resulted in reduced amplitudes of the stretch reflex and tendon-jerk reflex. Stiffness and reflex amplitudes were positively related to increasing age from 7–11 years. With increasing age, muscle spindle sensitivity also increased, although still less than adults. Children have also been shown to have a higher index of muscle coactivation which declines with age (Grosset *et al.*, 2005, 2007; Lambertz *et al.*, 2003). Coactivation of muscles may encourage the involved muscles to reduce the number of active cross-bridge attachments that develop during inactivity via the thixotropic properties of muscle (Enoka, 1994). The influence of improved tolerance to stretch has been suggested as a mechanism of enhanced flexibility in children, particularly in the context of using vibration simultaneously to reduce pain and potentially alter thixotropic properties (Sands *et al.*, 2005, 2006, 2008a).

The growth spurt has been implicated as a period during which range of motion is reduced or becomes stagnant (Falciglia *et al.*, 2009; Philippaerts *et al.*, 2007; Steinberg *et al.*, 2006; Yague and De La Fuente, 1998). Cross-sectional studies show this trend more clearly, but have critical flaws associated with accounting for variability in the tempo and timing of the growth and pubertal processes. It is postulated that flexibility could be reduced during this time as the bones grow in length prior to the muscles, leading to a temporary reduction in flexibility. Additionally, animal evidence supports structural changes to tendon and ligament tissue which increases stiffness with the onset of adolescence (McCormick and Thomas, 1998; Woo *et al.*, 1986). However, more research needs to be carried out in this area to confirm these ideas. In particular, longitudinal research is needed which tracks a number of flexibility measures that are not affected by changes in limb lengths associated with growth. The commonly used sit-and-reach test is affected by the discordant timing of growth in leg length followed by trunk length, for example. Based on available results it would be prudent to incorporate daily flexibility training for athletes aged 10–14 years in order to help prevent growth-associated losses of range of motion that may occur during this period.

Evidence for a direct association between flexibility enhancement and improvements in performance is lacking both in adult and youth populations. Instead, studies of athlete profiles at different performance levels provide support that flexibility is an important factor for performance, which varies depending on the sport in question. Geladas *et al.* (2005) found that in young female swimmers, greater shoulder flexibility was related to a faster 100m time, but this relationship was lower in young male swimmers. A study of baseball pitchers by Stodden *et al.* (2001) included three high school-aged players, and concluded that pitched ball velocity was significantly related to having greater pelvis and upper torso orientation at the point of maximal shoulder external rotation, indicating a component of flexibility to achieve such a position. In aesthetic sports the relationship is more obvious, as the scoring rubrics include components related to range of motion of executed skills. Since the optimal or necessary range of motion required for execution of various sports movements has not been identified, it is difficult for coaches to know how much flexibility is enough. Again, more research needs to be done to establish the relationships between enhancement of flexibility and performance. These relationships will be difficult to demonstrate given that sports skills most likely have an 'optimal' range of motion, and thus there is a ceiling effect on improvements (Corbin and Noble, 1980).

Both too little and too much flexibility have been implicated in injury, however, these connections are tenuous at best given the complex nature of defining and delineating both 'injury' and 'flexibility'. Virtually no data exists with regard to youth subjects. López–Miñarro and Alacid (2010) studied young elite paddlers and found that reduced hamstring extensibility affected spinal postures during maximal trunk flexion. Although no injury information was collected, the authors suggested that these postures might, in turn, influence injury potential by increasing vertebral and disc loads. A report from Mehdinasab and Fakoor (2005) supported previous research that demonstrated increased quadriceps tightness associated with Osgood-Schlatter's disease, however, these results must be viewed with caution since the subjects were tested after presenting with the injury. Kluemper *et al.* (2006) showed that a six-week stretching and strengthening programme for the shoulders improved forward-shoulder posture in adolescent swimmers, which has been implicated in 'swimmer's shoulder', however, the methods did not allow conclusions to be made regarding the relative influence of stretching versus strengthening exercises on the outcomes. Data from adult subjects has been unable to demonstrate clear relationships between flexibility levels and general and specific injury risk, and conclusions therefore remain elusive.

Practical recommendations

Aesthetic versus non-aesthetic sports

One of the first practical considerations in flexibility training application is to determine the goals of the training. Sports such as gymnastics, figure skating and diving have specific flexibility rules, requirements and established culture favouring the demonstration of large range of motion positions. Aesthetic sports also tend to involve early preparation and thereby begin at younger training ages (McNeal and Sands, 2006). Non-aesthetic sports use flexibility and range of motion as a mechanical advantage primarily to increase the distance and time through which forces can be applied or absorbed, thereby increasing mechanical impulse (McNeal and Sands, 2006). For example, the baseball bat swing begins with a windup that serves to increase the distance and time through which the bat is swung (Figure 10.2). The windup also serves to stretch muscles prior to their primary force production phase in the development of the motions of the swing. Forces absorbed over a greater distance and time tend to be decelerated more slowly and with greater control. Forces received abruptly tend to force the athlete to bear the brunt of the force quickly and thereby potentially more injuriously (McNeal and Sands, 2006). Thus, one will likely see a great deal more attention paid to stretching activities when the sport involves aesthetic or judged components based on body position. In non-aesthetic sports, emphasis should be placed on achieving an optimal range of motion and further emphasis on increasing that range of motion is simply unnecessary and may be detrimental. Siff and Verkhoshansky (1993) argued that additional training time devoted to stretching was not necessary if the dominant training was correctly planned and implemented. Training alone, in their view, was enough to develop and maintain appropriate ranges of motion.

Active versus passive range of motion

'Active range of motion' refers to the idea that a limb or body part is moved through its full range of motion by virtue of muscle tension from an agonist muscle (Luttgens and Wells, 1982). 'Passive range of motion' is characterized by non-contractile motion of a limb. For example, in a simple toe-touch exercise, if the athlete sits on the ground and then reaches forward via active hip and trunk flexion to touch their toes, there is a fair amount of hip and trunk flexor muscle activity required to achieve this position. If the same athlete stands and bends forward to touch their toes then gravity can assist in the hip and trunk flexion and thereby reduce the need for active muscle tension in order to achieve the extreme position.

FIGURE 10.2 Frames from a high-speed video showing the start and end positions of a baseball bat swing. Note the extraordinary range of motion at the trunk and shoulders required to decelerate the bat at the end of the swing (right)

Generally, active range of motion is more highly prized and much more difficult to achieve due to the length–tension relationship of the shortened agonist muscle. However, active range of motion is first trained via passive range of motion such that the athlete can simply achieve the position before strength in the new range of motion is developed. Of course, both characteristics can be trained simultaneously, such as limb motions against elastic resistance (Figure 10.3). In addition to passive stretching, children should be encouraged to develop strength and motor control throughout any range of motion. Moreover, sensitive periods of flexibility development should not neglect range of motion-specific strength training with considerable attention devoted to proper posture and alignment.

Stretching frequency

Children enjoy a period when flexibility improvements tend to come rapidly. When trained specifically, stretching should be undertaken at least 2–3 times per week (Beunen and Malina, 1996; Brodie and Royce, 1998). However, daily stretching is currently implemented in nearly all aesthetic sports, and it is generally accepted that frequency of stretching is important for maintaining continuing improvements. Santonja (2007) found that stretching four days per week was superior to two days per week in pre-pubescents. Deleterious side-effects of daily flexibility training have not been documented in children, and experience has shown that daily and even several stretching sessions per day have been used in children's training without injury.

FIGURE 10.3 A young athlete using elastic stretch material as resistance against which to lift her leg

Stretching duration

The consensus regarding the duration of application of a stretching stimulus indicates optimal results are achieved with durations of 10–30s per exercise (Malina, 2007). Typically, these stretch durations are repeated approximately three times per exercise. Longer durations of stretching result in increased gains, but there is a problem of diminishing returns. Moreover, longer duration stretching tends to result in greater weakening of connective tissues immediately following the stretching (Hutton, 1992), an effect that appears to diminish with rest (Enoka, 1994).

Stretching intensity

Stretching brings discomfort, and the greater the stretching stimuli, the greater the discomfort. Unfortunately, stretching intensity is an enigma in flexibility research. The level of stretching intensity that is achieved should be constrained by the discomfort of the position. When the discomfort crosses a self-determined line to pain, then the position should not be pushed further. Future research should be conducted specifically addressing the issue of stretching intensity. Stretching intensity appears to be related to changes in muscle stiffness and subsequent changes in muscle strength and power.

The effects of stretching on subsequent strength and power are known to depend on interim activities (Faigenbaum et al., 2006; Kinser et al., 2008). Faigenbaum et al. (2006), for example, compared static, dynamic and static with dynamic warm-ups in a group of adolescent youth, and showed that if static stretches are followed by a period of dynamic activities, various indicators of power performance were enhanced, compared with static stretching alone prior to testing. Based on adult data and limited investigations in youths, it is suggested that static stretches be avoided prior to sporting activities requiring high levels of strength and power, and that dynamic warm-ups and range of motion exercises be utilized instead.

Flexibility training mode

Static stretching is perhaps the most common, most understood and most easily implemented type of flexibility training method for children. In static stretching the athlete moves to a desired extreme position and increases the stretch slowly under self-selected control; the athlete holds this extreme position for 10–30s. Static stretching is well understood, and usually serves as the default type of stretch for all novice athletes. Static stretching, while common, may suffer due to the inherent self-limiting desire to avoid discomfort.

Ballistic stretching is commonly used by athletes when they achieve a position near the end of their functional range. At the end position, ballistic stretching involves small bounces or short and quick motions to achieve greater range of motion. Ballistic stretching among adults has been shown to be as effective as static stretching for increasing range of motion (Covert et al., 2010; Mahieu *et al.*, 2007). The less common use of ballistic stretching is due largely to a fear that bouncing-type stretching will invoke the myotatic stretch reflex, causing the target muscle to contract and thereby resist stretching stimuli. The application of ballistic stretching should be reserved for youth who are mature enough to keep the bouncing motions small and controlled. Despite these fears, very little information is known about the mechanisms of ballistic stretching and long-term benefits.

Proprioceptive neuromuscular facilitation (PNF), first described in the 1940s and 1950s, was developed to aid paralysis patients (Siff and Verkhoshansky, 1993). While there are a number of variations of PNF stretching, the basic principle is that a preceding activity can facilitate the acquisition of new range of motion. PNF stretching can be effective for children, but carries significant responsibilities on the partner or stretching facilitator (Sands, 1984). When children are stretched using PNF techniques, the partner has to be careful not to exceed the limits of the person being stretched (Figure 10.4). The partner has to be alert to body position and posture, and must be sensitive to the extreme positions that can be achieved. If an adult stretches the child then these kinds of problems are usually avoided. However, PNF stretching with children serving as partners is riskier due to the inattentiveness and playful nature of children. A clear paucity

FIGURE 10.4 Proprioceptive Neuromuscular Facilitation (PNF) stretching. Note that the athletes are performing three different positions: lifting a leg forward, lifting a leg sideward and lifting a leg rearward. The partners who are holding the legs provide support, resistance and postural feedback

of data using PNF techniques exists, however, simple observation of aesthetic sport training clearly indicates that coaches and athletes have used these techniques for decades (Sands, 1984).

Dynamic stretching involves larger ranges of motion achieved by swinging, gentle kicking and other movements that dynamically take a limb or body part through its full range of motion (Figure 10.5). The attraction of dynamic stretching is that skill rehearsal and warm-up can be built into the movements used for the dual purpose of achieving flexibility gains while also rehearsing and developing skills and/or specific athletic positions (Faigenbaum *et al.*, 2005).

Flexibility training via the addition of vibration (Figure 10.6) has been shown to enhance range of motion acquisition in children (Kinser *et al.*, 2008; Sands *et al.*, 2008b, 2009). The mechanism behind vibration induced enhanced flexibility is currently unknown, but good possible mechanisms include increased tissue temperatures due to increased blood flow (Issurin *et al.*, 1993), increased thixotropic activity within muscle and connective tissue cells (Hutton, 1992) and pain reduction (Kinser *et al.*, 2008; McNeal *et al.*, 2011; Sands *et al.*, 2008b, 2009). The results of vibration aided stretching have been impressive with up to 400 per cent range of motion improvement acutely and 100 per cent improvement chronically (Sands *et al.*, 2006).

FIGURE 10.5 Dynamic stretching is shown with athletes lifting a knee to their chest during a standing and rhythmic marching-type movement

FIGURE 10.6 Two young athletes using vibration stretching. The two positions shown are to be enhanced when seeking to improve a split position and running stride length. Note that the athlete on the left is stretching the forward leg by placing her heel on the vibrator while the athlete on the right is stretching her rear leg by placing her thigh on the vibrator and consciously leaning backwards

Key points

- Flexibility involves fluidity of motion not simply the range between end points of the joint angle.
- Children develop fluid motion via flexibility training at a faster rate than adults.
- Stretching exercises should last 10–30 s, and be performed from daily to twice weekly.
- Close attention should be paid to posture and alignment while stretching.
- Mobility is important in aesthetic sports in performing specific body positions, and in other sports for the development and arresting of high forces.

References

Beunen, G. and Malina, R. M. (1996). 'Growth and biological maturation: Relevance to athletic performance'. In: O. Bar-Or, *The Child and Adolescent Athlete* (pp. 3–24). Oxford: Blackwell Science.

Bouchard, C., Malina, R. M. and Perusse, L. (1997). *Genetics of Fitness and Physical Performance*. Champaign, IL: Human Kinetics.

Brodie, D. A. and Royce, J. (1998). 'Developing flexibility during childhood and adolescence'. In: E. Van Praagh, *Pediatric Anaerobic Performance* (pp. 65–93). Champaign, IL: Human Kinetics.

Burgess, D. J. and Naughton, G. A. (2010). 'Talent development in adolescent team sports: A review', *International Journal of Sports Physiology and Performance*, 5, 103–116.

Chandler, T. J., Kibler, W. B., Uhl, T. L., Wooten, B., Kiser, A. and Stone, E. (1990). 'Flexibility comparisons of junior elite tennis players to other athletes', *American Journal of Sports Medicine*, 18, 134–136.

Corbin, C. B. and Noble, L. (1980). 'Flexibility: A major component of physical fitness', *Journal of Physical Education & Recreation*, 51, 23–24, 57–60.

Covert, C. A., Alexander, M. P., Petronis, J. J. and Davis, D. S. (2010). 'Comparison of ballistic and static stretching on hamstring muscle length using an equal stretching dose', *Journal of Strength and Conditioning Research*, 24, 3008–3014.

Cribb, A. M. and Scott, J. E. (1995). 'Tendon response to tensile stress: An ultrastructural investigation of collage: proteoglycan interactions in stressed tendon', *Journal of Anatomy*, 187, 423–428.

Drabik, J. (1996). *Children & Sports Training*. Island Pond, VT: Stadion Publishing Co.

Enoka, R. M. (1994). *Neuromechanical Basis of Kinesiology*. Champaign, IL: Human Kinetics.

Faigenbaum, A. D., Bellucci, M., Bernieri, A., Bakker, B. and Hoorens, K. (2005). 'Acute effects of different warm-up protocols on fitness performance in children', *Journal of Strength and Conditioning Research*, 19, 376–381.

Faigenbaum, A. D., Kang, J., McFarland, J., Bloom, J. M., Magnatta, J., Ratamess, N. A. and Hoffman, J. R. (2006). 'Acute effects of different warm-up protocols on anaerobic performance in teenage athletes', *Pediatric Exercise Science*, 17, 64–75.

Falciglia, F., Guzzanti, V., Di Ciommo, V. and Poggiaroni, A. (2009). 'Physiological knee laxity during pubertal growth', *Bulletin of the NYU Hospital for Joint Diseases*, 67, 325–329.

Feit, H., Kawai, M. and Mostafapour, A. S. (1989). 'The role of collagen crosslinking in the increased stiffness of avian dystrophic muscle', *Muscle & Nerve*, 12, 486–492.

Gajdosik, R. L. (2001). 'Passive extensibility of skeletal muscle: Review of the literature with clinical implications', *Clinical Biomechanics*, 16, 87–101.

Geladas, N. D., Nassis, G. P. and Pavlicevic, S. (2005). 'Somatic and physical traits affecting sprint swimming performance in young swimmers', *International Journal of Sports Medicine*, 26, 139–144.

Grosset, J. F., Mora, I., Lambertz, D. and Perot, C. (2005). 'Reflex and stiffness of the triceps surae for pre-pubertal children of different ages', *Computer Methods in Biomechanics and Biomedical Engineering*, 8, 123–124.

Grosset, J. F., Mora, L., Lambertz, D. and Perot, C. (2007). 'Changes in stretch reflexes and muscle stiffness with age in pre-pubescent children', *Journal of Applied Physiology*, 102, 2352–2360.

Heyward, V. H. (1984). *Designs For Fitness: A Guide to Physical Fitness Appraisal and Exercise Prescription*. Minneapolis, MN: Burgess.

Hutton, R. S. (1992). 'Neuromuscular basis of stretching exercises'. In: P. V. Komi, *Strength and Power in Sport* (pp. 29–38). Oxford: Blackwell Scientific Publications.

Issurin, V. B., Liebermann, D. G. and Tenenbaum, G. (1993). 'Vibratory stimulation training: A new approach for developing strength and flexibility in athletes', 2nd Maccabiah-Wingate International Congress on Sport and Coaching Sciences, the Wingate Institute for Physical Education and Sport.

Kinser, A. M., Ramsey, M. W., O'Bryant, H. S., Ayres, C. A., Sands, W. A. and Stone, M. H. (2008). 'Vibration and stretching effects on flexibility and explosive strength in young gymnasts', *Medicine and Science in Sports and Exercise*, 40, 133–140.

Kluemper, M., Uhl, T. and Hazelrigg, H. (2006). 'Effect of stretching and strengthening shoulder muscles on forward shoulder posture in competitive swimmers', *Journal of Sport Rehabililtation*, 15, 58–70.

Lambertz, D., Mora, I., Grosset, J. F. and Perot, C. (2003). 'Evaluation of musculotendinous stiffness in pre-pubertal children and adults, taking into accout muscle activity', *Journal of Applied Physiology*, 95, 64–72.

López-Miñarro, P. A. and Alacid, F. (2010). 'Influence of hamstring muscle extensibility on spinal curvatures in young athletes', *Science & Sports*, 25, 88–93.

Luttgens, K. and Wells, K. F. (1982). *Kinesiology*. Philadelphia: CBS College Publishing.

Magnusson, S. P., Simonsen, E. B., Aagaard, P., Boesen, J., Johannsen, F. and Kjaer, M. (1997). 'Determinants of musculoskeletal flexibility: Viscoelastic properties, cross-sectional area, EMG and stretch tolerance', *Scandinavian Journal of Medicine and Science in Sports*, 7, 195–202.

Mahieu, N. N., McNair, P., De Muynck, M., Stevens, V., Blanckaert, I., Smits, N. and Witvrouw, E. (2007). 'Effect of static and ballistic stretching on the muscle-tendon tissue properties', *Medicine and Science in Sports and Exercise*, 39, 494–501.

Malina, R. M. (2007). 'Growth, maturation and development: Applications to young athletes and in particular to divers'. In: R. M. Malina and J. L. Gabriel, *USA Diving Coach Development Reference Manual* (pp. 3–29). Indianapolis: USA Diving.

Marey, S., Boleach, L. W., Mayhew, J. L. and McDole, S. (1991). 'Determination of player potential in volleyball: Coaches' rating versus game performance', *Journal of Sports Medicine and Physical Fitness*, 31, 161–164.

Marshall, J. L., Johanson, N., Wickiewicz, T. L., Tischler, H. M., Koslin, B. L., Zeno, S. and Meyers, A. (1980). 'Joint looseness: A function of the person and the joint', *Medicine and Science in Sports and Exercise*, 12, 189–194.

McCormick, R. J. (2003). 'The flexibility of the collagen compartment of muscle', *Meat Science*, 36, 79–91.

McCormick, R. J. and Thomas, D. P. (1998). 'Collagen crosslinking in the heart: Relationship to development and function', *Basic and Applied Myology*, 8, 143–150.

McNeal, J. R. and Sands, W. A. (2006). 'Stretching for performance enhancement', *Current Sports Medicine Reports*, 5, 141–146.

McNeal, J. R., Edgerly, S., Sands, W. A. and Kawaguchi, J. (2011). 'Acute effects of vibration-assisted stretching are more evident in the non-dominant limb', *European Journal of Sport Sciences*, 11, 45–50.

Mehdinasab, S. A. and Fakoor, M. (2005). 'Muscle tightness of the lower limb in Osgood-Schlatter disease', *British Journal of Sports Medicine*, 39, 396–397.

Miletic, D., Katic, R. and Males, B. (2004). 'Some anthropological factors of performance in rhythmic gymnastics novices', *Collegium Anthropologicum*, 28, 727–737.

Mirkov, D. M., Kukolj, M., Ugarkovic, D., Koprivica, V. J. and Jaric, S. (2010). 'Development of anthropometric and physical performance profiles of young elite male soccer players: A longitudinal study', *Journal of Strength and Conditioning Research*, 24, 2677–2682.

Nordez, A., McNair, P. J., Casari, P. and Cornu, C. (2010). 'Static and cyclic stretching: Their different effects on the passive torque-angle curve', *Journal of Science and Medicine in Sport*, 13, 156–160.

Norris, S. R. (2010). 'Long-term athlete development Canada: Attempting system change and multi-agency cooperation', *Current Sports Medicine Reports*, 9, 379–382.

Ochi, E., Nakazato, K., Song, H. and Nakajima, H. (2008). 'Aging effects on passive resistive torque in the rat ankle joint after lengthening contractions', *Journal of Orthopaedic Science*, 13, 218–224.

Philippaerts, R. M., Vaeyens, R., Janssens, M., Van Renterghem, B., Matthys, D., Craen, R., Bourgois, J., Vrijens, J., Beunen, G. and Malina, R. M. (2006). 'The relationship between peak height velocity and physical performance in youth soccer players', *Journal of Sports Sciences*, 24: 221–230.

Rost, K. and Schon, R. (1997). *Talent Search for Track and Field Events*. Leipzig: German Track and Field Association, translated by M. R. Hill, H. Nowoisky and N. N. Wegink. University of Utah, Salt Lake City, UT.

Sands, B. (1984). *Coaching Women's Gymnastics*. Champaign, IL: Human Kinetics.

Sands, W. A. (2002). 'Physiology'. In: W. A. Sands, D. J. Caine and J. Borms, *Scientific Aspects of Women's Gymnastics* (pp. 128–161). Basel: Karger.

Sands, W. A., McNeal, J. R. and Stone, M. H. (2009). 'Vibration, split stretching, and static vertical jump performance in young male gymnasts', *Medicine and Science in Sports and Exercise*, 41, S255.

Sands, W. A., McNeal, J. R., Stone, M. H., Haff, G. G. and Kinser, A. M. (2008a). 'Effect of vibration on forward split flexibility and pain perception in young male gymnasts', *International Journal of Sports Physiology and Performance*, 3, 469–481.

Sands, W. A., McNeal, J. R., Stone, M. H., Kimmel, W. L., Haff, G. G. and Jemni, M. (2008b). 'The effect of vibration on active and passive range of motion in elite female synchronized swimmers', *European Journal of Sport Science*, 8, 217–233.

Sands, W. A., McNeal, J. R., Stone, M. H., Russell, E. M. and Jemni, M. (2006). 'Flexibility enhancement with vibration: Acute and long-term', *Medicine and Science in Sports and Exercise*, 38, 720–725.

Sands, W. A., Stone, M. H., Smith, S. L. and McNeal, J. R. (2005). 'Enhancing forward split flexibility: USA synchronized swimming', *Synchro Swimming USA*, 13, 15–16.

Santonja, M. F. M., Canteras, J. M., Rodriguez, G. P. L. and López-Miñarro, P. A. (2007). 'Effects of frequency of static stretching on straight-leg raise in elementary school children', *Journal of Sports Medicine and Physical Fitness*, 47, 304–308.

Schmidt-Wiethoff, R. (2003). 'Kinematic analysis of internal and external rotation range of motion in professional tennis', *Medicine & Science in Tennis*, 8, 18–19.

Siff, M. C. and Verkhoshansky, Y. V. (1993). *Supertraining*. Johannesburg: School of Mechanical Engineering, University of Witwatersrand.

Smith, D. J. (2003). 'A framework for understanding the training process leading to elite performance', *Sports Medicine*, 33, 1103–1126.

Steinberg, N., Hershkovitz, I., Peleg, S., Dar, G., Masharawi, Y., Heim, M. and Siev-Ner, I. (2006). 'Range of joint movement in female dancers and nondancers aged 8 to 16 years', *American Journal of Sports Medicine*, 34, 814–823.

Stodden, D. F., Fleisig, G. S., McLean, S. P., Lyman, S. L. and Andrews, J. R. (2001). 'Relationship of pelvis and upper torso kinematics to pitched baseball velocity', *Journal of Applied Biomechanics*, 17, 164–172.

Sutherland, D. H., Olsen, R. A., Biden, E. N. and Wyatt, M. P. (1988). *The Development of Mature Walking*. Philadelphia: JB Lippincott.

Waugh, K. G., Mikel, J. L., Parker, R. and Coon, V. A. (1983). 'Measurement of selected hip, knee, and ankle joint motions in newborns', *Physical Therapy*, 63, 1616–1621.

Wong, S., Ada, L. and Butler, J. (1998). 'Differences in ankle range of motion between pre-walking and walking infants', *Australian Journal of Physiotherapy*, 44, 57–60.

Woo, S. L. Y., Orlando, C. A., Gomez, M. A., Frank, C. B. and Akeson, W. H. (1986). 'Tensile properties of the medial collateral ligament as a function of age', *Journal of Orthopaedic Research*, 4, 133–141.

Yague, P. H. and De La Fuente, J. (1998). 'Changes in height and motor performance relative to peak height velocity: A mixed-longitudinal study of Spanish boys and girls', *American Journal of Human Biology*, 10, 647–660.

Yamamura, C., Zushi, S., Takata, K., Ishiko, T., Matsui, N. and Kitagawa, K. (1999). 'Physiological characteristics of well-trained synchronized swimmers in relation to performance scores', *International Journal of Sports Medicine*, 20, 246–251.

PART 3

Contemporary issues in youth strength and conditioning

11

PERIODIZATION STRATEGIES FOR YOUTH DEVELOPMENT

G. Gregory Haff

Introduction

Periodization is fundamentally a planning paradigm in which training interventions are structured so as to maximize performance or adaptive responses in accordance with the athletes' needs (Haff and Haff 2012; Haff in press). While typically not considered to be a large part of the training practices of youth or developmental athletes, periodization as a planning paradigm should form the foundation of any long-term athlete development model. Long-term athlete development models clearly present time frames or periods in which specific targeted outcomes are emphasized along the athlete's developmental journey from early foundational developmental training towards high-performance competition that is targeted later in their athletic life. If we consider that these outcomes are the goals or emphasis of the training process it is evident that we can structure, or more precisely periodize, the athlete's training activities in accordance with these established parameters (Figure 11.1). Providing this type of a structural framework would then increase the effectiveness of the overall long-term athlete developmental model.

From a conceptual perspective we can consider the various stages of the athlete's development along a developmental pyramid in which the base of the pyramid is centred on fundamental movement skills, and the peak is when the highest level of performance is targeted with sport-specific training (Figure 11.2). Along this developmental pyramid, each level represents a key phase of the athlete's long-term development and serves as the basic structural guidelines from which the periodized training plan is crafted. Ultimately, periodizing a training plan for the youth athlete is no different than developing training structures for an elite athlete. Regardless of the targeted population, the overall plan is based upon the needs of the athlete, the athlete's developmental status and the athlete's overall strengths and weaknesses (Bompa and Haff 2009; Haff in press).

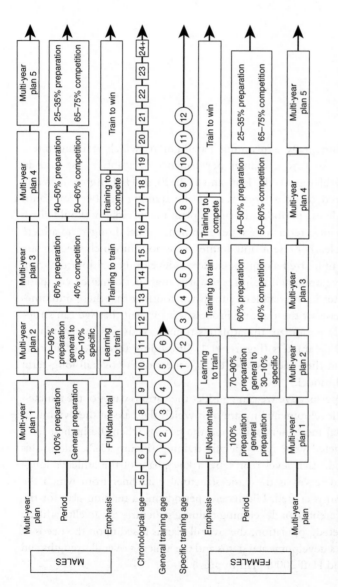

FIGURE 11.1 A hypothetical model for integrating periodization modelling and long-term athlete development

Source: adapted from Ford *et al.* (2011) and Balyi and Hamilton (2004).

Notes: multi-year training plan: a long-term planning structure that guides the focus of the young athlete's training. These structures are interlinked, with each plan building upon the plan that comes before it. Typically these plans contain 2–4 annual training plans, but this can be adapted to meet the individual athlete's needs. Period: training periods are used to divide the annual training into focused training targets that are constructed in accordance with the athlete's long-term developmental plan. Typically these are broken into preparatory, competitive and transition periods (see Figure 11.3). Specific training age: refers to the number of years the youth athlete has been participating in sport-specific training interventions. General training age: refers to the number of years the youth athlete has been participating in general or fundamental training activities. Emphasis: refers to the targeted training goals for the individual athlete. For the youth athlete there are five levels of emphasis that relate to the individual athlete's level of development (see Figure 11.2).

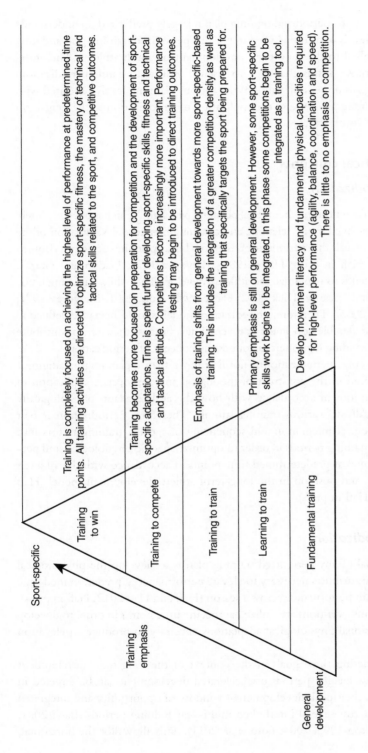

FIGURE 11.2 Theoretical long-term development pyramid with continuum of training focus

Source: adapted from Balyi and Hamilton (2004), Ford *et al.* (2011) and Jeffreys (2008).

The development of a periodized training plan is largely predicated on understanding the various levels of planning used to create a periodized training plan and how they can be applied to the long-term development of youth athletes. Therefore, the primary purpose of this chapter is to discuss: 1) how to define periodization; 2) the primary goals of periodization; 3) the various planning levels associated with a periodized training plan; and 4) the application of periodization to the long-term development of youth athletes.

Basic theoretical concepts

Defining periodization

Periodization is a practical and theoretical planning paradigm, which is often misinterpreted or misconceived in the scientific and coaching literature. Examination of the classic literature reveals that periodization is a non-linear planning paradigm (Bompa and Haff 2009; Haff in press; Harre 1982; Matveyev 1977; Nádori and Granek 1989), which intends to maximize the athlete's development, while removing training monotony and linearity (Dick 2002; Harre 1982; Kurz 2001; Matveyev 1977; Plisk and Stone 2003). Therefore, periodization models should never be defined as linear, non-linear, flexible non-linear or reverse linear because these terms contribute to the misunderstanding that often surrounds the concept of periodization.

While, at its core, periodization is nothing more than a planning paradigm, it must be considered in the construct of the logical and appropriate application of training interventions in accordance with how the athlete adapts physiologically and psychologically to various training stimuli. Therefore, periodization is best defined as the logical integration and sequencing of specific training factors into interdependent training periods in order to optimize specific physiological and performance outcomes at predetermined time points in accordance with the athlete's individual needs and position in the long-term athlete development model (Haff and Haff 2012; Haff in press).

Goals of periodization

The primary goal of any periodized training plan is to develop the physiological and performance attributes necessary to elevate performance at predetermined time points or maintain performance across a season (Haff and Haff 2012; Haff in press). Precise training interventions are utilized at specific time points in order to develop the multidimensional physiological adaptations necessary to produce an elevation in performance.

When considering these goals in the context of the long-term development of youth athletes, specific periods of accelerated development can be targeted in accordance with their peak developmental window of opportunity and integrated and sequenced across several interlinked multi-year training periods (Balyi 2001; Balyi and Hamilton 1993, 2004; Ford et al. 2011). This allows for the horizontal, sequential development which is at the core of any long-term athlete development model (Balyi 2001; Balyi and Hamilton 1993, 2004; Ford *et al.* 2011; Haff in press). If structured correctly, the application of training factors at each level of planning results in a balancing of stress, restoration and adaptation ultimately resulting in a reduction of overtraining potential or training monotony in young athletes, which is considered to be one of the goals of periodization.

Levels of planning

There are several distinct levels of planning that are central to the creation of a periodized training plan (Table 11.1). Each of these planning levels must be considered in the context of the overall training goals established for the athlete, and the level of physiological, chronological and performance development of the youth athlete (Bompa and Haff 2009). Generally, the levels of planning utilized in a periodized training structure spans from global or long-term structures, such as the multi-year training plan, to individual training units, which are very precise and contained in an individual day's workouts (Figure 11.3) (Haff and Haff 2012; Haff in press). The ability to horizontally sequence and vertically integrate these training structures is a central determining factor which dictates the ability of the periodized training plan to accomplish the training goals established for the youth athlete (Haff in press).

From a hierarchical standpoint, all periodized training plans contain eight interrelated levels of planning (Figure 11.3) which include: 1) multi-year training plan; 2) annual training plan; 3) macrocycle; 4) mesocycle; 5) microcycle; 6) training day; 7) training session; and 8) training unit.

Multi-year training plan

Central to the concept of long-term athlete development modelling is the multi-year training plan, as this structure dictates the pathway that all other levels of the periodization process are constructed (Bompa and Haff 2009; Haff in press). This plan is comprised of a series of interlinked annual training plans that direct the athlete toward specific developmental and performance targets (Haff *et al.* 2004a, 2004b). While most commonly used to direct athletes in their Olympic Games preparations (Bompa and Haff 2009; Counsilman and Counsilman 1994; Fry *et al.* 1991), the quadrennial training plan is ideally suited for the development of youth athletes (Jeffreys 2008). For example, Jeffreys (2008) presents a multi-year training plan for the youth football (soccer) athlete that integrates a quadrennial training structure into the four-year academic structure typically contained in high-school sports (Table 11.2). Each annual training plan is designed to establish specific aspects of the athlete's development, culminating with the optimization of the multi-year training structures targeted outcome. In this model, the athlete's quadrennial plan progresses from foundational development (general preparation) through to continued development to performance development, culminating in the optimization of performance in the last year of the multi-year training plan (Table 11.2).

TABLE 11.1 Components of a periodized training plan

Component	Duration	Description
Multi-year training plan	2–4 years	Contains multiple years of training, with the most traditional being the quadrennial plan.
Annual training plan	1 year	Also known as a yearly training plan. Often constructed with one or more macrocycles of training. Each annual training plan is a component of the multi-year training plan.
Macrocycle	Several months to a year	When the annual training plan contains only one macrocycle, the terms are used synonymously. Often the macrocycle is considered a season. Regardless each macrocycle is subdivided into preparatory, competitive and transition periods which are further subdivided into specific phases. The macrocycle forms the basis for the annual training plan.
Mesocycle	2–6 weeks	Considered a medium-sized training period and sometimes referred to as a block of training. While typically 4 weeks in duration, it generally lasts 2–6 weeks. From a structural standpoint the mesocycle forms the basis of the macrocycle.
Microcycle	Several days to 2 weeks	Considered the most important planning structure. Generally last around 7 days, but can range from several days to 2 weeks. The microcycle is comprised of the individual training days and is structured to meet the goals set forth by the mesocycle.
Training day	1 day	An individual training day, which can be comprised of multiple training sessions and units. Each training day is planned in accordance with the goals set forth in the microcycle plan.
Training session	Several hours	Generally consists of several hours of training. If a rest period between training units in the training session lasts more than 30 minutes the session should be considered as a multiple session.
Training unit	Several minutes to hours	A training unit is a dedicated focused activity. For example a training unit could be dynamic stretching in a warm-up or an agility component of a session. Several training units can be strung together to create a training session.

Source: based on Bompa and Haff (2009), Issurin (2008, 2009) and Stone *et al.* (2007).

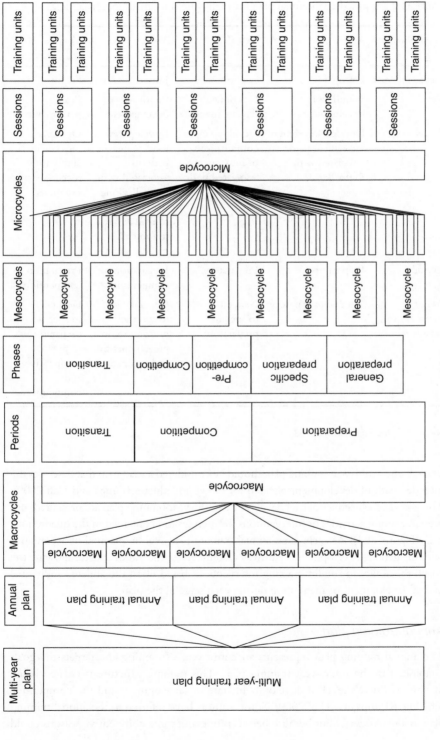

FIGURE 11.3 Structural relationship of the levels of planning contained in a periodized training plan

TABLE 11.2 Proposed quadrennial plan for high-school football (soccer) athletes

Annual training plan	Year 1	Year 2	Year 3	Year 4
Academic year	Freshman	Sophomore	Junior	Senior
Level	Foundation development	Continued development	Performance development	Peak performance
Goals	Develop key generic movement patterns associated with football	Develop key combinations of movements associated with football	Develop key movement patterns associated with football, along with the ability to read and react to football-specific stimuli	Optimize movement ability in soccer-specific situations
Period	Preparatory	Preparatory	Preparation to competition	Preparation to competition
Major periodization phases	General preparatory	General to specific preparatory	General to specific preparatory to pre-competitive and competitive	General to specific preparatory to pre-competitive and competitive

Source: adapted from Jeffreys, 2008.

Overall, the multi-year training plan should be considered a road map that describes the intended path of development planned for the youth athlete (Bompa and Haff 2009). The goals and objectives of each level of the multi-year training plan are presented, not precise training activities or interventions for each session contained in the quadrennial plan (Figure 11.1). As such, each annual training plan will be planned in accordance with the general developmental pathway established for the youth athlete, allowing the coach the ability to modify training interventions based upon the athlete's individual rate of development or maturation during each stage of the plan.

Annual training plan

The annual training plan represents an entire year of training and targets the goals established in the multi-year training plan. This training structure is created based upon the athlete's level of development, rate of development and the competitive schedule (Bompa and Haff 2009). Some authors have referred to the annual training plan as a macrocycle, but because between one and three competitive seasons could be contained in one training year, depending upon the sport (i.e. athletics has two seasons) or the number of sports a youth athlete participates in, it is probably better to consider the year of training as an annual training plan (Haff in press). Based upon this line of reasoning, the macrocycle, or season(s), would be a sub-component of the annual training plan and be another level of the planning hierarchy (Bondarchuk 1986; Rowbottom 2000). Much like multi-year training plans, the annual training plan is a generalized training structure that serves as a template from which other levels of planning are constructed (Bompa and Haff 2009; Viru 1988).

Macrocycle

Since an annual training plan can potentially contain several distinct competitive periods, the macrocycle should be considered as a planning structure that is representative of a season (Haff in press; Viru 1988). Various macrocycle structures can be employed in an annual training plan depending upon the youth athlete's needs (Figure 11.4). For example, a youth athlete might participate in a sport with only one season, and as such only one macrocycle would be planned for this athlete (Figure 11.4, models 1–4). Conversely, an athlete may compete in a sport, such as athletics, that might require two macrocycles in their annual training plan, which would prepare the athlete for the indoor and outdoor seasons (Figure 11.4, model 5). When working with youth athletes, it is very likely that they are participating in multiple sports and the annual training plan for these athletes would have interlinked macrocycles, which are structured around each sport's season. For example, the annual training plan might have a macrocycle that targets football through the summer and autumn months and athletics in the spring and summer months. This type of scenario would require a two to three macrocycle training structure (Figure 11.4, models 6–7). Additionally, it is important to consider how each macrocycle contributes to the athlete's overall developmental progression, how they are integrated with one another and how they align with the annual training plans goals.

Regardless of the number of macrocycles contained in an annual training plan all macrocycles are subdivided into three major periods which include the periods: 1) preparation; 2) competition; and 3) transition (Bondarchuk 1986; Fry *et al.* 1992; Rowbottom 2000). These key periods can occur multiple times throughout the training year depending upon the individual athlete's needs, the competitive schedule and the athlete's level of development.

Preparation period

This period is designed to target the development of the athlete's physiological, psychological and technical abilities in accordance with their level of development and sports requirements (Bompa and Haff 2009). Typically, between three and six months of the annual training plan are dedicated to the preparation period, but this can be shortened or extended depending upon the athlete's level of development (Bompa and Haff 2009; Haff in press). Younger athletes generally dedicate more time to this period

Developmental annual training plans with competitive season

Month	8	9	10	11	12	1	2	3	4	5	6	7
Model 1	Preparation period								Competition period			Transition period
	General preparation phase								Competition period			Transition phase
Model 2	Preparation period						Competition period					Transition period
	General preparation phase				Specific preparation phase		Pre-competition phase		Competition phase			Transition phase
Model 3	Preparation period							Competition period				Transition period
	General preparation phase					Specific preparation phase		Pre-competition phase	Competition phase			Transition phase
Model 4	Preparation period						Competition period					Transition period
	General preparation phase					Specific preparation phase		Pre-competition phase		Competition phase		Transition phase

(*Continued*)

Developmental annual training plans with multiple competitive season

Month	8	9	10	11	12	1	2	3	4	5	6	7
Model 5 (period)	Preparation period	Preparation period	Preparation period	Preparation period	Competition period	Competition period	Transition period	Preparation period	Competition period	Competition period	Competition period	Transition period
Model 5 (phase)	General preparation phase	General preparation phase	Specific preparation phase	Specific preparation phase	Pre-competition phase	Competition phase	Transition phase	Specific preparation phase	Pre-competition phase	Competition phase	Competition phase	Transition phase
Model 6 (period)	Preparation period	Preparation period	Competition period	Competition period	Transition period	Preparation period	Competition period	Transition period	Preparation period	Competition period	Competition period	Transition period
Model 6 (phase)	General preparation phase	General preparation phase	Pre-competition phase	Competition phase	Transition phase	Specific preparation phase	Competition phase	Transition phase	Specific preparation phase	Competition phase	Competition phase	Transition phase
Model 7 (period)	Preparation period	Competition period	Competition period	Preparation period	Preparation period	Preparation period	Preparation period	Competition period	Competition period	Transition period	Preparation period	Preparation period
Model 7 (phase)	Specific preparation phase	Pre-competition phase	Competition phase	General preparation phase	General preparation phase	Specific preparation phase	Specific preparation phase	Competition phase	Competition phase	Transition phase	General preparation phase	General preparation phase

FIGURE 11.4 Example of annual training plan structures for youth athletes

Source: adapted from Bondarchuk (1986), Counsilman and Counsilman (1994) and Haff and Haff (2012).

Notes: the various annual plan structures presented here represent different methods for sequencing the various periods that are contained in an annual plan. These are only examples as there are an infinite number of sequential structures that can be created. The sequence chosen is dictated by the individual athlete's level of development and training needs.

because they have a lower training base, while advanced athletes will not need to spend as much time in this period because they have established a greater training base.

Youth athletes who participate in one sport will generally have one long preparation phase, while athletes who participate in multiple sports will have preparation periods that are subdivided into each macrocycle contained in the annual plan. Regardless of the duration of the preparatory period, it will be subdivided into either a (i) general or (ii) specific preparation phase (Bompa and Haff 2009; Rowbottom 2000):

(i)   *General preparation phase:* this phase is generally placed in the early part of the overall preparation period and earlier in the annual training plan as it is designed to establish a general training base (Bompa and Haff 2009). Additionally, this phase has a larger contribution to the overall training that is contained in the early fundamental developmental periods of any long-term athlete development plan (Balyi 2001; Balyi and Hamilton 1993, 2004). Typically, this phase will contain a variety of training means designed to develop fundamental performance characteristics such as general motor abilities or fundamental skills development, skills and fitness which create the foundation of the youth athlete's training base (Issurin 2008, 2009; Matveyev 1977). Early in the youth athlete's development, this phase will make up a larger portion of the overall preparation period. As the athlete progresses from a developmental to advanced classification, this phase will be modulated in accordance with their individual rate of development.

(ii) *Specific preparation phase:* the second component of a preparation period is the specific preparation phase, which is designed to capitalize on the physiological adaptations established during the general preparation phase (Bompa and Haff 2009). Traditionally, this phase incorporates more sport-specific activities which are marked by higher training loads that are designed to elevate the athlete's performance capacity prior to transitioning into the competitive period. Additionally, there will be an increased emphasis on technical and tactical skill sets in order to lay a performance foundation prior to engaging in direct competitive development.

The contribution of the general and specific preparatory phases to the overall preparation period will largely be dependant upon the athlete's stage of development (Bompa and Haff 2009). Specifically, youth athletes who are in the early parts of the developmental process will spend larger amounts of time in the general preparatory phase in order to establish a greater training base, while the more developed athlete will capitalize on their existing training base by placing more emphasis on the specific preparation phase.

Competitive period

The central component of the competitive period is the actual competitive schedule and attempting to optimize the athlete's preparedness for this time period

(Bompa and Haff 2009; Haff and Haff 2012; Haff in press). This is accomplished by maintaining, or slightly improving, the athlete's physiological and sport-specific skills established during the preparatory period. Generally, this period is marked by a reduction in training workloads that target general preparation in conjunction with increasing the emphasis on training activities that target sport-specific fitness while elevating technical and tactical skills around the needs of the competitive schedule (Bompa and Haff 2009; Haff and Haff 2012). In the classic literature, this period is marked by fluctuations in both volume and intensity in accordance with the athlete's competitive schedule while accounting for travel, actual competitive stressors and the time needed to recover (Bompa and Haff 2009). With youth athletes it is also important to consider that their individual growth or maturation rates will influence the overall fluctuations of both volume and intensity that are appropriate for their development.

Two general phases are utilized in order to account for these issues, including the pre-competitive and main competitive phases:

(i) *Pre-competitive phase:* often considerd a linking phase, the pre-competitive phase serves to bridge between the sport-specific preparation phase and the main competitive phase. Traditionally this phase contains exhibition and unofficial competitions that serve to develop sport-specific fitness while allowing the coach to evaluate the inner workings of the team (Haff and Haff 2012; Haff in press). Classically the main objective of this phase is not competitive success but to use competitions as a means of preparation for the main competitive phase. For the youth athlete this phase is used as a developmental tool where game-based activities are used to develop skills. In order to account for the training stress of game play the focus of the periodized plan will shift in line with these changing objectives.

(ii) *Main competitive phase:* the primary objective of the main competitive phase is to optimize performance at predetermined time points, which are dictated by the athlete's actual competitive schedule. With the youth athlete the individual training age or stage of development will dictate how much emphasis will be placed upon the main competitive phase. With younger, less-developed athletes this phase will be used as a developmental tool, while with more experienced or developed athletes who have a higher training age the emphasis will shift towards competitive success. As the athlete moves through the competitive schedule, performance is either maintained or elevates culminating with an 8–12-day taper that targets the main competition established for this period. The success of this phase is largely dictated by the ability to modulate travel, training and competition stressors, while maximizing recovery.

Transition period

Conceptually a linking period, the transition period serves to bridge between two macrocycles, annual training plans or multi-year training structures (Bompa and

Haff 2009; Nádori and Granek 1989; Rowbottom 2000). This period is marked by a large reduction in training stressors and is designed to only be used to maintain fitness and technical skills, while allowing the athlete to recover from the previous training activities and allow them to be refreshed mentally and physically (Nádori and Granek 1989). Traditionally this period lasts between two and four weeks (Bompa and Haff 2009; Rowbottom 2000) depending upon its location in the annual training plan. In some instances, this period can be extended to six weeks depending upon the cumulative fatigue generated by the previous competitive period, macrocycle, annual plan or number of sports participated during the annual training plan (Bompa and Haff 2009). It is important to note that the longer the transition phase, the larger the reduction in the athlete's overall fitness and abilities which will need to be addressed by a longer preparation phase in the subsequent macrocycle.

Mesocycle

Considered a medium-duration training structure, the mesocycle is typically designed in two- to six-week blocks (Haff and Haff 2012; Haff in press; Issurin 2008). The most frequently used mesocycle length is four weeks because asymptotic effects generally begin to appear after this duration (Fry *et al.* 1992; Haff in press). These asymptotic effects are manifested as a state of involution, during which physiological and performance gains either stagnate or decline (Viru 1995). If the training focus or stress is altered, the involution effects can be avoided and the athlete can continue to develop.

Mesocycles, or blocks of training (Issurin 2008, 2009; Rowbottom 2000), are considered the crucial building blocks of the annual training plan (Rowbottom 2000). These blocks should logically sequence the development of specific attributes in order to allow the attributes developed in one block to serve as the foundation for subsequent blocks (Fry *et al.* 1992; Harris *et al.* 2000; Minetti 2002; Rowbottom 2000; Zamparo *et al.* 2002).

In the classic literature, a 3:1 (three increasing workload microcycles: 1 decreasing workload microcycle) loading structure is considered to be the most basic mesocycle format (Bompa and Haff 2009; Fry *et al.* 1992; Haff and Haff 2012; Haff in press). This basic structure is ideally suited for the developmental programme of a youth athlete because of its simplistic nature and ease for managing training stressors. Other loading structures can be used such as a 3:2, 4:1 or 4:2, which are also applicable for youth development programmes (Figure 11.5). The ratio of loading to recovery contained in the mesocycle is largely predicated by the athlete's training age and ability to recover from training stressors. For more information on mesocycle structures see Bompa and Haff (2009) or Haff and Haff (2012).

Microcycle

From a planning perspective, the microcycle is considered to be the most important structure as this is where the daily training structures are considered (Haff

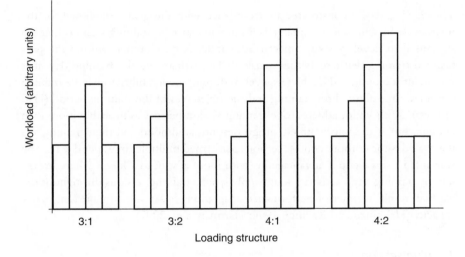

FIGURE 11.5 Example of mesocycle loading structures

and Haff 2012; Viru 1990). For the most part the microcycle is approximately seven days in duration, but can range from several days to one or two weeks (Fry *et al.* 1992; Haff and Haff 2012; Viru 1990) depending upon the overall needs of the training plan. The training activities chosen for the microcycle are dictated by the objectives set forth in the mesocycle, macrocycle and annual training plan.

Despite the repetitive nature of microcycles, it is obvious that, based upon the mesocycle structure, not all microcycles will contain the same content or objectives. There are numerous microcycle structures that can be employed (Rowbottom 2000; Viru 1990), but most are broadly classified as either: 1) developmental; 2) preparation; 3) competitive; or 4) restoration microcycles (Matveyev 1977; Viru 1990). These microcycle structures are typically used to modulate training stressors in accordance with the training goals. Regardless of the microcycle classification, variations in training load should occur across each microcycle in order to stimulate adaptation and recovery (Nádori and Granek 1989). It is important to note that youth athletes, especially those who have a lower training age, will not be able to tolerate the frequency, volume and intensity of training utilized with advanced athletes. Additionally, it is essential that individuals working with youth athletes should not train these athletes as mini adults because these athletes do not have the training base to handle adult training programmes (Faigenbaum *et al.* 2009). Microcycles can be structured with training and recovery days in a variety of formats including 1:1, 2:1, 3:1 or 5:2 training–recovery ratios (Viru 1990). For more information about microcycles see, Bompa and Haff (2009).

Training day

The training day is constructed in accordance with the goals established for the microcycle in which it is contained. Employing specific training sessions that are structured to develop a key aspect of the athlete's development within the pre-planned training day targets these goals. When structuring the training day, it is important to consider the athlete's level of development, ability to handle training activities, time allotted for training and the objectives of the training period (Haff in press). With youth athletes, one training session per day is probably more than enough, but as the youth athlete progresses into adulthood and their training age is elevated, shorter more concise sessions performed multiple times per day may be warranted. This tactic is advantageous with more advanced athletes where break-ing the training day's activities into evenly spaced training sessions throughout the day will result in superior performance adaptations as a result of increasing work capacity (Häkkinen and Kallinen 1994; Hartman et al. 2007).

Training session

A training session or workout is one of the smallest units of planning contained in a periodized plan (Haff in press; Haff and Haff 2012; Issurin 2008; Zatsiorsky 1995). A training session is typically defined as training activities, which contain less than 40 minutes between individual bouts of activity or training units (Haff in press; Haff and Haff 2012; Häkkinen et al. 1988a, b). Typically the training ses-sion will contain specific training units that target the development of a specific attribute.

Training unit

A training unit is a focused training activity that is used to create a training session (Haff in press). For example, a training session may contain a dynamic warm-up unit, agility unit, strength unit and a flexibility unit. The training units chosen are largely dictated by the focus of the training session and the athlete's developmental status. With youth athletes, the training units selected are largely dependent upon their training age, training emphasis and period of development. For example, in the early developmental years (training age one to four years) the primary training target of the youth athlete is focused on general or foundational training activities that are centred on the development of basic movement literacy.

Integration of periodization and long-term athlete development modelling

While actual scientific data investigating the effectiveness of which periodiza-tion models are best suited for youth athletes is limited (especially those in the early stages of development), a theoretical framework can be established for its utilization based upon the many long-term athlete development models presented in the scientific literature.

Long-term athlete development modelling is simply a multi-year training structure that is similar to the classic periodization modelling research (Balyi 2001; Balyi and Hamilton 1993, 2004; Ford *et al.* 2011). Based upon the work of Ford *et al.* (2011) and Balyi and Hamilton (1993, 2004), specific periods of development can be established (Figure 11.1) which can serve as the framework for the periodized training plan. While Figure 11.1 presents a basic framework for integrating periodization with the long-term athlete development model, it is important to realize that some youth athletes will be 'early maturers' while some may be 'late maturers' and the time frames presented are simply guidelines that must be tailored to the individual youth athlete's needs (Lloyd *et al.* 2012).

The individual periods of development can serve as the framework for the development of the periodization model. For example, in Figure 11.1 from the onset of training, in this case six years of age, the primary emphasis of the training plan is the establishment of fundamental movement skills (Ford *et al.* 2011) while de-emphasizing competition. This main emphasis is targeted until approximately the age of 10 for males and 9 for females. Based upon this recommendation, a 3–4-year, multi-year training plan can be established which targets this emphasis with the use of a large amount of general preparation training. Each successive annual training plan would be structured to develop these developmental processes based upon the principles of motor learning.

The foundation developed in the first multi-year training plan then serves as the base for the subsequent multi-year training structure, which can be revised as the athlete matures. In Figure 11.1 this part of the developmental model would start to incorporate specific preparation methods as well as developmental competitions in which sport-specific development is initiated. Balyi and Hamilton (2004) recommend a ratio of 70:30 of training or practice to competition during this phase of the developmental model. However, it is likely that this ratio may vary from 90:10 in the first annual training plan and then change to an 80:20 ratio in the second annual plan, culminating with a 70:30 ratio in the third annual training plan of this multi-year plan. It is likely that this ratio will vary depending upon the individual athlete's sport and level of development.

In the third multi-year training plan there is an increased emphasis on competition, but it is important to realize that too many competitions will reduce training time and ultimately reduce overall development (Balyi and Hamilton 2004). Typically, a ratio of 60:40 (training:competition) is often recommended during this multi-year plan, but will vary in accordance with the sport and level of development. While competitions become more prevalent during this plan of development the focus is not simply on winning. Continued development in training, further development of sport-specific skills and learning how to use these skills in competition become more important during this plan (Balyi and Hamilton 2004).

The onset of the fourth proposed multi-year training plan initiates a major shift in emphasis towards competition. During this period a greater emphasis is placed upon maximizing sport-specific fitness, skills and translation into competitive performance (Balyi and Hamilton 2004). Typically, a training:competition ratio of 50:50 is recommended, but it is more likely that a 40–50 per cent training to 50–60 per cent competition ratio should be used to ensure that the youth athlete continues to develop the requisite physiological adaptations and skills while still allowing for an increased emphasis on competitions.

Once the athlete is fully developed he or she would engage in additional multi-year training plans depending upon how long the athlete remains in the sport. At this time a 25–35 per cent training to 65–75 per cent competition ratio is likely. However, this ratio will vary depending upon how often the athlete needs or is able to compete.

While Figure 11.1 offers a possible model for integrating long-term athlete development theory with the concepts of periodization, it is important to remember that the actual means and methods of training youth athletes have not been presented in this chapter. While an example of how periodization can be used to structure long-term athlete development has been presented, it is important to note that regardless of the application of a periodized plan its success relies on individualizing the programme. The youth athlete's specific needs and rate of development must be considered when developing the plan in conjunction with integrating and sequencing specific training interventions in line with established planning structures in order to maximize the athlete's long-term development.

Key points

- Periodization is simply a planning paradigm that allows for the logical and systematic structuring of the training process. It is designed to remove linearity while systematically integrating and sequencing training factors in accordance with the athlete's developmental level.
- When employing long-term athlete development models, the process of periodizaton should be utilized to structure training interventions in line with periods of accelerated development in order to optimize the youth athlete's development.
- Utilizing long-term training structures such as the multi-year plan are key to the successive integration of periodization with long-term athlete development. Specifically, it is important to utilize these structures to outline the youth athlete's sequential development from developmental toward elite athlete status.
- Periodization should never be considered a rigid structure, it should be considered as a work in progress that can be altered in accordance with the level and rate of development of the youth athlete.

References

Balyi, I. (2001) *Sport System Building and Long-Term Athlete Development in British Columbia*, British Columbia: SportMed BC.

Balyi, I. and Hamilton, A. (1993) 'Long-term athlete development: trainability in childhood and adolescence', *Olympic Coach*, 16: 4–9.

Balyi, I. and Hamilton, A. (2004) *Long-Term Athlete Development: Trainability in Childhood and Adolescence. Windows of Opportunity, Optimal Trainability*, Victoria: National Coaching Institute British Columbia and Advanced Training and Performance Ltd.

Bompa, T. O. and Haff, G. G. (2009) *Periodization: Theory and Methodology of Training*, 5th edn, Champaign, IL: Human Kinetics.

Bondarchuk, A. (1986) 'Periodization of sports training', *Legkaya Atletika*, 12: 8–9.

Counsilman, J. E. and Counsilman, B. E. (1994) *The New Science of Swimming*, Englewood Cliffs, NJ: Prentice Hall.

Dick, F. W. (2002) *Sports Training Principles*, 4th edn, London: A & C Black.

Faigenbaum, A. D., Kraemer, W. J., Blimkie, C. J., Jeffreys, I., Micheli, L. J., Nitka, M. and Rowland, T. W. (2009) 'Youth resistance training: updated position statement paper from the National Strength and Conditioning Association', *Journal of Strength and Condition Research*, 23: S69–70.

Ford, P., De Ste Croix, M., Lloyd, R., Meyers, R., Moosavi, M., Oliver, J., Till, K. and Williams, C. (2011) 'The long-term athlete development model: physiological evidence and application', *Journal of Sports Sciences*, 29: 389–402.

Fry, R. W., Morton, A. R. and Keast, D. (1991) 'Overtraining in athletes: an update', *Sports Medicine*, 12: 32–65.

Fry, R. W., Morton, A. R. and Keast, D. (1992) 'Periodization of training stress: a review', *Canadian Journal of Sport Science*, 17: 234–240.

Haff, G. G. (in press) 'The essentials of periodization', in I. Jeffreys and J. Moody (eds) *Strength and Conditioning for Sports Performance*, London: Routledge.

Haff, G. G. and Haff, E. E. (2012) 'Training integration and periodization', in J. Hoffman (ed.) *Strength and Conditioning Program Design*, Champaign, IL: Human Kinetics.

Haff, G. G., Kraemer, W. J., O'Bryant, H. S., Pendlay, G., Plisk, S. and Stone, M. H. (2004a) 'Roundtable discussion: periodization of training: Part 1', *Strength and Conditioning Journal*, 26: 50–69.

Haff, G. G., Kraemer, W. J., O'Bryant, H. S., Pendlay, G., Plisk, S. and Stone, M. H. (2004b) 'Roundtable discussion: periodization of training: Part 2', *Strength and Conditioning Journal*, 26: 56–70.

Häkkinen, K. and Kallinen, M. (1994) 'Distribution of strength training volume into one or two daily sessions and neuromuscular adaptations in female athletes', *Electromyography and Clinical Neurophysiology*, 34: 117–124.

Häkkinen, K., Pakarinen, A., Alen, M., Kauhanen, H. and Komi, P. V. (1988a) 'Daily hormonal and neuromuscular responses to intensive strength training in 1 week', *International Journal of Sports Medicine*, 9: 422–428.

Häkkinen, K., Pakarinen, A., Alen, M., Kauhanen, H. and Komi, P. V. (1988b) 'Neuromuscular and hormonal responses in elite athletes to two successive strength training sessions in one day', *European Journal of Applied Physiology*, 57: 133–139.

Harre, D. (1982) *Principles of Sports Training*, Berlin: Sportverlag.

Harris, G. R., Stone, M. H., O'Bryant, H. S., Proulx, C. M. and Johnson, R. L. (2000) 'Short-term performance effects of high power, high force, or combined weight-training methods', *Journal of Strength and Conditioning Research*, 14: 14–20.

Hartman, M. J., Clark, B., Bembens, D. A., Kilgore, J. L. and Bemben, M. G. (2007) 'Comparisons between twice-daily and once-daily training sessions in male weight lifters', *International Journal of Sports Physiology and Performance*, 2: 159–169.

Issurin, V. (2008) 'Block periodization versus traditional training theory: a review', *Journal of Sports Medicine and Physical Fitness*, 48: 65–75.

Issurin, V. B. (2009) 'Generalized training effects induced by athletic preparation: a review', *Journal of Sports Medicine and Physical Fitness*, 49: 333–345.

Jeffreys, I. (2008) 'Quadrennial planning for the high school athlete', *Strength and Conditioning Journal*, 30: 74–83.

Kurz, T. (2001) *Science of Sports Training*, 2nd edn, Island Pond, VT: Stadion Publishing.

Lloyd, R. S., Oliver, J. L., Meyers, R. W., Moody, J. L. and Stone, M. H. (2012) 'Long-term athletic development and its application to youth weightlifting', *Strength and Conditioning Journal*, 34: 55–66.

Matveyev, L. P. (1977) *Fundamentals of Sports Training*, Moscow: Fizkultua i Sport.

Minetti, A. E. (2002) 'On the mechanical power of joint extensions as affected by the change in muscle force (or cross-sectional area), ceteris paribus', *European Journal of Appiedl Physiology*, 86: 363–369.

Nádori, L. and Granek, I. (1989) *Theoretical and Methodological Basis of Training Planning with Special Considerations within a Microcycle*, Lincoln, NE: NSCA.

Plisk, S. S. and Stone, M. H. (2003) 'Periodization strategies', *Strength and Conditioning Journal*, 25: 19–37.

Rowbottom, D. G. (2000) 'Periodization of training', in Garrett, W. E. and Kirkendall, D. T. (eds) *Exercise and Sport Science*, Philadelphia: Lippicott Williams and Wilkins.

Stone, M. H., Stone, M. E. and Sands, W. A. (2007) *Principles and Practice of Resistance Training*, Champaign, IL: Human Kinetics Publishers.

Viru, A. (1988) 'Planning macrocycles', *Modern Athlete and Coach*, 26: 7–10.

Viru, A. (1990) 'Some facts about microcycles', *Modern Athlete and Coach*, 28: 29–32.

Viru, A. (1995) *Adaptations in Sports Training*, Boca Raton, FL: CRC Press.

Zamparo, P., Minetti, A. E. and di Prampero, P. E. (2002) 'Interplay among the changes of muscle strength, cross-sectional area and maximal explosive power: theory and facts', *European Journal of Applied Physiology*, 88: 193–202.

Zatsiorsky, V. M. (1995) *Science and Practice of Strength Training*, Champaign, IL: Human Kinetics.

12

DISPELLING THE MYTHS OF RESISTANCE TRAINING FOR YOUTHS

Michael H. Stone, Kyle C. Pierce, Michael W. Ramsey, Margaret E. Stone and Satoshi Mizuguchi

Introduction

Strength training is a general term concerned with regular exercise used for enhancing strength and strength-related characteristics, such as muscle hypertrophy, maximum force production, strength endurance, rate of force development, power and speed. Strength training can be viewed from the aspect of the type of equipment used or the goal being pursued. Strength training can involve bodyweight exercises, resistance-producing devices, such as stretch bands, or various machines, free weights (weight training) or, more commonly, combinations of this equipment. Strength training can be part of an overall programme for health or part of the training for sport. From a sport perspective strength training encompasses the competitive aspects of bodybuilding, powerlifting and weightlifting. Because the number of participants engaging in strength training has been increasing (Thompson, 2011) among all levels and ages of the population, it becomes increasingly important to understand potential consequences of the training process. This is even more important when the consequences concern more vulnerable segments of the population, such as children. Therefore, the purpose of this chapter is to briefly review the potential repercussions of the training process as it affects children and adolescents, particularly as it pertains to training for the sport of weightlifting.

Strength training: potential injury among children and adolescents

There is little doubt that both long-term observation and recent research indicate that children and adolescents can benefit from strength training (see Chapter 5), however, injury potential has been a major focus of controversy, especially as it concerns sport. In the authors' experience, and that of others (Pierce *et al.*, 2008), this controversy is usually founded on opinion rather than solid evidence. Often well-meaning individuals in direct contact with youths mistakenly believe resistance training, and in particular weightlifting, is a dangerous activity. In this context it is quite common to find strength training and weightlifting facilities restricted for children and many adolescents (often restricted up to age 16–18 years). When considering Naim Süleymanoğlu, arguably the best weightlifter of modern times (Turkish three-time Olympic winner, seven-time World champion who has also set 46 world records), it is known that he began training at 10 years old and set his first world record at 16 years of age. Although he may be considered an exception, had he been in most Western countries it is likely that he would have still been waiting to get into a gym at 16 years of age, rather than lifting at international level. This raises the important consideration of chronological versus physiological age. Many times a child may be physiologically more advanced than their chronological age, therefore, hard and fast rules of training solely based on chronological age should be viewed with scepticism.

In the past strength training was generally regarded as 'unsafe' for children for many years (American Academy of Pediatrics, 1983, 1990, 2001), the misconceptions stemming from poorly designed and misinterpreted data from the 1960s and 1970s (Benjamin and Glow, 2003). These misconceptions have had serious negative impact for more than three decades. These papers concluded that resistance training should be used with extreme caution and that weightlifting has a high injury rate and should be avoided by pre-adolescents. Unfortunately, these papers were largely based on the rare occurrence of epiphyseal growth plate injuries at any age and the erroneous idea that strength training might 'stunt growth' (Falk and Eliakim, 2003; Hamill, 1994; Malina, 2006). Indeed, considerable research and experiential data concerning youth weightlifting, published or translated into English, has been available since at least the 1970s and 1980s (for example, Aján and Baroga, 1988; Dvorkin, 1975; Pierce *et al.*, 1999, 2008). Most of these studies and reviews (Aján and Baroga, 1988; Dimitrov, 1993; Dvorkin, 1975, 1992; Hamill, 1994) did not support the American Academy of Pediatrics proscription of these sports.

Recent literature reviews (Stratton *et al.*, 2004) and updates (American Academy of Pediatrics, 2008) have taken a less conservative tone. While these updated papers generally support strength training among children and adolescents, it is less clear as to what methods and loading schemes would be acceptable. Indeed, training with 'maximal weights' was generally proscribed. However, the term 'maximal weights' was not well defined and by implication would seem to constitute a position against strength training as part of sports training or competitive weightlifting for children and adolescents up to approximately 16 years old. However, these statements do not specifically address competitive sports including weightlifting (Stratton *et al.*, 2004), but did recommend against 'inter-individual competition', effectively precluding involvement in the sport of weightlifting.

By contrast, a number of reviews and studies of injury type and injury rates associated with strength training among youth and adults indicate that injury rates and incidence are not excessive and are less common than those associated with sports such as American football, basketball, gymnastics, football or rugby (Hamill, 1994; Stone *et al.*, 1994). Although serious injury can occur they are uncommon (Hamill 1994; Stone *et al.*, 1994). Injuries are generally the result of poor technique, excessive loading, overly fatigued training, poorly designed equipment, ready access to the equipment or, typically, lack of qualified supervision (Stone *et al.*, 1994). In a revised 2009 National Strength and Conditioning Association (NSCA) position stance (Faigenbaum *et al.*, 2009) and a position stance by the Canadian Society for Exercise Physiology (Behm *et al.*, 2008), weightlifting was deemed to be a safe sport and with proper coaching and good planning there is no reason to keep children from participating. To an extent lack of data has been an issue, however, alarmist responses by well-meaning physicians, educators and coaches result in disservice to weightlifting and the use of strength training as part of the training process for other sports. Indeed, weightlifting is often condemned by the uninformed as being particularly injurious.

Objective data indicates that resistance training, including the sport of weightlifting, is actually considerably safer than is generally believed. This is especially true if training and competition are appropriate for the age group and properly supervised (Byrd *et al.*, 2003; Pierce *et al.*, 1999). Considering that data indicates children and adolescents can physically and physiologically benefit from strength training and that strength training is a safe activity for these groups, we must develop appropriate training guidelines (Behm *et al.*, 2008; Faigenbaum *et al.*, 2009; Pierce *et al.*, 2008).

Guidelines for training/coaching children and adolescents

When training adolescents, and particularly children, there are several practical aspects that must be addressed before beginning the training process. Consider the points covered in the following four sections.

Strength training equipment

Equipment must be in proper working order and the equipment should be *regularly* inspected. Most machines are made for adults and are not necessarily adjustable for smaller bodies. Evidence indicates that free weights (barbells, dumbbells, associated racks and benches) produce superior results, especially in terms of transfer of training effect (Stone *et al.*, 2011). Multi-joint exercises (such as squats and pulling movements) are more easily and efficiently accomplished using free weights. These multi-joint exercises are quite similar to multi-joint activities of many sports and even daily living, thus it may be argued that mechanical specificity is greater using these exercises compared to machines.

Proper lifting technique

Appropriate technique is important for several reasons. Poor technique will result in limitations for adaptation, in turn, reducing performance gains and stagnating progress. In a sport context, good technique can markedly enhance the 'transferability' of the exercise. So, the potential for enhanced gains in sport performance activities, resulting from poor technique displayed in training exercises, is reduced. Poor technique can increase the potential for injury and, therefore, proper technique should be taught and learned initially in a child's development. This means that the coach has to understand proper technique and know how to teach it effectively to young athletes. Early development of technique is especially important for large muscle mass, multi-joint exercises such as squats or pulling movements. Initially developed technique (poor or not) that is used for long periods (i.e. several years) may be difficult if not impossible to change later. Establishment of good technique from the start of a training programme is paramount to safety, enhanced progress and greater satisfaction. In this context, lack of sufficient strength will limit technique acquisition (Lloyd *et al.*, 2012; Potts, 2009). Thus, maximum strength should be enhanced simultaneously (or perhaps before) moving to technically difficult strength training exercises.

Reasonable safety standards and spotting techniques

Although injuries can occur, compared with most physical activities and sports, free weight training results in a relatively low incidence and rate of injury (Hamill, 1994). Arguably, most injuries occur as a result of poor fatigue management. However, the acute injuries produced in training often result from poor technique or lack of adherence to simple safety procedures, including reasonable supervision (Pierce *et al.*, 2008; Stratton *et al.*, 2004). Injury potential can be reduced by implementing some logical safety guidelines that include the following:

1 Make sure that all participants are educated in good safety procedures.
2 Appropriate emergency assistance procedures should be in place in case of an injury.
3 Make sure the training area is kept clean, neat and that no obstacles are present.
4 Make sure that all participants warm up before each training session.
5 Allow participants to have ready access to fluids during and after training.
6 Make sure that participants understand proper breathing techniques and that these techniques can reduce injury.
7 Some exercises, particularly squats and bench press exercises require spotters. Make sure that proper spotting techniques are known and used.
8 In weightlifting movements, the athlete should be taught how to avoid injury during a missed lift.
9 Make sure that each session is properly supervised.

Types of strength training programmes

Various strength training programmes have been suggested for children. Most of these programmes indicate that higher repetitions (10–15 reps/set) should be used. However, it is very important to realize that this type of training for any age should be initiated only after good technique has been established. Technique is best established with one-on-one supervision and by performing repetitions one at a time with feedback from the coach after each repetition. Loading for this approach should be sub-maximal, allowing proper execution of each repetition. If proper technique is not being used, corrections should be made before going on to the next repetition. This 'one repetition at a time' approach is especially important in learning the technique of complex, multi-joint movements, such as jumping, squatting, snatches or cleans, or their derivatives. Only when good technique is established for each exercise should multiple repetitions/sets be allowed. If good technique is not established initially, the multiple repetition approach simply promotes poor technique development.

After learning proper technique, age and goals should be considered when selecting the type of programme used. When dealing with children (8–10 years) early training protocols should use higher repetitions per set (8–12 reps/set), use a training session frequency of 2–3 days per week and include a variety of exercises (Lloyd *et al.*, 2012). The exception might be in the use of semi-ballistic movements such as weightlifting pulling movements, where higher repetitions could result in acute fatigue-induced technique failure and increased injury potential. While not appropriate in a competitive sport context, motivation and programme adherence can be improved by allowing the children and young adolescents to take part in planning the programme (e.g. choose some exercises). Although initial training (the first 2–3 weeks) might use one set per exercise, training should rapidly progress towards a periodized training programme and use of multiple sets (Pierce *et al.*, 2008). The periodization process includes heavy and light days, 'unload' weeks and active rest periods, which can promote fatigue management, enhance recovery and increase training adaptation. When using strength training in a sport context, this aspect of training must be properly integrated into the overall training process, otherwise optimum gains and performance improvements may stagnate and the potential for injury and overtraining will increase (Plisk and Stone, 2003; Stone *et al.*, 1994).

Differences in training male and female children and adolescents

Women and girls have broken with traditional cultural norms and now engage in a variety of strength training activities. Among adolescents, gains in maximum strength and related characteristics can be greater than in children and the absolute gains do reflect some significant sex differences. Qualitative adaptations to strength training in adolescents and young women (and by assumption female children) are largely similar to men. However, genetic and hormonal differences appear to create enough variance to warrant alterations in the training of adolescent females in order to concentrate on specific mechano-physiological differences.

Perhaps the most profound difference between the sexes deals with anabolic and catabolic hormones. Androgens, in particular testosterone, influence a variety of sex-characteristic-linked physiological differences, such as lean body mass, maximum strength, peak rate of force development and power output (Hakkinen *et al.*, 2000; Hansen *et al.*, 1999). These differences are accentuated upon reaching adolescence (Ramos *et al.*, 1998). Indeed, higher testosterone concentrations not only appear to be related to strength and explosive strength performances between men and women, but also may explain intra-sex differences (Cardinale and Stone, 2006). Furthermore, the rate of training-induced adaptation can also be influenced by differences in resting testosterone concentrations, thus women or girls with higher concentrations may progress at a faster rate (Hakkinen *et al.*, 2000).

There are sex differences that become more apparent in adolescents (Behringer *et al.*, 2010) that can result in training outcome differences or necessitate programming differences. For example, women have relatively less lean body mass and muscle in their upper bodies compared to men. This difference might be reflected in lower absolute and relative strength measures for women compared with men (Stone *et al.*, 2001). Upper-body differences may necessitate additional upper-body exercises during specific phases of training or for specific activities in which the upper body is primarily engaged (such as throwing and aspects of weightlifting). This difference is of particular importance as the upper body is the link between many lower-body activities and the performance outcome, for example squats in which a load is placed on top of the upper body. Thus, a weak upper body could limit squatting ability as the necessary support for holding the bar along the shoulder girdle is reduced. It is possible that early recognition and intervention will obviate this potential problem.

Maximum strength is defined as the greatest force that can be generated under a given set of circumstances, and explosive strength as rate of force development (RFD). Many sports depend upon both maximum strength, explosiveness and high-power outputs. For success and to produce reasonable performances in these 'explosive strength sports' it would be desirable to enhance maximum RFD development and peak power outputs. Compared with men, electromechanical delay, contraction times, RFD and power output are typically lower in women (Garhammer and Gregor, 1992; Winter and Brookes, 1994) and these differences may partially be accounted for by androgen differences (Cardinale and Stone, 2006) and, as the child reaches puberty, by menstrual cycle factors. These sex-linked characteristics may be related to performance- and injury-rate differences between men and women. For example, in terms of performance, maximum strength is a major factor in weightlifting, 'explosiveness' and power output are also key elements for success (Stone *et al.*, 2005). Although relatively common among elite male weightlifters, few women have lifted more than twice their body mass in the clean and jerk. Compared with men, women's peak power during weightlifting movements are approximately 65 per cent. Although men and women weightlifters generally train in a similar manner, many coaches recognize sex-linked characteristics that can result in performance problems, such as differences in upper-body strength, electromechanical delay, skeletal muscle contraction time and menstrual cycle characteristics. As a result, initiation of, often subtle, training alterations at specific points developmentally or during specific phases of a periodized programme, such as additional upper-body work during preparation, can address these potential problems. For example, mature females may be more at risk of injury compared to males, particularly ACL injury, due to differences in electromechanical delay, force absorption, active-joint stabilization and biomechanical factors. Reduction in these sex-related differences in performance and injury potential have been shown to occur in young women as a result of strength training, as well as specific neuromuscular training altering landing patterns after jumping (Hoff and Almasbakk, 1995). Thus, it is likely that specific training programmes may promote performance gains, decreasing the gap between men and women as well as reducing injury potential. Similar arguments concerning strength training can be made for a variety of sports requiring high levels of maximum strength, explosive strength and power.

Adaptation to training also depends upon a number of psycho-physiological factors, such as chronological versus physiological age, physical and mental maturity and environmental/cultural conditions such as current involvement with sport, prior participation in activities that develop coordination, agility, balance and flexibility. Generally, the training programmes for females should follow the same process as those for males at all stages of development. However, in some instances, particularly in terms of training for sport, specific training differences can be incorporated; these can include a greater emphasis on upper-body strength, particularly during early season and preparation phases, on explosiveness and on neurological factors associated with jumping and landing. These differences in training should be recognized as the result of sex-linked traits that become more obvious developmentally (e.g. child to adolescent). Arguably, the earlier they are addressed the less of a problem they become as the child develops into an adult.

A case in point: weightlifting

Weightlifting is a competitive sport consisting of the snatch and clean and jerk. Training for weightlifting consists of using a variety of large muscle-mass exercises, such as squats and variations, snatch and clean and jerk and variations. Weightlifting training has been used to examine potential effects of strength–power training on a number of performance and physiological variables among children and adolescents (Byrd et al., 2003; Dvorkin, 1975). For example, a series of studies carried out in the Soviet Union beginning in the 1950s and continuing through the 1980s examined the effects of weightlifting training on the physical development, physiology and performance of children and adolescents. The results of these studies have been discussed in detail by Dvorkin (1975). The data gleaned from these studies indicates that from 12–22 years of age, weightlifting training can produce positive alterations in body composition, cardio-respiratory variables such as resting heart rate, blood pressure and physical work capacity (e.g. the PWC-170 fitness test), and increases in a variety of motor fitness parameters (e.g. jumping and sprinting), as well as competitive weightlifting performance.

Considering the observational, correlation and longitudinal data as a whole, there can be little doubt that resistance training, particularly weightlifting training, can improve strength and strength-related variables (e.g. RFD, power, strength-endurance, etc.) among children and adolescents. These studies also offer evidence for the efficacy of strength gain alone in producing positive alterations in skill-related variables among children and adolescents. Furthermore, the data indicates that, with appropriate training there is good reason to believe that sports performance can be positively enhanced.

Weightlifting, based on entries by country in the Olympics, is one of the most popular sports around the world. Considerable study has been devoted to its effects on performance, performance transfer to other sports and injury potential (Stone *et al.*, 1994, 2006a, 2006b). While the potential benefits of strength training are now recognized by most medical/scientific groups dealing with children and adolescents, the controversial aspects tend to re-appear when dealing with training for sport, particularly weightlifting (Pierce *et al.*, 1999). Over the past 20 years weightlifting has come under increased scrutiny and has been more controversial than any other aspect of resistance training for young people. For example, the use of ballistic movements, such as weightlifting movements and plyometric exercises, and particularly the sport of weightlifting, have been criticized in opinion articles as producing excessive injury rates (Brzycki, 1994). Although, injuries in weightlifting and related activities can occur, the incidence and rate of injury appears to be relatively low and severe injury is uncommon (Hamill, 1994; Levallee and Balam, 2010). Indeed, most injuries among children and adolescents associated with strength training activities appear to be preventable accidents that could be greatly reduced with better supervision and coaching (Myer *et al.*, 2009). Unfortunately, controversy concerning weightlifting and youth still exists even though information is available indicating that, under proper supervision, these activities are no more (and usually less) injurious than other sports (Hamill, 1994; Stratton *et al.*, 2004). In fact, it can be argued that weightlifting training and related strength training activities can enhance health-related characteristics and in fact reduce injury potential for some activities and sports (Hamill, 1994; Stone *et al.*, 1994).

Weightlifting in the Soviet Union was a very popular and fairly competitive sport, and considerable study was devoted to the effects of weightlifting training, particularly among the young. Studies reported by Dvorkin (1975) are particularly compelling as, in many cases, large groups were tracked continuously from age 13–19 years and compared with control groups of non-exercising peers or similar age groups involved in track and field sports. These studies indicated that weightlifting training produced positive improvements in body composition, cardio-respiratory characteristics and general well-being. Furthermore, there was no indication that weightlifting training 'stunted' growth.

In addition, weightlifting injury rate can be lower than other forms of resistance training (Hamill, 1994). Weightlifting, over a year's competition and training performed by 70 male and female children ranging in age from 7–16 years (mean age: 15 girls = 12.3 ± 2.6 y, 55 boys = 11.6 ± 2.0 y), resulted in no days of training lost from injuries (Pierce *et al.*, 1999). Maximal and near-maximal lifts in competition were allowed as long as correct technique was maintained. Both males and females showed increased strength measured by weightlifting performance (Pierce *et al.*, 1999). Similar results were found in a more detailed follow-up study of three females (13.7 ± 1.2 y) and eight males (12.5 ± 1.6 y) across a year's competition (534 competition lifts), and both the boys and girls showed substantial increases in weightlifting performance and no injuries requiring medical attention or loss of training time occurred (Byrd *et al.*, 2003). The conclusion from these two observations was that, if training and competition are appropriate for the age group and properly supervized, weightlifting training and competition are considerably safer than has been generally believed. The authors (Byrd *et al.*, 2003; Pierce *et al.*, 1999) emphasized that these results must be viewed in the context of a scientific approach to training and competition. Only under these conditions do the authors suggest that resistive training or weightlifting is appropriate for children – a factor that should be true for all sports.

Understanding developmental factors is absolutely essential when training children and adolescents. According to Balyi and Hamilton (2004), 8–12 years of training is necessary for a talented athlete to reach elite levels, and there are 'windows of opportunity' or critical ages at which specific types of training can yield the greatest benefits. Although this model has been accepted by many coaches, the scientific evidence for 'windows of opportunity' has been questioned (Ford *et al.*, 2011). Despite ambiguity surrounding this model, there appears to be a physiological basis for improvements in motor performance throughout childhood and adolescence (Bass, 2000; Dimitrov, 1993; Malina *et al.*, 2004). Thus, these windows may present unique training opportunities to maximize strength, power and speed gains for young athletes. To some extent this progression can be noted in American football and basketball with three years' participation in middle school, four years in high school and, generally, 4–5 years in college before playing professional sports. However, it may be argued that specialization often occurs too early and, unfortunately, well-meaning but overzealous coaches and parents often try to hurry the developmental process in many sports, including weightlifting.

Evidence indicates that physical ability involves the development of proficiency in fundamental movement skills (walking, running and jumping) and fundamental sport skills (catching, hopping and galloping), which, when combined, allows skillful operation in various sporting situations (Higgs *et al.*, 2008). Previous research indicates that peak brain maturation occurs between the ages of 6–8 years and 10–12 years (Rabinowickz, 1986), and that there can be a simultaneous accelerated development of the neuromuscular system (Blimkie, 1989). Indeed, by 12 years of age most of the neural pathways for fundamental movement skills will be defined. This evidence suggests that the pre-pubertal years are likely a critical time frame for introduction and development of skills and techniques, including those associated with weightlifting (Lloyd *et al.*, 2012).

In the evaluation of reasonable starting ages for children and the development of appropriate training plans it is logical that the opinions of coaches dealing directly with children be carefully considered. In the authors' opinion the appropriate starting age for weightlifting can be as early as 10–11 years, provided that the biological age of the child and the maturity of the child are reasonable. Initially the ratio of technique work to strength and conditioning should be approximately 50 per cent light technique, 25 per cent basic strength training and 25 per cent basic conditioning training. This opinion is supported by the observations of other scientists and coaches, for example, Aján and Baroga (1988) indicate that the 'initial stage of training' for weightlifting should take place between the ages of 11 and 16. Starting at the ages of around 11 or 12, they strongly indicate that the aim of training should focus on general physical preparation (development of biomotor abilities) and that specialized training should not comprise more than 40 per cent of the total training plan. Accordingly, a variety of dynamic exercises and exercises to assist in the development of movement characteristics necessary for weightlifting (and sport in general) development should be included. Activities associated with basic gymnastics and track and field, along with games such as basketball and volleyball, are recommended as part of the training at this age. Additionally, the use of free weight exercises aimed at general strengthening should be used. Aján and Baroga also suggest that the aims and objectives in the second year of training (ages 12–13) should be on general physical development (50 per cent) and stress 'correct habits of execution' when learning the technique of the competition exercises. Specialized training should be added gradually in subsequent years, and to optimize long-term results, each phase of training should be built on the previous phase. Specialized training should dominate (80–90 per cent) the programme by the third or fourth year.

In Bulgaria, the starting age for weightlifting training decreased by an average of two years from 1983 to 1993 such that 10–11 year olds were 'selected' for inclusion in weightlifting programmes. In this small country that has been highly successful in weightlifting, the recommended age to begin training is 10 years, and similar programmes were set up in other Eastern European countries (Dimitrov, 1993). Furthermore, it should be noted that many (and likely most) of the athletes participating in many Eastern European weightlifting programmes were initially selected, based primarily on a comprehensive talent identification search (Dimitrov, 1993).

At these recommended ages children should, initially, deal with general physical development that is compatible with sport-specific fitness and this emphasis should continue for at least 2–3 years (Aján and Baroga, 1988). For example, weightlifting developmental fitness for children would include considerable training dealing with basic body strengthening (e.g. weight training, gymnastics, tumbling), strength-endurance factors and enhancing cardio-respiratory ability, mobility and range of motion. However, evidence among adults and adolescents indicates that emphasis on cardiovascular endurance that includes typical aerobic exercise (e.g. long-distance running, swimming, cycling, etc.) should be limited or avoided as this may compromise the ability to gain strength and particularly explosiveness (Hakkinen *et al.*, 2003). Tables 12.1 and 12.2 show a typical timeline for a child's development and a typical training programme that might be used with a beginning weightlifter.

From Table 12.1, basic strength training should include body-weight movements in the youngest age group (e.g. gymanastics), progressing to the use of free weights in older groups (e.g. squats, pulls). Technique training should use age- and size-appropriate bars with minimal loading (see Figure 12.1). The aim of this should be to develop skill proficiency in the snatch and clean and jerk, and will overlap with strength training. Basic conditioning should include components such as flexibility, sprints, bounding, hopping, and games such as soccer, basketball and gymnastics.

TABLE 12.1 Timeline for children's development as a weightlifter, assuming reasonable biological maturity

Age (years)	Basic strength (%)	Technique (%)	Basic conditioning (%)
8–10	70	5	25
10–12	25	50	25
12–15	40	40	20
16–18	70	20	10

TABLE 12.2 Example of a daily training schedule for beginners aged 10–12 years

	Monday	Tuesday	Wednesday	Thursday	Friday	Saturday	Sunday
Week 1	WT Tech	Cond	WT Tech	Cond	WT	Games	Rest
Week 2	WT Tech	Cond	WT Tech	Cond	WT Tech	Games	Rest
Week 3	WT Tech	Cond	WT Tech	Cond	WT Tech	Games	Rest
Week 4	WT	Cond	WT	Cond	WT	Games	Rest

Notes
WT = weight training; Tech = technique training; Cond = other conditioning activities (e.g. sprints, agility, ball throws, etc.).

FIGURE 12.1 Example of bar progression within a technical exercise for athletes of different age, size and training history

Source: Lloyd *et al.*, 2012.

The training programme displayed in Table 12.2 assumes availability six days per week. Exercises would always be performed with between one and three warm-up sets before progressing to the target weight. Weight and technical training would introduce exercises such as the squat, front squat, jerk technique and bench press using single repetitions for a set of 10 in the first couple of weeks and then progressing to multiple sets (progressing to three sets of 10 repetitions by week four). The clean would be introduced after a few weeks of basic training. Conditioning would include exercises such as sprints, walking twists, foot strengthening exercises, agility tasks and ball throws. Again, the aim should be to progress to three sets of 10 repetitions by week four. Each session should conclude with flexibility work.

Summary and recommendations

With any physical activity or sport, reasonable safety measures and appropriate supervision should be in place, otherwise training should not be carried out. Although it is clear that the potential for injury is an issue that requires ongoing scientific study, current evidence indicates that, in typical supervised environments, the potential for strength training-associated injury is quite low. Supervision in training and competition should be carried out by well-qualified professionals who possess an understanding of generic sports science and the growth and maturational intricacies specifically related to paediatric exercise science. Furthermore, the coach/instructor should have good coaching skills for this age group, with the ability and drive to apply this knowledge. Finally, in support of resistance training for children and adolescents involved in sport, motivation would be minimal without some form of competition in which the role of strength training is clearly defined. For weightlifting, this competition could deal with technique competitions at early ages (≤ 11–12 years), in which the judges rate the technique of the child much like gymnastics.

Key points

- Strength training exercises would appear to facilitate enhanced development throughout childhood across a wide spectrum of performances. Due to the complex motor control/force characteristics required of movements such as squats, snatches, cleans, jerks and derivations, the use of large muscle mass, multi-joint exercises likely facilitate both muscle development and superior neural activation patterns.
- Injuries can occur, however, strength training including the sport of weightlifting has not been shown to result in excessive injury rates, and catastrophic injuries are quite rare, particularly when well supervised by knowledgeable trainers and coaches.
- All educators and active coaches should be required to demonstrate, through *testing, certification* and *regular updates*, knowledge of safety and proficiency in the sports sciences (physiology, biomechanics, psychology, human development and motor learning, etc.), particularly as they relate to strength training.
- Sport governing bodies should recognize the importance of strength and conditioning in the overall developmental process and implement evidence-based frameworks for athlete development that address the need for youth-oriented strength and conditioning. Programmes should aim to develop a high level of movement literacy in younger ages, develop sport-specific skills, including gymnastic and weight-training exercise techniques, between the ages of 8 and 11, and train and deploy well-trained strength coaches and weightlifting coaches to further develop technique and strength in children across a range of sports after approximately 11 years of age.

References

Aján, T. and Baroga, L. (1988) *Weightlifting: Fitness for all Sports*, Budapest: International Weightlifting Federation.

American Academy of Pediatrics. (1983) 'Weight training and weight lifting: Information for the pediatrician', *Physician and Sportsmedicine*, 11: 157–161.

American Academy of Pediatrics. (1990) 'Strength training, weight and power lifting, and body building by children and adolescents', *Pediatrics*, 86: 801–803.

American Academy of Pediatrics. (2001) 'Strength training by children and adolescents', *Pediatrics*, 107: 1470–1472.

American Academy of Pediatrics. (2008) 'Strength training by children and adolescents', *Pediatrics*, 121: 835–840.

Balyi, I. and Hamilton, A. (2004) 'Long-term athlete development: Trainability in childhood and adolescence', *Olympic Coach*, 16: 4–8.

Bass, S. L. (2000) 'The pre-pubertal years: A uniquely opportune stage of growth when the skeleton is most responsive to exercise?' *Sports Medicine*, 30: 73–78.

Behm, D. G., Faigenbaum, A. D., Falk, B. and Klentrou, P. (2008) 'Canadian Society for Exercise Physiology position paper: Resistance training in children and adolescents', *Applied Physiology Nutrition and Metabolism*, 33: 547–561.

Behringer, M., van Heede, A., Youe, Z. and Mester, J. (2010) 'Effects of resistance training and adolescents: A meta-analysis', *Pediatrics*, 126: e1199–e1210.

Benjamin, H. J. and Glow, K. M. (2003) 'Strength training for children and adolescents: What role can physicians play', *Physician and Sports Medicine*, 31: 19–25.

Blimkie, C. J. (1989) 'Age- and sex-associated variation in strength during childhood: Anthropometric, morphologic, neurological, biomechanical, endocrinologic, genetic and physical activity correlates', in C. Gisolfi and D. Lamb (eds) *Perspectives in Exercise Science and Sports*, Indianapolis: Benchmark.

Brzycki, M. (1994) 'Speed of movement an explosive issue', *Nautilus*, Spring, 8–11.

Buchheitt, M., Mendez-Villanueva, A., Delhomel, G., Brughelli, M. and Ahmaidi, S. (2010) 'Improving sprint ability in young elite soccer players: Repeated shuttle sprints vs. explosive strength training', *Journal of Strength and Conditioning Research*, 24: 2715–2722.

Byrd, R., Pierce, K., Reilly, L. and Brady, J. (2003) 'Young weightlifters' performance across time', *Sport Biomechanics*, 2: 133–140.

Cardinale, M. and Stone, M. H. (2006) 'Is testosterone influencing explosive performance?' *Journal of Strength and Conditioning Research*, 20: 103–110.

Dimitrov, D. (1993) 'Age to begin with weightlifting training', in A. Lukácsfalvi and F. Takacs (eds) *Proceedings of the International Weightlifting Symposium*, Budapest: International Weightlifting Federation.

Dvorkin, L. S. (1975) 'The training of young weightlifters 13–16 years old', in *The 1975 Russian Weightlifting Yearbook* (translated by B.W. Scheithauer), Moscow: Fiskultura I Sport Publishing.

Dvorkin, L. S. (1992) *Weightlifting and Age: Scientific and Pedagogical Fundamentals of a Multi-Year System of Training Junior Weightlifters* (translated by A. Charniga Jr), Livonia, MI: Sportivny Press.

Faigenbaum, A., Kraemer, W. J., Blimkie, C. J. R., Jeffries, I., Michelli, L. J., Nitka M. and Rowland, T. W. (2009) 'Youth resistance training: Updated position statement from the National Strength and Conditioning Association', *Journal of Strength and Conditioning Research*, 23: S60–S79.

Falk, B. and Eliakim, A. (2003) 'Resistance training, skeletal muscle and growth', *Pediatric Endocrinology Reviews*, 1: 120–127.

Ford, P., De Ste Croix, M., Lloyd, R., Meyers, R., Moosavi, M., Oliver, J., Till, K. and Williams, C. (2011) 'The Long-Term Athlete Development model: Physiological evidence and application', *Journal of Sports Sciences*, 29: 389–402.

Garhammer, J. and Gregor, R. (1992) 'Propulsion forces as a function of intensity for weightlifting and vertical jumping', *Journal of Strength and Conditioning Research*, 6: 129–134.

Hakkinen, K., Pakarinen, A., Kraemer, W. J., Newton, R. U. and Alen, M. (2000) 'Basal concentrations and acute responses of serum hormones and strength development during heavy resistance training in middle-aged and elderly men and women', *Journal of Gerontology*, Series A, 55: B95–B105.

Hakkinen, K., Alen, M., Kraemer, W. J., Gorostiaga, E., Izquierdo, M., Rusko, H., Mikkola, J., Hakkinen, A., Valkeinen, H., Kaarakainen, E., Romu, S., Erola, V., Ahtianen, J. and Paavolainen, L. (2003) 'Neuormuscular adaptations during concurrent strength and endurance training versus strength training', *European Journal of Applied Physiology*, 89: 42–52.

Hamill, B. (1994). 'Relative safety of weightlifting and weight training', *Journal of Strength and Conditioning Research*, 8: 53–57.

Hansen, L., Bangsbo, J., Twisk, J. and Klausen, K. (1999) 'Development of muscle strength in relation to training level and testosterone in young male soccer players', *Journal of Applied Physiology*, 87: 1141–1147.

Higgs, C., Balyi, I., Way, R., Cardinal, C., Norris, S. and Bluechardt, M. (2008) *Developing Physical Literacy: A Guide for Parents and Children aged 0 to 12*, Vancouver: Canadian Sports Centre.

Hoff, J. and Almasbakk, B. (1995) 'The effects of maximal strength training on throwing velocity and muscle strength in female team-handball players', *Journal of Strength and Conditioning Research*, 9: 255–258.

Lavallee, M. E. and Balam, T. (2010). 'An overview of strength training injuries: Acute and chronic', *Current Sports Medicine Reports*, 9: 307–313.

Lloyd, R. S., Oliver, J. L., Moody, J., Meyers, R. W. and Stone, M. H. (2012) 'Long-term development of youth weightlifting', *Strength and Conditioning Journal*, 34: 55–66.

Malina, R. M. (2006) 'Weight training in youth – growth, maturation and safety: An evidenced based review', *Clinical Journal of Sports Medicine*, 16: 478–487.

Malina, R. M., Bouchard, C. and Bar-Or, O. (2004) *Growth, Maturation, and Physical Activity*, Champaign, IL: Human Kinetics.

Myer, G. D., Quatman, C. E., Khoury, J., Wall, E. J. and Hewett, T. E. (2009) 'Youth versus adult "weightlifting" injuries presenting to United States emergency rooms: Accidental versus nonaccidental injury mechanisms', *Journal of Strength and Conditioning Research*, 23: 2054–2060.

Pierce, K. C., Brewer, C., Ramsey, M. W., Byrd, R., Sands, W. A., Stone, M. E. and Stone, M. H. (2008) 'Youth resistance training', *Professional Strength and Conditioning Journal*, 10: 9–23.

Pierce, K., Byrd, R. and Stone, M. H. (1999) 'Youth weightlifting: Is it safe?' *Weightlifting USA*, 17: 5.

Plisk, S. and Stone. M. H. (2003) 'Periodization strategies', *Strength and Conditioning*, 25: 19–37.

Potts, N. (2009) 'An investigation into the influence of learning strategy on the acquisition of the clean', Doctoral dissertation, University of Edinburgh.

Rabinowickz, T. (1986) 'The differentiated maturation of the cerebral cortex', in F. Falkner and J. Tanner (eds) *Human Growth: A Comprehensive Treatise, Vol. 2, Postnatal Growth: Neurobiology*, New York: Plenum.

Ramos, E., Fronterea, W. R., Liopart, A. and Felicianao, D. (1998) 'Muscle strength and hormonal levels in adolescents: Gender related differences', *International Journal of Sport Medicine*, 19: 526–531.

Sands, W. A. (1994) 'Physical abilities profiles: 1993 National TOP's testing', *Technique*, 14: 15–20.

Stone, M. H. and Stone, M. E. (2011) 'Resistance training modes: A practical perspective', in M. Cardinale, R. Newton and K. Nosaka (eds) *Strength and Conditioning*, Oxford: Wiley-Blackwell.

Stone, M. H., Triplett-McBride, N. T. and Stone, M. E. (2001) 'Strength training for women: Intensity, volume and exercise factors: Impact on performance and health', in W. E. Garret and D. T. Kirkendall (eds) *Women in Sports and Exercise*, Rosemont, IL: American Academy of Orthopaedic Surgeons Publications.

Stone, M. H., Pierce, K. C., Sands, W. A. and Stone, M. E. (2006a) 'Weightlifting Part 1: A brief overview', *Strength and Conditioning Journal*, 28: 50–66.

Stone, M. H., Pierce, K. C., Sands, W. A. and Stone, M. E. (2006b) 'Weightlifting Part 2: Program Design', *Strength and Conditioning Journal*, 28: 10–17.

Stone, M. H., Fry, A. C., Ritchie, M., Stoessel-Ross, L. J. L. and Marsit, J. L. (1994) 'Injury potential and safety aspects of weightlifting movements', *Strength and Conditioning Journal*, 16: 15-24.

Stone, M. H., Sands, W. A., Pierce, K. C., Carlock, J., Cardinale, M. and Newton, R. U. (2005) 'Relationship of maximum strength to weightlifting performance', *Medicine and Science in Sports Exercise*, 37: 1037–1040.

Stratton, G. Jones, M., Fox, K.R., Tolfrey, K., Harris, J., Maffulli, N., Lee, M. and Frostick, S. P. (2004) 'BASES Position Statement on Guidelines for Resistance Exercise in Young People', *Journal of Sports Sciences*, 22: 383–390.

Szasz, T. (1994) 'Diagnoses are not diseases', *Skeptic*, 2: 86–89.

Thompson, W. (2011) 'World survey of fitness trends for 2012', *ACSM Health and Fitness Journal*, 15: 9–18.

Winter, E. M. and Brookes, B. C. (1994) 'Electromechanical response times and muscle elascticty in men and women', *European Journal of Applied Physiology*, 63: 124–128.

13

NUTRITIONAL STRATEGIES TO OPTIMIZE YOUTH DEVELOPMENT

David H. Fukuda, Kristina L. Kendall, Robert P. Hetrick and Jeffrey R. Stout

Introduction

An increased interest in youth sporting events has led to a proliferation of training and competition opportunities for children and adolescents. The benefits of physical activity throughout physiological development are well documented and may have long-term effects on overall health and quality of life (Malina, 2009). Adequate nutrition and the instilment of appropriate habits with regard to food selection and timing are of particular importance when building the foundation for a healthy lifestyle as well as a competitive athletic experience during childhood and adolescence (Meyer *et al.*, 2007). With childhood obesity becoming a growing problem worldwide, increased physical activity and participation in sports may provide a solution to this issue that may be reaching epidemic proportions (Malina, 2009; Pate *et al.*, 2006). Nutrition can be used to enhance performance and will be the specific emphasis of this chapter, but it is important to note that proper dietary habits may be associated with youth participation in sporting activities (Pate *et al.*, 2000). Specific areas of focus when considering the nutritional needs of young athletes are the maintenance of proper growth and development, the prevention and management of injuries as well as overreaching or overtraining, and the regulation of energy balance and availability. This chapter will examine nutritional strategies from the approach of three individual, but overlapping, sets of domains, including the Long-Term Nutritional Development (LTND) model, the Daily Nutrition model and a more applied approach using nutrient timing.

Basic theoretical concepts

Long-Term Nutritional Development (LTND) model

A consequence of growing participation in sports by children and adolescents has been greater focus on training and competition. In order to manage this emphasis on youth athletes and to temper an increasingly competitive environment, the Long-Term Athlete Development (LTAD) model has been proposed as a means of combining the cultivation of 'athletic potential' with the concerns of 'biological growth' (Balyi and Hamilton, 2004; Ford *et al.*, 2011). By identifying 'windows of opportunity', or sensitive periods of growth and development (Balyi and Hamilton, 2004), the LTAD model can provide an outline for specific nutritional considerations (Table 13.1). For the purpose of this chapter, we will term the nutritional approach to youth athlete development with the use of the LTAD framework, the LTND model. The LTND model should be considered, at minimum, a companion to the growing and well-deserved attention garnered by the LTAD model or, possibly, a necessary precursor that would allow for the participation of young athletes in their respective activities. The general domains or stages of the proposed LTND model would include: *Eat to develop, Learn to eat, Eat to grow, Eat to train* and *Eat to win*. Similar to previous convention and for the sake of convenience, chronological age will be used to describe these stages, but it is important to remember that these windows of opportunity are not simply demarcated by years and that both biological and training age must also be considered.

The first two stages of the LTND model coincide with general growth and development as well as a period of increasing physical literacy (Ford *et al.*, 2011). *Eat to develop* is associated with the time period of 6–9 years of age, while *Learn to eat* is associated with the age of 9–12 years old, both of which have been related to periods of peak brain maturation (Balyi and Hamilton, 2004; Borms, 1986; Ford *et al.*, 2011; Rabinowicz, 1986). With regard to the *Eat to develop* stage, it is important that all children, especially those with heightened activity levels, meet the necessary requirements for the macro- and micro-nutrients. Basic nutrition at home and school should be strictly emphasized to meet the demands of the various

TABLE 13.1 Comparison of the LTAD and LTND models

Developmental focus	Typical age span	Long-term athlete development model	Long-term nutritional development model
Physical literacy	Males: 6–9 years old Females: 6–8 years old	FUNdamentals	Eat to develop
	Males: 9–12 years old Females: 8–11 years old	Learning to train	Learn to eat
Physical and mental capacity	Males: 12–16 years old Females: 11–15 years old	Training to train	Eat to grow
	Males: 16–23 years old Females: 15–21 years old	Training to compete	Eat to train
High performance	Males: 19 years and older Females: 18 years and older	Training to win	Eat to win

development processes tied to this age span. The habit of consuming breakfast to start the day should be highlighted with the benefit of improved cognitive performance and a decreased likelihood for obesity (Hoyland *et al.*, 2009; Rampersaud *et al.*, 2005; Szajewska and Ruszczynski, 2010). The *Learn to eat* stage typically coincides with pre-pubescence, a period of development previously associated with the development of more complex movement skills and cognitive processes, including motor development (Ford *et al.*, 2011). This stage should include an element of nutritional education and ownership of dietary choices for children (Oliver *et al.*, 2011). Education should be comprised of proper food selection, primarily balance among different types of healthy foods, as well as the concepts of moderation, portion control and proper snacking, which will lead to improved decision-making in future sporting (and life) endeavours.

The lessons learned in the *Learn to eat* stage are crucial to support the numerous physiological changes associated with puberty and sexual maturation during the *Eat to grow* stage. The *Eat to grow* stage occurs between the ages of 12 and 16 years old and coincides with accelerated growth (peak height and weight velocity) as well as emotional and cognitive development (Ford *et al.*, 2011). The LTAD model characterizes this period as the *Training to train* stage (Balyi and Hamilton, 2004) and specific attention should be devoted to meeting or exceeding energy expenditure requirements through nutrient-dense caloric intake in order to support both the increased developmental processes and augmented physical training loads (Oliver *et al.*, 2011; Petrie *et al.*, 2004). An additional 500 kilocalories per day has been recommended during times of rapid growth in adolescents (Hoch *et al.*, 2008). This increase in energy intake should be addressed through the consumption of nutrient-rich food choices as opposed to 'empty calories', such as refined sugars or saturated fats. In particular, calcium for bone growth and iron to support hemoglobin production should be attained through the diet during this sensitive period of development (American Academy of Pediatrics, 2000). The LTAD model is characterized by a developmental adjustment with girls approaching this stage prior to boys, however, the daily nutrition and energy recommendations should be similar regardless of sex.

During the *Eat to train* stage, it is helpful to distinguish between energy balance and energy availability. The *Eat to train* stage encompasses the age span between 16 and 20 years old. Energy balance is the trade-off between energy expenditure and energy intake throughout the day, while energy availability is the difference between energy intake and the energy needed for physical activity in the form of exercise (Loucks *et al.*, 2011). Energy balance should be maintained during this transition period, which is associated with concomitant increases in the rate of muscular development due to changes in the hormonal milieu and physical training loads (Ford *et al.*, 2011; Janssen, 2007; Petrie *et al.*, 2004). Energy availability is of concern due to the benefits of nutrient timing on training and recovery in young athletes. Nutrient timing recommendations may need to be adjusted to support individual training needs and will be discussed in greater detail in this chapter.

The *Eat to win* stage, occurring between the ages of 18 and 22 years old, is the final stage of the LTND model and provides the foundation for a healthy and successful athletic career. Increased competitive opportunities and typically a higher level of commitment to training characterize this stage. Nutritional adaptations during the *Eat to win* stage might include changes in energy balance to either gain or lose weight while attempting to maintain energy availability to achieve quality training sessions (Loucks *et al.*, 2011; Petrie *et al.*, 2004). The habits developed with regard to nutrient timing during the *Eat to train* stage should continue to be practised. At this point in the chain of development, nutritional supplements to support dietary intake and enhance training stimuli may also be considered on an individual basis.

Daily nutrition model

Children and adolescents require adequate energy intake to allow for proper growth, development and maturation (Hoch *et al.*, 2008). Active youth will have needs in excess of this level due to greater energy expenditure from participating in sports. Physical training requires additional calories to assist with growth and support an increased basal metabolic rate (Hoch *et al.*, 2008; Petrie *et al.*, 2004). Among 9–13-year-old children, the energy requirements range from 1,415 kilocalories per day for the sedentary up to 3,000 kilocalories per day for the very active (Petrie *et al.*, 2004). This value increases to 3,800 kilocalories per day for adolescents, age 14–18 years old (Petrie *et al.*, 2004). In addition to basic energy requirements, the domains of the Daily Nutrition model include the macronutrients (carbohydrates, protein and fat) and micronutrients (vitamins and minerals).

Carbohydrates

It is thought that children lack fully developed glycolytic capacity, therefore, an increased reliance on fat, rather than carbohydrate, as an energy substrate to support performance is hypothesized (Boisseau and Delamarche, 2000). This difference may disappear during the adolescent period, as little or no difference has been seen in muscle glycolytic enzymes in adolescents 13–15 years old compared with adults (Haralambie, 1982). It is still unclear whether young athletes need as many carbohydrates as adults per body weight, but because of the importance of carbohydrates as substrates for high-intensity training, it is recommended that young athletes consume around 55–60 per cent of their total daily energy intake as carbohydrates (Montfort-Steiger and Williams, 2007). Grain-based foods, vegetables and fruit provide adequate amounts of carbohydrates to be used as fuel for exercise. In addition, fibre, minerals and vitamins may contribute to the muscle glycogen restoration processes needed for training and competition.

Protein

Children and adolescents have higher protein needs per kg of body weight than adults to support growth (Bar-Or, 2001). Protein is required for hormone and enzyme production, nutrient transfer in blood and repair of tissue in response to exercise. It is recommended that the adolescent athlete obtain at least 12–15 per cent of their dietary energy from protein for the maintenance and development of lean body mass (Petrie *et al.*, 2004). Young athletes who train at higher intensities may have greater protein needs and may benefit from consuming up to 1.7 g per kg of body weight per day (Meyer *et al.*, 2007). Suggested foods include lean cuts of meat, poultry and fish, as well as eggs, beans, nuts, low-fat milk, yogurt and cheese.

Fat

Children utilize more fat than carbohydrates compared with adults during and after exercise (Duncan and Howley, 1999); however, the transition from mid- to late puberty changes substrate metabolism and the reverse, similar to what is seen in adults, becomes more prevalent (Haralambie, 1982). Despite the indication that children rely more on fat as an energy source during exercise, ingestion of high-fat foods before exercise may reduce the magnitude of growth hormone secretion by up to 40 per cent, limiting muscle adaption and growth (Galassetti *et al.*, 2006). Although there is no adequate intake (AI) for total fat intake, it has been recommended that 25–30 per cent of total daily calories come from fat (Butte, 2000). Unsaturated fats should contribute the most, with saturated fats providing no more than 10 per cent of the total daily calories. The AI levels for boys aged 9–13 years are 12 g per day and 1.2 g per day for linoleic acid and alpha-linolenic acid (essential fatty acids: omega-6 and omega-3) respectively. For adolescent boys (14–18 years), the levels slightly increase to 16 g per day and 1.6 g per day. For young girls, AI levels are 10 g per day and 1.0 g per day for linoleic and alpha-linolenic acid respectively, while adolescent girls have AI levels of 11 g per day and 1.1 g per day (Petrie *et al.*, 2004). Restricting fat intake in children could impair growth and development and lead to insufficient intake of essential fatty acids and fat soluble vitamins. Sources of healthy fats include olive oil, flaxseed, peanut butter, nuts, avocados and milk.

Micronutrients

In children and adolescents, iron and calcium are two minerals frequently identified as being deficient, possibly affecting health and physical performance (Clarkson and Haymes, 1995). With up to 90 per cent of peak bone mass achieved by 18 years of age (Pettinato *et al.*, 2006), calcium intake during childhood and adolescence is critical in preventing or minimizing the risk of stress fractures and osteoporosis (Greer and Krebs, 2006). Milk provides the greatest amount of calcium in the diets of adolescents, aiding bone strength. Additionally, supplementing with vitamin D supports the absorption of calcium in the gastrointestinal tract and kidneys, promoting bone growth and remodelling. Children and adolescents require around 800–1,200 mg (9–10 years old) and 1,200–1,500 mg (11–18 years old) of calcium (Baker *et al.*, 1999) and a minimum of 600 IU of vitamin D each day (Ross *et al.*, 2011). In addition, food sources of calcium citrate might be an appropriate choice for young athletes prone to anemia because citrate aids iron absorption (Tenforde *et al.*, 2010). It is important to note that there is no differentiation between calcium recommendations for boys and girls, but girls are less likely to meet their daily needs, which is specifically detrimental due to heightened consequences when considering increased hormonal interactions during puberty (Albertson *et al.*, 1997). One of the often cited factors for limited calcium intake in female children and adolescents, along with lifestyle and lactose intolerance, is the negative perception of dairy products and their association with dietary fat (Albertson *et al.*, 1997). In opposition to this common belief, Chan *et al.* (1995) showed an increase in consumption of dairy products to meet the recommended dietary allowance for calcium over the course of a 12-month period did not increase total or saturated fat intake in pubertal girls.

Iron requirements also peak during adolescence due to rapid growth and the expansion of blood volume and muscle mass (Anttila *et al.*, 1997); however, inadequate iron intake and iron deficiency are commonly reported in athletes (Deakin, 2000). The onset of menstruation imposes additional iron needs for girls. Low iron intake could be a potential cause of poor performance, especially in females when the menstrual cycle has started. Inadequate iron intake may decrease physical and mental performance in youth, with chronic inadequate intake leading to low stores of iron that can impair muscle metabolism (Beard, 2001) and affect cognitive function (Grantham-McGregor and Ani, 2001). Dietary consumption of vitamins and minerals via food sources is preferable (Miller *et al.*, 2001) and consultation with a physician may be warranted prior to supplementation by other means.

Clinical/practical applications

Nutrient timing

If young athletes are training consistently and following a balanced nutrition plan, then they are probably ready to incorporate nutrient timing as part of their overall performance plan. Nutrient timing is one of the easiest things they can do to modify their nutrition programme and perhaps improve performance and recovery. Briefly, nutrient timing refers to eating the right nutrients, in the right amounts, at the right time before, during and after exercise, so as to optimize the young athlete's performance goals. The domains of nutrient timing include the time frame prior to commencing exercise, the duration of time committed to exercise and the recovery period following the exercise session (Ivy, 2008).

Metabolic profile of youth athletes during exercise

Children and adolescents tend to metabolize more fat than carbohydrate for energy compared to adults when exercising at the same relative intensity (Aucouturier *et al.*, 2008; Timmons *et al.*, 2007). Furthermore, young athletes have a limited anaerobic capacity compared to adults because of their reduced ability to generate energy through glycolysis (Kaczor *et al.*, 2005). Sports scientists speculate that this metabolic response during exercise in youth may serve as a method to conserve the limited glycogen stores demonstrated in young athletes (Lee *et al.*, 2011). However, Timmons and colleagues (2003) reported that young athletes are able to utilize blood glucose at a faster rate for energy during exercise than adults. Therefore, supplementing carbohydrate before and during exercise may be more beneficial for young athletes than in adults. In support, several studies have demonstrated that supplementing carbohydrate before and during prolonged exercise contributes significantly to energy demands and performance compared to placebo in young athletes (Phillips *et al.*, 2010; Riddell *et al.*, 2001). In fact, several studies have reported that consuming a 6 per cent carbohydrate-electrolyte (6% CHO-E) solution before and during intense intermittent exercise or competition improves performance and may help maintain hydration (Wilk *et al.*, 1998). This includes numerous studies that have reported positive benefits of CHO supplementation before and during exercise on performance in adolescent multiple-sprint sport athletes (Dougherty *et al.*, 2006; Lee *et al.*, 2011; Phillips *et al.*, 2010, 2012a, 2012b).

Post-exercise recovery

Recovery nutrition has been studied extensively in young adults (Saunders, 2011). Data suggests that the consumption of a fluid containing carbohydrate and protein, like chocolate milk, has been shown to accelerate glycogen replenishment, stimulate protein synthesis, attenuate protein catabolism and rehydrate post-intense training (Saunders, 2011). Unfortunately, no study has examined the effects of post-exercise nutrition on recovery in children or adolescent athletes. Without direct scientific observation in this population, recommendations from data on young adults suggesting the importance of post-exercise nutrition should be considered.

The three key elements of a post-workout drink

1   Drink fluids that contain electrolytes:
    Fluid and electrolyte replenishment are perhaps the most important part of recovery. Also, maintaining a well-hydrated state helps to accelerate recovery (Roy, 2008).
2   Restore muscle fuel stores by consuming carbohydrates and protein:
    Recent evidence has shown that, during the post-exercise period, adding protein to the carbohydrate mix is even better than carbohydrates alone for

glycogen repletion, especially during normal training and competition (Ivy *et al.*, 2008; Saunders, 2011).

3 Consume carbohydrates and protein to enhance muscle recovery:
Immediately following intense exercise it is recommended to consume a carbohydrate and protein snack, such as chocolate milk or a peanut butter and jam sandwich, to initiate skeletal muscle recovery (Witard and Tipton, 2012). However, skeletal muscle can remain sensitive to the anabolic effects of protein several hours post exercise (Witard and Tipton, 2012). Therefore, to maximize muscle recovery, the young athlete should consume adequate carbohydrate and protein post exercise and at every meal over the course of a 12–24-hour period. Proper post-exercise nutrition may accelerate the recovery process in young athletes thus enabling them to be ready for successive practices, matches or competitions.

According to data reported on young adults, approximately 1.0 g of high glycemic carbohydrate per kg of body weight should be consumed within 15–30 minutes after high-intensity and/or prolonged exercise (Saunders, 2011). Furthermore, glycogen stores have been shown to replenish with greater efficiency when protein is added to the mix (Ivy *et al.*, 2008). Protein should be a part of the post-exercise meal in a 3:1 ratio of carbohydrates to protein, similar to what is found in chocolate milk. The use of chocolate milk improves upon the 1.5:1 ratio of carbohydrates to protein found in standard white milk. As is the case with typical carbohydrate-based sports drinks, chocolate milk consumption should be reserved for periods following heightened physical activity.

As mentioned previously, post-workout recommendations outlined here are based on findings in young adults (Saunders, 2011). Initial recovery after an intense workout should happen over a two-hour period with a fluid-based nutritional snack. The young athlete should consume a recovery drink immediately after training, and then again two hours later. Table 13.2 describes how much total carbohydrate and protein the young athlete is recommended to consume over the

TABLE 13.2 Suggested post-workout (within two hours) carbohydrate to protein ratios by body weight

Body weight (kg)	Carbohydrates (g)	Protein (g)	Estimated volume of chocolate milk (litres)
40	40	13	0.5
50	50	17	0.6
60	60	20	0.7
70	70	23	0.8
80	80	26	0.9
90	90	30	1.0

two-hour period. For example, a 50 kg athlete should consume 25 g of carbohydrates and 8.5 g of protein (~0.3 litres of chocolate milk) after training, and then again two hours later.

Ingestion of a 6% CHO-E solution immediately before and throughout intense training sessions has been shown to enhance intermittent, high-intensity endurance capacity and maintain hydration in adolescent athletes (Wilk and Bar-Or, 1996). Many 6% CHO-E solutions are commercially available and should be incorporated into young athletes' training programmes and competitions. While no data exists on the benefits of post-exercise nutrition in children and adolescent athletes, sufficient data does exist in young adults (18–22 years) to recommend it as an important strategy. Therefore, the authors recommend that young athletes engaging in intense, high-volume training regimens should consume a post-exercise solution that contains carbohydrate and protein as suggested previously.

From a nutritional, decision-making standpoint, the use of food diaries provides a conventional method of tracking daily energy consumption and nutrient composition for young athletes. During the early stages of the aforementioned LTND model (*Eat to develop, Learn to eat* and, possibly, *Eat to grow*), parents may choose to utilize food diaries to aid in an effort to make informed dietary choices for their children. The food diary can be used to determine energy balance and availability as well as the ability of the current diet regimen in meeting the recommendations noted in the Daily Nutrition model. A number of popular commercial software programmes are available for mobile phones that make the maintenance of food diaries relatively uncomplicated. As children reach the *Eat to train* stage, or whenever they are ready to handle the additional demands, the responsibility of managing a food diary can be shifted to them as part of an increased ownership of both general health and training goals.

Summary

The proper nutritional approach with regard to nutrition in youth athletes has been reviewed on an activity-specific level via nutrient timing, on a daily basis via nutrient recommendations and throughout the developmental stages of childhood and adolescence. The domains set forth within each of these approaches should be considered in order to optimize athletic potential and biological maturation. Nutritional education and ownership of dietary choices are key to adequate nutrition, and are fundamental when building the foundation for a healthy experience in youth sporting activities. Table 13.3 provides a review of the nutritional approaches, domains and key points covered throughout this chapter.

TABLE 13.3 Review of nutritional approaches, domains and key points

Approach	Domains	Key points
Long-term nutritional development model	Eat to develop 6–9 years	• All children, especially those with heightened activity levels, should meet the necessary requirements for the macro- and micro-nutrients. • Consume breakfast to improve cognitive performance and a decreased likelihood for obesity.
	Learn to eat 9–12 years	• Education should be comprised of proper food selection, primarily balanced among different types of healthy foods, as well as the concepts of moderation, portion control and proper snacking. • Reinforcement of good nutritional habits.
	Eat to grow 12–16 years	• Specific attention should be devoted to meeting or exceeding energy expenditure requirements through nutrient-dense caloric intake. • Focus on calcium consumption from nutrient-dense foods for bone growth and iron to support hemoglobin production.
	Eat to train 16–20 years	• Energy balance should be maintained. • Nutrient timing adjusted to support individual training needs.
	Eat to win 18–22 years	• Changes in energy balance to either gain or lose weight while attempting to maintain energy availability. • Nutritional supplements to support dietary intake and enhance training stimuli.
Daily nutrition	Carbohydrate	• Substrates for high-intensity training. • 55–60% of their total daily energy intake as carbohydrates. • Grain-based foods, vegetables and fruit.
	Protein	• Hormone and enzyme production, nutrient transfer in blood and repair of tissue in response to exercise. • 12–15% of their dietary energy from protein for the maintenance and development of lean body mass. • Lean cuts of meat, poultry and fish, as well as eggs, beans, nuts and dairy products.

Approach	Domains	Key points
Daily nutrition	Fat	• Children utilize more fat than carbohydrates compared to adults during and after exercise. • Puberty changes substrate metabolism towards CHO. • 25–30% of total daily calories come from fat (specific attention to essential fatty acids). • Healthy fats include olive oil, flaxseed, peanut butter, nuts, avocados and milk.
	Vitamins and minerals	• 90% of peak bone mass is achieved by age 18. • 800–1,200 mg (9–10y), 1,200–1,500 mg (11–18y) of calcium and 600IU of vitamin D. • Inadequate iron intake and iron deficiency are commonly reported in athletes.
Nutrient timing	Pre/during exercise	• Young athletes are able to utilize blood glucose at a faster rate for energy during exercise than adults. • Consuming a 6% CHO-E solution right before and during intense intermittent exercise or competition improves performance and may help maintain hydration.
	Post-exercise	• Drink fluids that contain electrolytes. • Consume carbohydrates and protein to restore muscle fuel stores and enhance muscle recovery.

Key points

Child and youth athletes have unique requirements with regard to nutrition. A number of different approaches and associated strategies have been outlined throughout this chapter. In summary:

- From a developmental perspective, young athletes progress through stages according to physiological and biological growth. These domains include *Eat to develop*, *Learn to eat*, *Eat to grow*, *Eat to train* and *Eat to win*.
- Day-to-day nutrition for youth athletes requires particular focus on energy balance and the intake of the energy-yielding macro-nutrients and key micro-nutrients, including iron and calcium.
- Training and competition in child and adolescent athletes can be enhanced through the proper timing and composition of nutrients.

References

Albertson, A. M., Tobelmann, R. C. and Marquart, L. (1997) 'Estimated dietary calcium intake and food sources for adolescent females: 1980–92', *Journal of Adolescent Health*, 20: 20–26.

American Academy of Pediatrics (2000) 'Intensive training and sports specialization in young athletes', *Pediatrics*, 106: 154–157.

Anttila, R., Cook, J. D. and Siimes, M. A. (1997) 'Body iron stores in relation to growth and pubertal maturation in healthy boys', *British Journal of Haematology*, 96: 12–18.

Aucouturier, J., Baker, J. S. and Duche, P. (2008) 'Fat and carbohydrate metabolism during sub-maximal exercise in children', *Sports Medicine*, 38: 213–238.

Baker, S. S., Cochran, W. J., Flores, C. A., Georgieff, M. K., Jacobson, M. S., Jaksic, T. and Krebs, N. F. (1999) 'American Academy of Pediatrics. Committee on Nutrition. Calcium requirements of infants, children, and adolescents', *Pediatrics*, 104: 1152–1157.

Balyi, I. and Hamilton, A. (2004) *Long-Term Athlete Development: Trainability in Childhood and Adolescence. Windows of Opportunity, Optimal Trainability*, Victoria: National Coaching Institute British Columbia and Advanced Training and Performance Ltd.

Bar-Or, O. (2001) 'Nutritional considerations for the child athlete', *Canadian Journal of Applied Physiology*, 26 Suppl: S186–S191.

Beard, J. L. (2001) 'Iron biology in immune function, muscle metabolism and neuronal functioning', *Journal of Nutrition*, 131: 568S–580S.

Boisseau, N. and Delamarche, P. (2000) 'Metabolic and hormonal responses to exercise in children and adolescents', *Sports Medicine*, 30: 405–422.

Borms, J. (1986) 'The child and exercise: An overview', *Journal of Sports Sciences*, 4: 3–20.

Butte, N. F. (2000) 'Fat intake of children in relation to energy requirements', *The American Journal of Clinical Nutrition*, 72: 1246S–1252S.

Chan, G. M., Hoffman, K. and McMurry, M. (1995) 'Effects of dairy products on bone and body composition in pubertal girls', *The Journal of Pediatrics*, 126: 551–556.

Clarkson, P. M. and Haymes, E. M. (1995) 'Exercise and mineral status of athletes: Calcium, magnesium, phosphorus, and iron', *Medicine and Science in Sports and Exercise*, 27: 831–843.

Deakin, V. (2000) 'Iron depletion in athletes', in L. Burke and V. Deakin (eds) *Clinical Sports Nutrition* (2nd edition), Boston, MA: McGraw-Hill.

Dougherty, K. A., Baker, L. B., Chow, M. and Kenney, W. L. (2006) 'Two percent dehydration impairs and six percent carbohydrate drink improves boys basketball skills', *Medicine and Science in Sports and Exercise*, 38: 1650–1658.

Duncan, G. E. and Howley, E. T. (1999) 'Substrate metabolism during exercise in children and the "crossover concept"', *Pediatric Exercise Science*, 11: 12–21.

Ford, P., De Ste Croix, M., Lloyd, R., Meyers, R., Moosavi, M., Oliver, J., Till, K. and Williams, C. (2011) 'The long-term athlete development model: Physiological evidence and application', *Journal of Sports Sciences*, 29: 389–402.

Galassetti, P., Larson, J., Iwanaga, K., Salsberg, S. L., Eliakim, A. and Pontello, A. (2006) 'Effect of a high-fat meal on the growth hormone response to exercise in children', *Journal of Pediatric Endocrinology and Metabolism*, 19: 777–786.

Grantham-McGregor, S. and Ani, C. (2001) 'A review of studies on the effect of iron deficiency on cognitive development in children', *Journal of Nutrition*, 131: 649S–668S.

Greer, F. R. and Krebs, N. F. (2006) 'Optimizing bone health and calcium intakes of infants, children, and adolescents', *Pediatrics*, 117: 578–585.

Haralambie, G. (1982) 'Enzyme activities in skeletal muscle of 13–15 years old adolescents', *Bulletin Europeen de Physiopathologie Respiratoire*, 18: 65–74.

Hoch, A. Z., Goossen, K. and Kretschmer, T. (2008) 'Nutritional requirements of the child and teenage athlete', *Physical Medicine and Rehabilitation Clinics of North America*, 19: 373–398.

Hoyland, A., Dye, L. and Lawton, C. L. (2009) 'A systematic review of the effect of breakfast on the cognitive performance of children and adolescents', *Nutrition Research Reviews*, 22: 220–243.

Ivy, J. L. (2008) 'Nutrition before, during, and after exercise for the endurance athlete', in J. Antonio, D. Kalman, J. R. Stout, M. Greenwood, D. S. Willoughby and G.G. Haff (eds) *Essentials of Sports Nutrition and Supplements*, Totowa, NJ: Humana Press.

Ivy, J. L., Ding, Z., Hwang, H., Cialdella-Kam, L. C. and Morrison, P. J. (2008) 'Post exercise carbohydrate-protein supplementation: Phosphorylation of muscle proteins involved in glycogen synthesis and protein translation', *Amino Acids*, 35: 89–97.

Janssen, I. (2007) 'Physical activity guidelines for children and youth', *Canadian Journal of Public Health*, 98 Suppl 2: S109–S121.

Kaczor, J. J., Ziolkowski, W., Popinigis, J. and Tarnopolsky, M. A. (2005) 'Anaerobic and aerobic enzyme activities in human skeletal muscle from children and adults', *Pediatric Research*, 57: 331–335.

Lee, J. D., Sterrett, L. E., Guth, L. M., Konopka, A. R. and Mahon, A. D. (2011) 'The effect of pre-exercise carbohydrate supplementation on anaerobic exercise performance in adolescent males', *Pediatric Exercise Science*, 23: 344–354.

Loucks, A. B., Kiens, B. and Wright, H. H. (2011) 'Energy availability in athletes', *Journal of Sports Sciences*, 29: S7–S15.

Malina, R. M. (2009) 'Children and adolescents in the sport culture: The overwhelming majority to the select few', *Journal of Exercise Science and Fitness*, 7: S1–S10.

Meyer, F., O'Connor, H. and Shirreffs, S. M. (2007) 'Nutrition for the young athlete', *Journal of Sports Sciences*, 25 Suppl 1: S73–S82.

Miller, G. D., Jarvis, J. K. and McBean, L. D. (2001) 'The importance of meeting calcium needs with foods', *Journal of the American College of Nutrition*, 20: 168S–185S.

Montfort-Steiger, V. and Williams, C. A. (2007) 'Carbohydrate intake considerations for young athletes', *Journal of Sports Science and Medicine*, 6: 343–352.

Oliver, J. L., Lloyd, R. S. and Meyers, R. W. (2011) 'Training elite child athletes: Promoting welfare and well-being', *Strength and Conditioning Journal*, 33: 73–79.

Pate, R. R., Trost, S. G., Levin, S. and Dowda, M. (2000) 'Sports participation and health-related behaviors among US youth', *Archives of Pediatrics and Adolescent Medicine*, 154: 904–911.

Pate, R. R., Davis, M. G., Robinson, T. N., Stone, E. J., McKenzie, T. L. and Young, J. C. (2006) 'Promoting physical activity in children and youth: A leadership role for schools. A scientific statement from the American Heart Association Council on Nutrition, Physical Activity, and Metabolism (Physical Activity Committee) in collaboration with the Councils on Cardiovascular Disease in the Young and Cardiovascular Nursing', *Circulation*, 114: 1214–1224.

Petrie, H. J., Stover, E. A. and Horswill, C. A. (2004) 'Nutritional concerns for the child and adolescent competitor', *Nutrition*, 20: 620–631.

Pettinato, A. A., Loud, K. J., Bristol, S. K., Feldman, H. A. and Gordon, C. M. (2006) 'Effects of nutrition, puberty, and gender on bone ultrasound measurements in adolescents and young adults', *Journal of Adolescent Health*, 39: 828–834.

Phillips, S. M., Turner, A. P., Gray, S., Sanderson, M. F. and Sproule, J. (2010) 'Ingesting a 6% carbohydrate-electrolyte solution improves endurance capacity, but not sprint performance, during intermittent, high-intensity shuttle running in adolescent team games players aged 12–14 years', *European Journal of Applied Physiology*, 109: 811–821.

Phillips, S. M., Turner, A. P., Sanderson, M. F. and Sproule, J. (2012a) 'Beverage carbohydrate concentration influences the intermittent endurance capacity of adolescent team games players during prolonged intermittent running', *European Journal of Applied Physiology*, 112: 1107–1116.

Phillips, S. M., Turner, A. P., Sanderson, M. F. and Sproule, J. (2012b) 'Carbohydrate gel ingestion significantly improves the intermittent endurance capacity, but not sprint performance, of adolescent team games players during a simulated team games protocol', *European Journal of Applied Physiology*, 112: 1133–1141.

Rabinowicz, T. (1986) 'The differentiated maturation of the cerebral cortex', in F. Falkner, and J. Tanner (eds) *Human Growth: A Comprehensive Treatise, Vol. 2, Postnatal Growth: Neurobiology*, New York: Plenum.

Rampersaud, G. C., Pereira, M. A., Girard, B. L., Adams, J. and Metzl, J. D. (2005) 'Breakfast habits, nutritional status, body weight, and academic performance in children and adolescents', *Journal of the American Dietetic Association*, 105: 743–760.

Riddell, M. C., Bar-Or, O., Wilk, B., Parolin, M. L. and Heigenhauser, G. J. (2001) 'Substrate utilization during exercise with glucose and glucose plus fructose ingestion in boys ages 10–14 yr', *Journal of Applied Physiology*, 90: 903–911.

Ross, A. C., Manson, J. E., Abrams, S. A., Aloia, J. F., Brannon, P. M., Clinton, S. K., Durazo-Arvizu, R. A., Gallagher, J. C., Gallo, R. L., Jones, G., Kovacs, C. S., Mayne, S. T., Rosen, C. J. and Shapses, S. A. (2011) 'The 2011 report on dietary reference intakes for calcium and vitamin D from the Institute of Medicine: What clinicians need to know', *J Clin Endocrinol Metab*, 96: 53–58.

Roy, B. D. (2008) 'Milk: The new sports drink? A Review', *Journal of the International Society of Sports Nutrition*, 5: 15.

Saunders, M. J. (2011) 'Carbohydrate-protein intake and recovery from endurance exercise: Is chocolate milk the answer?' *Current Sports Medicine Reports*, 10: 203–210.

Szajewska, H. and Ruszczynski, M. (2010) 'Systematic review demonstrating that breakfast consumption influences body weight outcomes in children and adolescents in Europe', *Critical Reviews in Food Science and Nutrition*, 50: 113–119.

Tenforde, A. S., Sayres, L. C., Sainani, K. L. and Fredericson, M. (2010) 'Evaluating the relationship of calcium and vitamin D in the prevention of stress fracture injuries in the young athlete: A review of the literature', *PM & R*, 2: 945–949.

Timmons, B. W., Bar-Or, O. and Riddell, M. C. (2003) 'Oxidation rate of exogenous carbohydrate during exercise is higher in boys than in men', *Journal of Applied Physiology*, 94: 278–284.

Timmons, B. W., Bar-Or, O. and Riddell, M. C. (2007) 'Influence of age and pubertal status on substrate utilization during exercise with and without carbohydrate intake in healthy boys', *Applied Physiology, Nutrition and Metabolism*, 32: 416–425.

Wilk, B. and Bar-Or, O. (1996) 'Effect of drink flavor and NaCL on voluntary drinking and hydration in boys exercising in the heat', *Journal of Applied Physiology*, 80: 1112–1117.

Wilk, B., Kriemler, S., Keller, H. and Bar-Or, O. (1998) 'Consistency in preventing voluntary dehydration in boys who drink a flavored carbohydrate-NaCl beverage during exercise in the heat', *International Journal of Sport Nutrition*, 8: 1–9.

Witard, O. C. and Tipton, K. D. (2012) 'Postexercise nutrient timing with resistive activities', in C. M. Kerksick (ed.) *Nutrient Timing: Metabolic Optimization for Health, Performance, and Recovery*, Boca Raton, FL: CRC Press.

14

OVERUSE INJURIES AND INJURY PREVENTION STRATEGIES FOR YOUTHS

Patria Hume and Keith Russell

Introduction

This chapter focuses on overuse injuries specific to young athletes that are due to training and the effects of growth and maturation. We outline the incidence, nature, possible mechanisms, risk factors and injury prevention strategies for overuse injuries in young athletes. Common injuries likely to be encountered by strength and conditioning practitioners are highlighted.

The overuse injury problem

Youths are at increased risk of overuse injury due to the biomechanics of their immature musculoskeletal structures. Overuse injuries are common when a skeletally immature athlete is exposed to high training loads (Hutchinson and Nasser, 2000) especially during periods of rapid growth. Growth plates are unique to young athletes and include both epiphyseal growth plates near the ends of long bones (which are mainly subjected to compression forces) and apophyseal growth plates between tendon attachments and bone shafts (which are mainly subjected to traction forces). Common epiphyseal growth plate injuries occur at the distal radial physis (wrist) and distal femoral physis (just above the knee), whereas Osgood-Schlatter's disease (tibial apophysitis) and Sever's disease (calcaneal apophysitis) are common apophyseal growth-plate injuries. Scoliosis (lateral curvature of the spine) is another condition thought to be exacerbated by overuse.

Overuse injuries are complex, given the multifactorial risk factors, and consequently the strength and conditioning practitioner should be aware of multiple injury prevention strategies. In a review of rib stress fractures in rowing (McDonnell *et al.*, 2011), joint hypomobility, vertebral malalignment, low bone mineral density or poor technique, in combination with increases in training volume, were associated with rib stress fractures. Training volume alone, however, can have less effect on injury than other factors. Large differences in seat and oar handle velocities, sequential movement patterns, gearing, higher elbow-flexion to knee-extension strength ratios, higher seat-to-handle velocity during the initial drive or higher shoulder angle excursion may result in rib stress fractures. Increased risk may also be due to low calcium, low vitamin D or eating disorders. Some evidence shows injury prevention strategies in young rowers should focus on strengthening the serratus anterior, strengthening leg extensors, stretching the lumbar spine and increasing hip joint flexibility both in extension and flexion, reducing excessive protraction, training with ergometers on slides, and calcium and vitamin D supplementation.

Training of young athletes has undergone dramatic changes in recent years with decreases in the age of initiating training and increases in training time, training loads and skill level. Because of increases in training time, and specialization, there are more repetitions of fewer movement patterns. However, the authors believe that young athletes can safely train at and even beyond the relative training stimuli possible in adult athletes. Strength training is effective in pre-puberty and moderate hypertrophy is possible (e.g. gymnasts). All tissue (muscle, ligament, tendon, bone) quickly adapts to training or detraining. Excessive training perturbs the body's homeostasis in musculoskeletal, metabolic, endocrine, immune and psychological domains, however, it appears that individual tolerance of high exercise volume and susceptibility to overtraining is highly individualistic (Hume and Stewart, 2012). Training is a balance issue, in that the training load must be enough to result in skill proficiency and consistency, but not so much that the athlete becomes overly fatigued or injured. There must be careful selection of strength training practices to prevent injury. For example, high repetitions of impact loading need to be monitored to eliminate overuse injuries. While exercises such as trunk extension and straight legs lifting/hip flexion can be useful to develop strength, they need to be carefully administered and monitored in youths to ensure safe training and sports participation. A more critical appraisal of exercises is required from a biomechanical perspective, including an analysis of strains sustained by internal structures, to reduce the risk of injury.

Basic theoretical concepts

Growth and development and overuse injury risk

There is highly variable tempo and timing of growth of different body systems. The nervous system is almost completely developed in pre-puberty whereas the reproductive system has not even begun to develop at that stage. Variability even exists within specific body systems, for example in the skeletal system where bones of the lower limbs do not grow at the same rate (Figure 14.1). The proximal femoral growth plate and distal tibial growth plate account for only one-third of total leg growth. Two growth plates bracketing the knee (distal femur and proximal

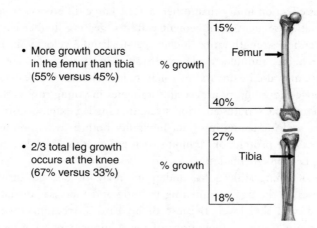

FIGURE 14.1 Different growth rates occur for the leg bones

Image courtesy of Dr. Don Bailey, Saskatchewan Growth Study.

tibia) account for two-thirds of total leg growth. Muscle strength increases during growth, but it may not increase in proportion to limb inertial properties (Hawkins and Metheny, 2001). Understanding such variability in growth can be important for predicting and preventing overuse injuries to circum-pubertal athletes.

By understanding the growing child, the strength and conditioning practitioner will be able to appreciate individual needs, provide a training programme that results in fewer injuries, provide a more interesting and enjoyable training programme, and help lead young athletes to a higher level of performance.

Growth and development considerations

During puberty marked physical changes in height, weight and strength occur. Bone grows first, which stretches muscle, which then grows in response to being stretched. These changes can be very rapid and can result in short periods of decreased coordination. Whole-body movement predominates over the fine control of feet, hands and the head. Fine control required for good technique is slow to develop, so do not expect too much too soon. Cater for individual abilities as youths mature at different rates and therefore have differences in their ability to perform various movement tasks. Youths younger than seven years generally have poor 'movement memory' and take time to learn movement sequences.

Excessive physical loading may cause skeletal injury so plan well so overuse injuries do not occur. Provide a balance between activity and rest and split longer training times into two shorter ones. Check minor pain carefully, especially near growth plates. Early overuse injury warning signs may indicate a too intensive programme for an individual, inadequate physical preparation, overly-hard equipment surfaces or a growth problem.

Incidence, mechanisms and signs and symptoms of overuse injuries in young athletes

Incidence rates of overtraining injuries in young athletes are not well understood given there have been no comprehensive studies reporting the epidemiology of overuse injury in youths. There have been no injury prevention intervention studies for overuse injuries in youths. Where overuse injuries have been reported, occurrence rates have represented injuries spanning varying lengths of time, making comparison between studies difficult.

The mechanism of injury is the physical action or cause of injury. Examples include the strong force of muscle actions acting on bone via the tendon, compression at a joint and accumulation of damage, and repeated impact forces on bone or cartilage resulting in damage. Exercise-induced muscle fatigue can also cause alterations in movement patterns and distribution of stress resulting in excess force transmitted to focal sites along the bone. Most people think of overuse injury being when tissues are injured due to repetitive sub-maximal loading (DiFiori, 2010). As we discuss common overuse injuries in young athletes we will outline the mechanisms of injuries and how strength and conditioning coaches can recognize the signs and symptoms for the injuries. Coaches need to be able to recognize the signs and symptoms for common overuse injuries to young athletes, such as stress fractures, growth-plate injuries and tendon injuries.

Stress fractures

Accumulation of repetitive forces and microdamage over time can overwhelm the body's reparative processes which can lead to the development of stress fractures. These injuries mostly occur in the lower leg and feet of athletes and are usually associated with localized pain, tenderness and swelling. Pain will typically persist as a dull ache even without activity and in some cases throughout the night. Early diagnosis of stress fractures is critical, as delayed diagnosis may result in prolonged rehabilitation and significant time away from sport.

Stress fractures occur from an imbalance between the rate of bone resorption (where osteoclasts break down old bone) and bone formation (ossification) in the process of bone remodelling. Mechanical stress (load per unit area) leads to bone strain (deformation), and repetitive bouts of mechanical loading can lead to bone microdamage. Bone typically responds by adapting its structure and getting stronger according to Wolff's law. Appropriate bone stress is important to instigate the osteogenic response. However, if the strain rate, or magnitude or frequency of mechanical loading, exceeds the ability of the bone to adapt, an accumulation of microdamage occurs, leading to a stress fracture. Given that bone has the ability to alter its size, shape and structure to meet the mechanical demands placed on it, exercises that stress growing bones should not necessarily be avoided in the strength and conditioning room but should be carried out carefully. Improper programming and excessive loading can contribute to overuse injury. Risk of stress fracture has also been attributed to low calcium and vitamin D intake as well as eating disorders, therefore strength and conditioning coaches need to be cognisant of the effects of poor nutrition on risk of injury. Strain rate, magnitude of force and the number of loading cycles may contribute to microdamage formation and result in the development of stress fractures. Stress fractures are typically traced to changes in training volume (duration or distance) and intensity.

Stress fractures of pars interarticularis (spondololysis and spondylolisthesis)

Spondololysis is a small hairline fracture in one of the vertebra of the lower back. Such fractures are believed to occur as a result of repetitive episodes of truck hyper-extension, especially if combined with rotation. If undetected, or not cared for, the hairline fracture can worsen to become a displaced fracture where the posterior part of the vertebra separates from the anterior part and compromises the spinal cord. Spondylolisthesis refers to the forward (anterior) shift of a fractured vertebra on another (usually L5 on S1). Athletes will usually complain of low back pain which is aggravated by trunk extension, with or without leg pain. This condition most commonly results from untreated or poorly managed stress fractures and a lack of preparatory conditioning. Although these fractures can occur suddenly, the onset is usually gradual. Spondylolisthesis has the potential to be career threatening, and must be considered seriously.

General growth-plate injuries

Epiphyseal growth plates (physes) are areas of developing tissue near the ends of long bones, between the shaft of the bone and the end of the bone in youths. Long bones do not grow from the middle out; instead they grow from each end around the area of the growth plate. Growth plates are the last portion of the bone to harden (ossify) which makes them vulnerable to fracture, especially when youths are exposed to inappropriate training loads. Epiphysitis refers to inflammation of growth plates, a condition that can result in permanent damage. However, if man-aged correctly, it will resolve when the bone ossifies.

Growth-plate injuries occur in youths as the growth plate tends to be the weakest link in their growing skeleton. Circum-pubertal youths are especially vul-nerable, as this is the age of rapid growth. During a growth spurt the bones grow at different rates to the muscles, possibly causing increased musculotendon tight-ness. Range of motion losses can result in an athlete having difficulty performing skills that previously did not pose a problem. It is important to increase flexibility training during these periods to reduce the tractioning caused by tight muscles, otherwise the risk of injury is increased.

Apophyseal growth plates occur between tendon attachments and bone shafts and are usually injured (apohysitis) by repetitive or excessive traction forces, and are also vulnerable to being avulsed (pulled away). Avulsion factures can have long-term complications, so immediate medical attention is required. Youths' bones heal rapidly so it is imperative that immediate treatment is sought before the bone begins to heal in an abnormal position, resulting in limbs that are misaligned or unequal in length.

Small aches and pains, such as a 'sore wrist' over time may be the signs of a potential growth-plate injury and should be monitored carefully. Any child experiencing persistent pain that affects athletic performance, or is painful with pressure, should be referred to a medical professional. Although some aches and pains can be expected from youths participating in athletic activity, a child's complaint always deserves careful attention. A child should never be allowed nor expected to 'work through the pain'. Since growth plates are mostly near joints, or deep to the large bony bumps of muscle attachments, attention should be focused there.

Specific growth-plate injuries

Osgood Schlatter's disease (tibial apophysitis) is a growth disorder that occurs at the apophyseal growth plate immediately below the knee, and is common in young athletes between 10 and 15 years old – synonymous with the timing of the adolescent growth spurt. Through overuse the traction-induced strain at the quadriceps tendon and tibial tuberosity junction results in inflammation and pain. With repeated trauma, new bone grows back during healing, which may cause a bony lump at the tibial tuberosity. Tenderness and pain is typically worse during and after exercise. Pain often occurs when contracting the quadriceps against resistance or when contracting the muscles with the leg straight. Osgood Schlatter's disease is seen more often in youths involved with running and jumping activities, which result in larger stresses on the quadriceps tendon. Given sufficient recovery time, the condition will settle and management usually consists of activity modification until the athlete becomes pain-free. Age-appropriate strength and conditioning provision is essential to reduce the risk of growth plate injuries.

Sever's disease (calcaneal apophysitis) is a growth disorder of pain and tenderness where the Achilles tendon joins the heel bone (calcaneous). During rapid growth the bones become longer more quickly than the soft tissues, which places stress on the relatively shorter muscles and tendons. The pain from Sever's, like other apophysitis sites, decreases as the growth plates fuse. It can, however, persist for several years and become very painful if the causes are not ameliorated quickly. Some contributing factors can be overtraining, poor footwear, malalignment, joint stiffness and so on. Early detection and good management should allow athletes to continue training at a reduced or modified level.

Non-growth-plate injuries

Osteochondritis dissecans is a defect in the growth and maturation of bone and adjoining articular cartilage in a joint, and can occur in the elbow and wrist. It is not well understood, but it is believed that it is induced by repetitive shear and compressive forces. Unless treated early, it can be a career-ending injury.

Tendon injuries

Epicondylar (elbow) overuse injuries in sports with overhead or repetitive arm actions are frequent and often severe (Hume *et al.*, 2006). Epicondylosis develops over time from repetitive forces and results in structural changes in the tendon. Epicondylalgia refers to elbow pain at either the medial or lateral epicondyle of the elbow, related to tendinopathy of the common flexor or extensor tendon origins at these points. Pain is usually associated with gripping, resisted wrist extension and certain movements such as in tennis and golf, hence the common terms 'tennis elbow' (lateral epicondylosis) and 'golfer's elbow' (medial epicondylosis). 'Golfer's elbow' is a flexor pronator epiconylopathy (medial epicondyle) pronation and wrist flexion resulting in medial pain. 'Tennis elbow' results from wrist extension and external rotation/supination action resulting in pain over the lateral epicondyle. 'Handball goalie's elbow' has been defined as pain due to repetitive forced hyper-extension of the elbow.

Achilles tendons are the largest and strongest tendons in the human body and play a key role in running and jumping movements. Mechanically, Achilles tendons are optimized to withstand high tensile forces. However, Achilles tendons are lead causes of lower leg pain and loss of function in athletes using repetitive stretch–shorten cycle activity. Muscle imbalance within the triceps surae complex or weakness of stabilizing muscles such as the tibialis posterior overload the medial gastrocnemius to compensate for the imbalance, causing significant shearing forces within the Achilles tendon. Targeted strength training to reduce weaknesses could therefore be a viable means of reducing Achilles tendon injury in athletes. Limited ankle dorsiflexion range of motion, ankle joint pronation and torsion have been implicated in the onset of Achilles tendon injury. Flexibility training may reduce the tensile load through the tendon, preventing overloading. There is a suggested link between eccentric training and increased lower extremity stiffness, indicating that tendon stiffness can influence the risk of Achilles tendonosis via altering tensile loading of the tendon.

Joint injuries

Joint injuries in youths mimic very closely joint injuries in adults. However, there are complications from growth-plate involvement. Injuries that would cause a liga-ment or tendon rupture in adults, in youths will often result in an avulsion fracture of a piece of bone (apophysial growth plate) to which the tendon is attached.

The labrum is a ring of cartilage that surrounds and helps to stabilize the shoulder joint. The shoulder can rotate 360°, but it is not designed to do so while support-ing the entire body weight, as occurs in gymnastics manoeuvres. Shoulder range of motion in swimming and cricket also places considerable strain on the shoulder structures. Tearing of the labrum from its bony attachment usually occurs as a result of chronic traction and compression. Tearing can occur in isolation, or in conjunc-tion with other shoulder injuries such as subluxation. Rotator cuff tendonosis is where the rotator cuff tendons become swollen and painful. Repetitive overhead stress to the shoulder can cause cumulative micro trauma to the tendons, stimulating a cycle of chronic inflammation. This problem can be further exacerbated by shoulder muscle imbalances or shoulder instability.

The most common tissues involved in wrist pain are the small intercarpal ligaments that run between the carpal wrist bones. Initial aching may indicate impingement of the dorsal wrist structures is occurring. Intervention at an early stage can prevent further damage, but if the action is continued without changes, instability, subluxation (joint moving out of place) or even stress fractures may occur in youths.

Landings in sport movements can be stressful to the lower back due to increased compression and extension. In the early stages repetitive stress can result in vertebral ring apophysis inflammation. If rested and managed appropriately the injury can be resolved, but if excessive stress is continued, fractures and eventually excessive vertebra displacement can occur. Youths can be at greater risk of developing spinal injuries if they have weak lower abdominal muscles. Youths are more likely to compensate for weak abdominals by using the lumbar spine as a fulcrum or pivot point, which places greater compressive forces on the vertebrae. Excessive rotational or torsional stress can damage the small zygapophyseal joints on the vertebral arches that help link one vertebra with the next. Although only a relatively small amount of movement occurs at each joint, damage at one vertebra can result in a weak link in the spinal column 'chain'.

Risk factors for overuse injuries in youths

Risk factors differ from the mechanism of injury and are predisposing factors that combined with the mechanism of injury may make youth athletes more prone to injury. Potential injury risk factors that strength and conditioning coaches need to be cognisant of are exercise time (frequency and duration) volume, intensity, gender, age, level of performance, anatomical factors (bone structure and density, muscle fibre types, joint range of motion, hormonal factors and anatomical alignment), prior injury, poor conditioning, growth, improper training methods, poor technique, poor conditioning, lack of suitable equipment, poor surfaces and poor nutrition. Altering strength in one muscle group can alter length–tension relationships and inertial properties, and may destabilize joints and lead to injury.

Although focus is usually on external factors, such as training regimes, equipment, coaching techniques and the repetitive nature of some sports activities, the role of psychological factors that may influence the vulnerability or resiliency to injury in sports is also important. Stress-injury models suggest that potentially stressful events undergo cognitive appraisals and associated physiological and attentional changes (stress response) that may result in increased injury risk. Stress responses are moderated by personality, history of stressors and coping resources.

Practical applications

Injury prevention strategies to reduce the risk of overuse injuries to young athletes

Targeted injury prevention strategies, based on epidemiology (incidence, nature and mechanisms of injury) and risk factor analyses, have the potential to help reduce the incidence and severity of injuries. Periodization involving gradual and logical progression of training loads is a key injury prevention principle that has been outlined in Chapter 11. Given the complexity of overuse injuries, the most effective injury prevention strategies will be multifaceted. Hume and Potts (1999) developed a multifaceted, 10-point action plan for sport injury prevention. The resulting model, named *SportSmart* (Figure 14.2), and educational resources have physical conditioning as a key component (Hume *et al.*, 2005). Resources are available at the New Zealand Accident Compensation Corporation injury prevention education website (www.acc.co.nz/preventing-injuries).

Football coaches reported that they changed the way they coached after participating in the pilot of the FIFA 'The 11' resources as part of the *SportSmart* programme in New Zealand (Gianotti and Hume, 2009). Although 96 per cent of the coaches reported 'The 11' programme was useful, the DVD was reported as more useful (78 per cent) than the poster (40 per cent) (Gianotti *et al.*, 2008). After the education intervention, 96 per cent of football coaches changed the way they coached warm-up/cool-down and stretch (65 per cent), technique (63 per cent),

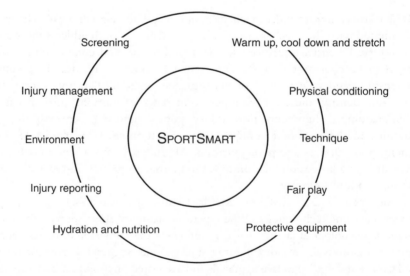

FIGURE 14.2 The SportSmart 10-point plan for community sports injury prevention

Image courtesy of Dr. Simon Gianotti.

fitness/strength and conditioning (60 per cent) and nutrition/hydration (58 per cent) practices (Gianotti *et al.*, 2008). Given the role and influence that strength and conditioning practitioners have with coaches, it is important they are cognisant of injury prevention strategies and actively promote and implement them.

A soccer-specific neuromuscular training programme including dynamic stretching, eccentric strength, agility, jumping and balance (including a home-based balance training programme using a wobble board) was protective of all injuries and acute onset injury in youth soccer athletes (380 training and 364 control) (Emery and Meeuwisse, 2010). The control programme was a standardized warm-up (static and dynamic stretching and aerobic components) and a home-based stretching programme. The injury rate in the training group was lower than in the control group (2.08 versus 3.35 injuries per 1,000 athlete hours). Studies designed in this manner are needed to ascertain the effectiveness of interventions to reduce specific overuse injuries.

Cost–benefit (time and money) evaluation of injury prevention initiatives needs to be conducted to ensure that effort and resourcing are well spent and so that maximum potential to reduce injury risk is achieved. The FREED (funding, resources, environment, evaluation and delivery) framework for community sports injury prevention is the outcome of extensive analysis of the results of community sports injury programmes implemented in New Zealand that have shown a decrease in the number and costs of injuries (Gianotti, 2009). This framework may be useful for other countries to use in developing injury-prevention programmes.

Ensure good technique

Incorrect mechanics during movement patterns can increase inappropriate loading. There are a number of screening protocols that can help identify movement dysfunction or technique faults. A whole-body functional movement competency screen (MCS) that challenges fundamental movement patterns of the body-weight squat (Kritz *et al.*, 2009a), the body-weight lunge and twist (Kritz *et al.*, 2009b), the push-up, the body-weight bend and pull (Kritz *et al.*, 2010) and the single-leg squat has been developed for use by sport and health professionals. The strength and conditioning coach videorecords the athlete performing five repetitions of each MCS movement task from the front and side, and then rates segment movement quality for the head, shoulders, lumbar, hips, knees, ankles and feet, and rates quality of balance and joint range of movement. Initial evidence showed MCS scores could predict trunk injury for male and female elite athletes (Kritz, 2012). Having screening movements that can help predict performance or injury will enable strength and conditioning practitioners to monitor and prescribe exercises for athletes to enhance their performance and reduce their injury risk.

Impact attenuation describes how efficiently the energy from an impact is absorbed. Insufficient impact attenuation is linked to an increased injury risk as a result of overloading in tissues (Steffen *et al.*, 2007). Vertical force impact peak and the maximal vertical loading rate may contribute to overuse injuries in runners

(Hreljac *et al.*, 2000). Maximal rate of rearfoot pronation and touchdown supination angle are also likely to increase injury in runners. There are important principles (e.g. segment alignment, distributing the forces over time, using a large base of support) related to landings that strength and conditioning coaches can teach to young athletes. Aiming for a 'soft' (or quiet) landing means that attenuation of energy will help to reduce injury risk. Both technique and physical preparation for controlled landings should be taught at a young age, practised often and continue throughout athletes' participation in the sport.

Summary

Understanding specific overuse injuries and their modifiable risk factors is essential for the strength and conditioning coach to reduce the risk of injury. Strength and conditioning coaches have an important role in educating athletes and coaches about the nature, risk and injury prevention strategies for overuse injuries. More emphasis by medical and sport science personnel working with coaches and athletes needs to be placed on prevention of overuse injury in sport through improved joint strength, biomechanically sound sport technique and use of appropriate sport equipment. It will be the skill of strength and conditioning coaches in interpreting evidence-based research and tracking and reporting their own injury prevention strategies that will make the difference in reducing the risk of overuse injury in young athletes, while maximizing opportunities to improve performance. Take a long-term view and prevent long-term injuries.

Key points

- Monitor your athletes for signs and symptoms of injury to help determine the incidence of overuse injuries in youths. Include a pre-participation injury history. Periodically ask young athletes if they are having any pain or aches. Be aware of the common regions of the body where the effects of stress appear and recognize signs and symptoms of specific overuse injuries. Advise young athletes to obtain medical diagnosis early where repeated pain is reported. Put injury management strategies in place quickly if an overuse injury occurs. Ensure proper medical referral is sought.
- Identify and monitor risk factors for specific overuse injuries. Evaluate which risk factors would be most effectively addressed. Think of ways to reduce likely risk factors. Reduce training loads and rotate training strains on body joints and tissue structures to reduce the risk of injury, particularly during rapid growth.
- Structure training sessions appropriately. Periodize training, reduce repetition of the same tasks in training sessions, distribute motor skills and work periods interspersed with frequent rest periods, use random practice so the same movement patterns are not repeated excessively, gradually increase workload progression, reduce workload when changing surfaces, use cross-training to

maintain adequate training volume while helping to reduce fatigue of specific musculoskeletal structures, provide at least one day physical rest each week, individualize training and skill development, reduce training loads and delay skill progressions for athletes experiencing rapid growth, alternate loading types during workouts, train athletes in a cyclically progressive manner and emphasize quality of workouts rather than repetitiveness and avoid assisted stretching techniques with beginning athletes.

- Teach correct landing techniques early and practise often. To reduce risk of injury maximize the time spent in the landing phase by using a 'toe-heel' landing pattern and bend the hips, knees and ankles. Ensure athletes maintain correct alignment of knees over toes throughout landing and they land evenly on both feet with a large base of support. Ensure young athletes have appropriate technique and strength before they jump from heights. Ensure appropriate surfaces are used for training and be more vigilant when training after changes of surfaces.

References

DiFiori, J. P. (2010) 'Overuse injuries in children and adolescents', *Current Sports Medicine Reports*, 9: 372–378.

Emery, C. A. and Meeuwisse, W. H. (2010) 'The effectiveness of a neuromuscular prevention strategy to reduce injuries in youth soccer: A cluster-randomised controlled trial', *British Journal of Sports Medicine*, 44: 555–562.

Gianotti, S. (2009) 'The FREED framework for community sports injury prevention implementation in New Zealand', *Sport Performance Research Institute New Zealand*, doctoral thesis, Auckland, AUT University.

Gianotti, S. M. and Hume, P. A. (2009) 'The implementation of "The 11" in New Zealand', FIFA medical conference, Zurich.

Gianotti, S. M., Hume, P. A. and Tunstall, H. (2008) 'Efficacy of injury prevention related coach education within netball and soccer', *Journal of Science and Medicine in Sport*, 13: 32–35.

Hawkins, D. and Metheny, J. (2001) 'Overuse injuries in youth sports: Biomechanical considerations', *Medicine and Science in Sports and Exercise*, 33: 1701–1707.

Hreljac, A., Marshall, R. N. and Hume, P. A. (2000) 'Evaluation of lower extremity overuse injury potential in runners', *Medicine and Science in Sports and Exercise*, 32: 1635–1641.

Hume, P. A. and Potts, G. (1999) *SportSmart: The 10-point Plan for Sports Injury Prevention: An Educational Resource*, Wellington: Accident, Rehabilitation and Compensation Insurance Corporation of New Zealand.

Hume, P. A. and Stewart, A. D. (2012) 'Body composition change'. In Stewart, A. D. and Sutton, L. (eds) *Body Composition in Sport, Exercise and Health*. London: Taylor & Francis.

Hume, P. A., Gianotti, S. and Brooks, D. (2005) 'The New Zealand SportSmart injury prevention programme', *British Journal of Sports Medicine*, 39: 391.

Hume, P. A., Reid, D. and Edwards, T. (2006) 'Epicondylar injury in sport: Epidemiology, type, mechanisms, assessment, management and prevention', *Sports Medicine*, 36: 151–170.

Hutchinson, M. R. and Nasser, R. (2000) 'Common sports injuries in children and adolescents', *Medscape Orthopaedics & Sports Medicine eJournal*. Online. Available at: http://www.medscape.com/viewarticle/408524_4 (accessed 14 March 2013).

Kritz, M. (2012) 'Development, reliability and effectiveness of the Movement Competency Screen (MCS)', *Sport Performance Research Institute New Zealand*, doctoral thesis, Auckland, AUT University.

Kritz, M., Cronin, J. and Hume, P. A. (2009a) 'The body-weight squat: A movement screen for the squat pattern', *Strength and Conditioning Journal*, 31: 76–85.

Kritz, M., Cronin, J. and Hume, P. A. (2009b) 'Using the body-weight lunge to screen an athletes' lunge pattern', *Strength and Conditioning Journal*, 31: 15–24.

Kritz, M., Cronin, J. and Hume, P. A. (2010) 'Screening the upper-body push and pull patterns using body weight exercises', *Strength and Conditioning Journal*, 32: 72–82.

McDonnell, L. K., Hume, P. A. and Nolte, V. (2011) 'Rib stress fractures among rowers: Definition, epidemiology, mechanisms, risk factors and effectiveness of injury prevention strategies', *Sports Medicine*, 41: 883–901.

Steffen, K., Andersen, T. E. and Bahr, R. (2007) 'Risk of injury on artificial turf and natural grass in young female football players', *British Journal of Sports Medicine*, 41: i33–i37.

15

WELL-BEING OF YOUTH ATHLETES

Jon L. Oliver, Abbe Brady and Rhodri S. Lloyd

Introduction

This book has shown the many benefits that youths can gain from participating in various types of strength and conditioning exercise throughout childhood. However, it also needs to be realized that sports participation is not without its risks and that child athletes should be viewed as a vulnerable population. Consequently, strength and conditioning coaches need to take responsibility for helping to ensure the child athlete has positive experiences during their involvement in sport. Reflecting this view the International Olympic Committee consensus statement on training elite child athletes states that the entire sports process should be pleasurable and fulfilling (Mountjoy *et al.*, 2008). A statement that should apply equally to all children involved in strength and conditioning programmes. For the purposes of this chapter a child will be considered as anyone under 18 years old, reflecting the definition of the United Nations. Consequently, the strength and condition coach could be considered to have legal, ethical and moral responsibilities for maintaining and promoting the well-being of this vulnerable population.

Well-being has been defined as a positive and sustainable state that allows individuals, groups or nations to thrive and flourish (Huppert *et al.*, 2004). Sports participation has been recognized as a vehicle that can facilitate improved well-being among children (Steptoe and Butler, 1996). Similarly, it is hoped that strength and conditioning programmes can help to promote well-being in children. However, a risk of sports participation is that it may, directly or indirectly, have a negative impact on a child's well-being, in terms of physical, social and psychological development (Oliver *et al.*, 2011). By understanding and controlling the factors that can influence well-being, the strength and conditioning coach can help maximize the enjoyment and development of the child athlete.

Positive or negative experiences within sport are likely to increase or decrease a child's sense of well-being, respectively. It is believed that the coach–athlete relationship is one of the most important influences on athlete motivation and sub-sequent application in training (Mageau, 2003), and the strength and conditioning coach must work hard to develop this relationship. In a recent report, Alexander *et al.* (2011) surveyed 6,000 young adults regarding their experiences as children in organized sport in the UK. Results of that survey showed that 75 per cent of respondents reported having experienced emotional harm and 25 per cent had experienced physical harm. This chapter will aim to identify possible threats to well-being, both physical and non-physical, and ways to maximize the develop-ment of a sense of well-being in youth athletes.

Basic theoretical concepts

While participation in sport is known to have a number of positive health and psy-chological benefits for the child athlete (Oliver *et al.*, 2011), it also presents various risks that will interact with the growth, maturation and emotional development of the child. These risks may include factors such as inappropriate training, over-training, injury, inadequate nutrition and internal and external psycho-social stress. These risks may be broadly categorized into physical risk factors and non-physical (psycho-social) risk factors, although in reality they will often overlap.

Physical factors in well-being

The physical demands placed on child athletes and the way in which they train is likely to have a primary role in determining their enjoyment of the training pro-cess. It is accepted that children are not miniature adults and that any conditioning programme needs to consider the unique way in which children will respond and adapt to training (Faigenbaum *et al.*, 2009; Mountjoy *et al.*, 2008). However, coaches need to look beyond the planning of single sessions to consider suitable progression, variation and overall training load within the training programme and how this allows for holistic development. Fundamental movement skills should be developed as a priority in the early stages of training, which has been a consistent theme throughout this book and in recent literature. As well as improving physi-cal abilities, the development of fundamental movement skills is associated with physical and psychological health benefits in children, such as an increased self-perception of competence (Lubans *et al.*, 2010).

Children naturally engage in varied, spontaneous and intermittent play-like physical activity (Oliver *et al.*, 2011). It has been suggested that resistance training provides a good reflection of the brief, intermittent type of exercise that children regularly perform (Faigenbaum and Westcott, 2007). However, long-term pro-grammes may not allow for the variation and spontaneity that is inherent to natural play activities, and the use of adult-like, highly structured and prescriptive training programmes may do little to meet the developmental needs of child athletes (Oliver *et al.*, 2011). This situation could be exacerbated by a training programme that focuses solely on physical development and ignores psycho-social development. A tendency to predominantly focus on physical development is common given the maturational and performance benefits that can be observed with this approach in childhood, and this approach is promoted in the widely adopted, long-term athlete development model (Balyi and Hamilton, 2004). However, some authors have suggested that developing psychological skill plays a more decisive role in realizing the talent of young athletes (Bailey *et al.*, 2010). Furthermore, recent evidence also shows that athletes who achieved an elite status as an adult spent less time training as young children than their near-elite counterparts, although they did increase their training volume in late adolescence (Moesch *et al.*, 2011). Therefore, well-being and performance may be optimized with training programmes that promote holistic development of the child athlete, with training volumes increased in the mid-teenage years for those striving to achieve an elite level (Moesch *et al.*, 2011).

A quarter of participants in organized youth sport have reported an experience of physical harm in their sport, with over half of these reporting being made to train when injured or exhausted or experiencing overly aggressive treatment (Alexander *et al.*, 2011). The incidence rate of these negative experiences increased as performance level moved towards the elite. Such situations should be avoidable providing that the strength and conditioning coach can follow good practice, be able to identify risks to physical well-being and, most importantly, recognize their influence and responsibility when working with youths. Limited evidence suggests that approximately 30 per cent of young athletes overtrain (Matos and Winsley, 2007) and that overuse and fatigue are primary risk factors of injury in adolescent athletes (Olsen *et al.*, 2006). These findings support the suggestion that coaches would be better to under- rather overtrain young athletes (Faigenbaum and Medors, 2010). Further information on potential risk factors contributing to overtraining in youth athletes is provided in Chapter 2. If injured, the child athlete should be referred to a clinician, although some form of suitable training is likely to be useful in rehabilitation (American Academy of Pediatrics, 2000). Preferably strength and conditioning programmes should contain prehabilitation exercises to help minimize injury risk in the first place, as suffering an injury may in itself have a negative impact on well-being.

The strength and conditioning coach must ensure that any training is in the best interests of the child. Recently, the term 'forced physical exertion' has been offered to denote movement from legitimate physical conditioning to abusive practice (Kerr, 2010). Suggested criteria to identify forced physical exertion include exercise that could cause potential harm, where there is no actual or perceived benefit, where there is an absence of consent or where exercise is used as a form of punishment (Kerr, 2010). Previous literature has clearly identified the existence of forced physical exertion with youth athletes (Clarkson, 2006).

As discussed in Chapter 13, nutrition is a key consideration when working with child athletes. A particular concern with regards to well-being is a state of continued negative energy balance. This is likely to be more prevalent in sports where slenderness or body image are important (particularly in female athletes), or where there are high training volumes that may result in rapid weight loss (Oliver *et al.*, 2011). Other symptoms primarily associated with female athletes include eating disorders, irregular menstrual cycles and osteopenia/osteoporosis, the effects of which may be difficult to reverse if not identified during adolescence. Any athlete showing early signs of any of these symptoms should be referred to a clinician.

Psycho-social factors in well-being

When designing the sporting environment to reduce psycho-social risks to well-being and maximize the potential for youth development, it is helpful if the coach has awareness of desirable personal qualities associated with young athletes' well-being. Qualities the strength and conditioning coach should encourage are: a growth mindset, self-determined motivation, perceived competence, confidence and resilience. The coach should also promote children's awareness of their acquisition of such capacities because these are valuable and highly transferable life skills (Danish *et al.*, 2004). In order to promote these qualities in their young athletes the coach should consider the importance of understanding children's participation motives and sources of enjoyment, the motivational climate, positive coach behaviours, peer friendship, social support and the importance of a sport–life balance.

Dweck (2006) introduced the concept of mindsets to explain how an individual's beliefs about their ability can assist or hamper their motivation to learn and their chances of experiencing success. A child with a growth mindset believes that with purposeful practice, time, guidance and above all effort, they can develop sporting ability and experience success. By contrast, a child with a fixed mindset believes that sporting ability is something that they either have or do not have, and consequently effort and practice are less important for success. Praising giftedness and winning (rather than effort and persistence) has been shown to encourage a fixed mindset as it focuses on factors beyond the child's effortful control. A growth mindset facilitates the development of adaptive behaviours such as problem solving, patience and enjoyment of learning, which are more appropriate for facilitating children's social and psychological well-being in sport.

When children participate in sport because they cherish its inherent enjoyment, pleasure and challenge, it is described as being intrinsically motivated and self-determined, which are strong predictors of well-being (Ryan and Deci, 2000). Encouraging self-determined motivation occurs when coaches interact with young athletes in ways that provide opportunities to satisfy basic needs to feel competent, autonomous and connectedness with significant others (Gagné *et al.*, 2003; Reinboth *et al.*, 2004). An autocratic coaching style and over-emphasis on winning and outperforming others encourages children to become more extrinsically oriented, which may reduce feelings of self-determination. Lower self-determination in children is more commonly associated with less enjoyment, lower adherence, less adaptive motivational behaviours and greater attrition (Wang and Biddle, 2007).

A primary aim of the coach should be to promote a sense of competence in the young athlete, as perceived competence has been recognized as a crucial factor influencing the psychological well-being of the child athlete (Reinboth *et al.*, 2004).

Compared to those with low perceptions of sport-related competence, children who have high perceptions of competency experience many benefits, including more positive feelings in sport situations, fewer emotional and behavioural problems, an internal locus of control, and a tendency to be intrinsically motivated and sustain interest for continued involvement in sport (Donaldson and Ronan, 2006; Horn and Harris, 1996).

It is vital to recognize that externally rated competence, for instance by a judge or a coach, is not as strongly related to psycho-social well-being and the benefits described above, as is the child's self-perception of competence. Two children may have the same level of technical ability in a skill but may have very different perceptions of their ability, and so it is important that the strength and conditioning coach does not assume that absolute performance achievement is equivalent to perceived competence. Whereas effort is equated with competence in those under six years of age, the increasing use of social comparison occurs between 7 and 14 years. Children under the age of ten are often not able to easily distinguish between their own performance and that of the team, which emphasizes the issue of young children's lack of cognitive and emotional readiness for competition (Passer, 1997). Between 13 and 18 years of age, athletes move from using mainly evaluative coach and peer feedback to include self-referenced performance evaluation to judge ability (Horn and Harris, 1996). By providing age-appropriate, constructive and positively framed instructions and feedback, the coach can contribute to the development of self-perceived competence.

Confidence is highly valued in sport because it has strong associations with positive emotions, positive self-perceptions, resilience, concentration, reduced performance anxiety and also successful performance (Vealey and Chase, 2008). Confidence can be an elusive quality and so understanding how to cultivate it in children is an important objective for many coaches. As well as using developmentally appropriate and individualized mental skills training to develop children's confidence, strength and conditioning coaches should be contributing to the ongoing confidence of children in everyday coaching interactions. Coaches can do this by keeping enjoyment on the agenda, helping children understand how to prepare well, prioritize process-focused (rather than outcome) goals and by providing clear feedback to the child about sport-related accomplishments.

Learning how to cope with challenges and setbacks in sport, such as illness, injury, slow progress, team conflict, non-selection or poor or inconsistent performance are important developmental experiences for young athletes. Resilience is the ability to adapt to adverse or changing situations while maintaining relatively stable levels of physical and psychological functioning (Luthar, 2006). The strength and conditioning coach can facilitate athletes' resilience by setting appropriate challenges (i.e. neither too difficult or too easy), providing encouragement, social support and creating a climate in which such setbacks are recognized as a part of the challenge in sport. The coach may also support the young athlete with age-appropriate mental skills training which has been shown to enhance resilience in young performers (Gucciardi et al., 2009).

Understanding that children have many motives for taking part in sport will help coaches design appropriate sporting environments to meet the needs for fun, friendship, autonomy, excitement, challenge, skill-development, fitness and success. Drop-out in youth sport has been closely associated with a lack of these features (Weiss and Ferrer-Caja, 2002). Though fun and enjoyment are often the main reasons children cite for taking part in sport (Weiss, 2000), research shows that some coaches have a poor understanding of what fun and enjoyment mean to children, and perceive that having fun can conflict with skill development (Bengoechea et al., 2004). Children report enjoying many experiences in sport such as: feeling a sense of mastery; achievement of skills; having support and involvement from parents, coaches and peers; positive social interactions; learning and demonstrating skills; and movement sensations (Scanlan and Simons, 1992). Thus, a challenge for the coach is to broaden ideas about enjoyment and create opportunities for the varied sources of experience from which it emanates.

Motivational climate is a helpful way of thinking about how particular features of the sporting environment influence participants' motivation and sport-related behaviours. A performance or ego-involving motivational climate is one that promotes competition, focuses on outcomes, rewards high achievers and punishes failure. By contrast, a mastery or task-involving motivational climate is one that rewards effort, focuses on improvement, recognizes the contribution of each athlete and encourages cooperation. Considerable research in youth sport has shown that a task-mastery climate is associated with positive outcomes for children, such as increased enjoyment, self-determination, perceived competence and belief that effort creates success (Smith et al., 2009; Theeboom et al., 1995; Wells et al., 2006). An ego-involving performance climate is associated with less desirable outcomes, such as increased boredom, aggressive behaviour, belief that innate ability and deception cause success in sport and decreased enjoyment. Establishing a task-involving mastery motivational as opposed to a 'win at all costs' achievement climate is most likely to facilitate the well-being of young athletes.

Three-quarters of participants in youth sport have reported experiencing emotional harm, of which one-third of these recalled negative experiences involving a coach (Alexander et al., 2011). The most common cause of emotional harm is reported to be criticism of performance. Research has shown that, compared to children whose coaches did not receive specialist training in how to communicate appropriately with children, those whose coaches did receive training had greater self-esteem, evaluated their coaches and the team more positively, experienced greater performance enjoyment and reported a stronger desire for continued future involvement (Smith et al., 1979). The coaches who had been trained learned about how to praise and reward effort, give clear and brief instructions in a positive way, offer encouragement, create clear expectations and boundaries for behaviour, and not to punish mistakes (Smith et al., 1979).

Peer friendship is also a major contributor to children's psycho-social development and is a key reason youths cite for involvement in sport (Smith, 2007; Weiss et al., 1996). Friendships are important because they provide emotional and social support as well as self-esteem affirmation (Weiss, 2000). Children who feel their peer group likes them experience greater enjoyment, higher motivation, less anxiety and are motivated to continue participation to maintain their friendships (Weiss, 2000). A challenge for coaches is to ensure that they provide time and opportunities for social interaction and cooperation to occur. Involving children in peer-group activities such as problem-solving and team-building activities are helpful for promoting sport-relevant social interactions.

Social support is considered important for young athletes' well-being by both protecting the child from the harmful effects of stress, and increasing the chances of positive feelings and shared resources for coping via social integration in supportive networks of family, friends, teachers and sports personnel (Rees, 2007). Coaches are recognized as providing social support in many ways, for example boosting children's self-esteem, giving advice, helping in tangible ways via equipment and resources, being trustworthy and showing care for the young athlete. Other ways the coach offers social support is by encouraging healthy behaviours and sport–life balance. Sport–life balance is an important consideration, especially when children have frequent and intense training loads on top of school, family and other life demands. Over-investment in sport at the expense of other activities has been found to produce fewer benefits to well-being than being involved in sport and non-sporting activities (Linver *et al.*, 2009).

Practical applications

The overall goal of the strength and conditioning coach should be to create an environment that enables the child athlete to flourish by developing a sense of well-being. This may be achieved by empowering the athlete to achieve their individual goals, and by developing a sense of competence and self-awareness. The coach should also be able to recognize potential hazards that may reduce well-being. These hazards reflect different forms of stress (physical and psycho-social) that need to be managed to maintain a positive state of well-being. To achieve this the strength and conditioning coach should be able to monitor training, the athlete and the coaching process, and importantly be able to react in a proactive manner.

Training and non-training stressors may have a negative influence on well-being, and importantly it may be the accumulation and interaction of these factors that may change the balance from a positive to a negative stress response. Having an appreciation of an athlete's lifestyle may help identify risk factors and at the very least will give the coach a better understanding of their athlete. For instance, a child may have many competing demands to balance; training, competition, travel, academic work, socializing, sleep, which, when considered together, may help identify possible threats to well-being. For example, youth athletes who specialize in individual sports have high training volumes, do not engage in other sports and dedicate little time to school or social activities are more likely to suffer from overtraining (Matos *et al.*, 2011). Figure 15.1 provides an example of a weekly schedule of an athlete, with each 30 minutes of the day accounted for. This type

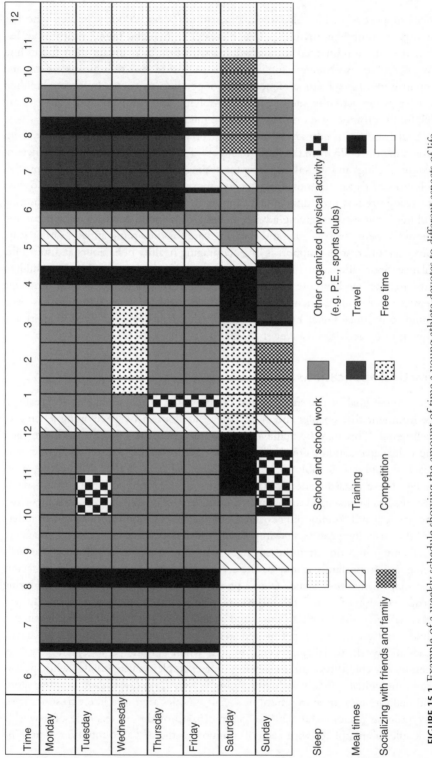

FIGURE 15.1 Example of a weekly schedule showing the amount of time a young athlete devotes to different aspects of life

of presentation can help both the athlete and the coach realize the demands that are being placed on the athletes' time, and how they are managing different aspects of their life. An athlete training solely for one sport, with very little free time, and managing limited sleep could be considered high risk. However, it should be noted that these are only risk factors and individual athletes may respond differently to similar demands in their life.

A greater depth of information and more continual monitoring can be obtained by asking a child athlete to keep a training diary. An example page from a training diary is shown in Figure 15.2. The diary records information on sleep, training, diet, provides space for any other comments, and includes a very brief well-being questionnaire. The well-being questionnaire was developed by McLean *et al.* (2010) and was shown to be able to track recovery of elite senior rugby league players in the days following a match. For each question a score of five equals the most positive response and a score of one equals the most negative response. While acutely lowered well-being scores may be expected post-competition or after a particularly demanding training session, an unexpectedly low score or continually depressed score in one or more of the categories may provide an indication of a more chronic problem. In all circumstances some sort of positive action should be taken, which might be as simple as lowering training loads post-competition and including recovery strategies, to a more in-depth discussion of any underlying issues with the athlete and some follow-up actions (e.g. a longer rest period, referral to a clinician).

All athletes will experience peaks and troughs in training and competition, however, it is important that the strength and conditioning coach does not over-react to such a situation in a negative manner. Rather than immediately increasing training loads to try to compensate for a poor performance, the coach should try to seek to understand any underlying causes that may be responsible. Early performance decrements may reflect a lack of interest and motivation and a feeling that training and competition no longer have a fun element. In a survey of 8,000 children the most commonly cited reasons for dropping out of sport included the feeling that the sport was no longer fun and that the coach was 'playing favourites' (Seefeldt *et al.*, 1992). Coaches should recognize the need to provide the youth athlete with a varied and stimulating programme to help avoid such a situation.

An important feature of good coaching practice involves engaging in reflective practice to promote mindfulness and learning, which in turn have the potential to inform the coach's behaviour. When coaching is looked at as a simple instructional activity, it fails to recognize that coaches are developing and learning too. An example of one issue that warrants reflection by youth coaches is understanding what being athlete-centred means. This can mean quite different things according to whether the performance-success or child-development aspect of 'athlete' is emphasized. Therefore, it is vital that the strength and conditioning coach reflects upon their actions, extends thinking beyond the practical or technical domains and considers assumptions about the goodness of sport and the coach's role in enhancing the well-being of the young athlete.

Date: _____

Number of hours sleep: _____

Quality of sleep: _____

How am I feeling today? (rate 1 to 5)

Sleep	Fatigue	Soreness	Stress	Mood	Total

Diet (*include time and what you ate*)

Breakfast:

Lunch:

Dinner:

Training (*to include competition and any other exercises*)

Type: Type:

Duration: Duration:

Intensity: Intensity:

Content: Content:

Other comments (*e.g. What else is going on in my life? How am I feeling?*)

FIGURE 15.2 Example page for a youth athlete diary

Key points

- The strength and conditioning coach should aim to create an environment in which the young athlete is able to flourish and develop a sense of well-being. Ultimately the coach should ensure that the entire sports process for the young athlete is developmentally appropriate, challenging, pleasurable and fulfilling.
- Although the benefits of sports participation are believed to outweigh the risks, negative experiences can occur and these may reduce the well-being of child athletes. Three-quarters of those involved in sport as children reported experiencing emotional harm and one-quarter experienced physical harm; in both instances the coach was implicated in some of these negative experiences.
- Physical and psycho-social factors may contribute to stress and a reduced sense of well-being. Having an awareness of potential threats to well-being and having systems in place to help identify these threats should enable the coach to be proactive in promoting a sense of well-being.
- Keeping training sessions and programmes varied and fun, providing positive feedback to promote a sense of perceived competence and focusing on process goals and individual development should help to ensure that youth athletes remain motivated to train and develop through sport.

References

Alexander, K., Stafford, A. and Lewis, R. (2011) *Summary Report: The experiences of children participating in organized sport in the UK*, London: NSPCC.

American Academy of Pediatrics (2000) 'Intensive training and sports specialization in young athletes', *Pediatrics*, 106: 154–157.

Bailey, R., Collins, D., Ford, P., MacNamara, A., Toms, M. and Pearce, G. (2010) *Participant Development in Sport: An academic review*, Leeds: SportsCoach UK.

Balyi, I. and Hamilton, A. (2004) *Long-Term Athlete Development: Trainability in Childhood and Adolescence. Windows of Opportunity, Optimal Trainability*, Victoria: National Coaching Institute British Columbia and Advanced Training and Performance Ltd.

Bengoechea, E. G., Strean, W. and Williams, D. J. (2004) 'Understanding and promoting fun in youth sport: coaches' perspectives', *Physical Education and Sport Pedagogy*, 9: 197–214.

Clarkson, P. M. (2006) 'Case report of exertional rhabdomyolysis in a 12-year-old boy', *Medince and Science in Sports and Exercise*, 38: 197–200.

Danish, S., Forneris, T., Hodge, K. and Heke, I. (2004) 'Enhancing youth development through sport', *World Leisure Journal*, 46: 38–49.

Donaldson, S. J. and Ronan, K. R. (2006) 'The effects of sports participation on young adolescents' emotional well-being', *Adolescence*, 41: 369–388.

Dweck, C. S. (2006) *Mindset: The new psychology of success*, New York: Random House.

Faigenbaum, A. D. and Medors, L. (2010) 'A coaches dozen: 12 FUNdamental principles', *Strength and Conditioning Journal*, 32: 99–101.

Faigenbaum, A. D. and Westcott, W. (2007) 'Resistance training for obese children and adolescents', *President's Council on Physical Fitness and Sport Research Digest*, 8: 1–8.

Faigenbaum, A. D., Kraemer, W. J., Blimkie, C. J., Jeffreys, I., Micheli, L. J., Nitka, M. and Rowland, T. W. (2009) 'Youth resistance training: updated position statement paper from the national strength and conditioning association', *Journal of Strength and Conditioning Research*, 23: S60–S79.

Gagné, M., Ryan, R. M. and Bargmann, K. (2003) 'Autonomy support and need satisfaction in the motivation and well-being of gymnasts', *Journal of Applied Sport Psychology*, 15: 372–390.

Gucciardi, D.F., Gordon, S. and Dimmock, J. A. (2009) 'Evaluation of a mental toughness training program for youth-aged Australian footballers: I. A quantitative analysis', *Journal of Applied Sport Psychology*, 21: 307–323.

Hardman, A., Jones, C. and Jones, R. (2010) 'Sports coaching, virtue ethics and emulation', *Physical Education and Sport Pedagogy*, 15: 345–359.

Horn, T. and Harris, A. (1996) 'Perceived competence in young athletes: research findings and recommendations for coaches and parents', in F. L. Smoll and R. E. Smith (eds) *Children and Youth in Sport: A biopsychosocial perspective*, Madison, WI: Brown and Benchmark Publishers.

Huppert, F. A., Baylis, N. and Keverne, B. (2004) 'Introduction: why do we need a science of well-being?' *Philosophical Tranactions of the Royal Society B: Biological Sciences*, 359: 1331–1332.

Kerr, G. (2010) 'Physical and emotional abuse of elite child athletes: the case of forced physical exertion', in C. H. Brackenridge and D. Rhind (eds) *Elite Child Athlete Welfare: International perspectives*, London: Brunel University Press.

Kristiansen, E. and Roberts, G. C. (2010) 'Young elite athletes and social support: coping with competitive and organizational stress in "Olympic" competition', *Scandinavian Journal of Medicine and Science in Sports*, 20: 686–695.

Linver, M. R., Roth, J. L. and Brooks-Gunn, J. (2009) 'Patterns of adolescents' participation in organized activities: are sports best when combined with other activities?' *Developmental Psychology*, 45: 354–367.

Lubans, D. R., Morgan, P. J., Cliff, D. P., Barnett, L. M. and Okely, A. D. (2010) 'Fundamental movement skills in children and adolescents: review of associated health benefits', *Sports Medicine*, 40: 1019–1035.

Luthar, S. S. (2006) 'Resilience in development: a synthesis of research across five decades', in D. Cicchetti and D. J. Cohen (eds) *Developmental Psychopathology: Risk, disorder, and adaptation*, New York: Wiley.

Mageau, G. A. and Vallerand, R. J. (2003) 'The coach-athlete relationship: a motivational model', *Journal of Sports Sciences*, 21: 883–904.

Matos, N. and Winsley, R. J. (2007) 'Trainability of young athletes and overtraining', *Journal of Sports Science and Medicine*, 6: 353–367.

Matos, N. F., Winsley, R. J. and Williams, C. A. (2011) 'Prevalence of nonfunctional overreaching/overtraining in young English athletes', *Medicine and Science in Sports and Exercise*, 43: 1287–1294.

McLean, B. D., Coutts, A. J., Kelly, V., McGuigan, M. R. and Cormack, S. J. (2010) 'Neuromuscular, endocrine, and perceptual fatigue responses during different length between-match microcycles in professional rugby league players', *International Journal of Sports Physiology and Performance*, 5: 367–383.

Moesch, K., Elbe, A. M., Hauge, M. L. and Wikman, J. M. (2011) 'Late specialization: the key to success in centimeters, grams, or seconds (cgs) sports', *Scandinavian Journal of Medicine and Science in Sports*, 21: e282–e290.

Mountjoy, M., Armstrong, N., Bizzini, L., Blimkie, C., Evans, J., Gerrard, D., Hangen, J., Knoll, K., Micheli, L., Sangenis, P. and Van Mechelen, W. (2008) 'IOC consensus statement: training the elite child athlete', *British Journal of Sports Medicine*, 42: 163–164.

Ntoumanis, N. and Biddle, S. J. H. (1999) 'A review of motivational climate in physical activity', *Journal of Sports Sciences*, 17: 643–665.

Oliver, J. L., Lloyd, R. S. and Meyers, R. W. (2011) 'Training elite child athletes: welfare and well-being', *Strength and Conditioning Journal*, 33: 73–79.

Olsen, S. J., Fleisig, G. S., Dun, S., Loftice, J. and Andrews, J. R. (2006) 'Risk factors for shoulder and elbow injuries in adolescent baseball pitchers', *American Journal of Sports Medicine*, 34: 905–912.

Passer, M. (1996) 'At what age are children ready to compete? Some psychological considerations', in F. L. Smoll, and R. E. Smith (eds) *Children and Youth in Sport: A biopsychosocial perspective*, Madison, WI: Brown and Benchmark Publishers.

Reinboth, M., Duda, J. L. and Ntoumanis, N. (2004) 'Dimensions of coaching behavior, need satisfaction, and the psychological and physical welfare of young athletes', *Motivation and Emotion*, 28: 297–313.

Rees, T. (2007) 'Influence of social support on athletes', in S. Jowett and D. Lavallee (eds) *Social Psychology in Sport*, Champaign, IL: Human Kinetics

Ryan, R. M. and Deci, E. L. (2000) 'Self-determination theory and the facilitation of intrinsic motivation, social development, and well-being', *American Psychologist*, 55: 68–78.

Scanlan, T. K. and Simons, J. P. (1992) 'The construct of sport enjoyment', in G.C. Roberts (ed.) *Motivation in Sport and Exercise*, Champaign, IL: Human Kinetics.

Seefeldt, V., Ewing, M. and Walk, S. (1992) *Overview of Youth Sports Programmes in the United States*, Washington, DC: Carnegie Council on Adolescent Development.

Smith, A. L. (2007) 'Youth peer relationships in sport', in S. Jowett, and D. Lavallee (eds) *Social Psychology in Sport*, Champaign, IL: Human Kinetics.

Smith, R. E., Smoll, F. L. and Cumming, S. P. (2009) 'Motivational climate and changes in young athletes' achievement goal orientations', *Motivation and Emotion*, 33: 173–183.

Smith, R. E., Smoll, F. L. and Curtis, B. (1979) 'Coach effectiveness training: a cognitive behavioral approach to enhancing relationship skills in youth sport coaches', *Journal of Sport Psychology*, 1: 59–75.

Steptoe, A. and Butler, N. (1996) 'Sports participation and emotional well-being in adolescents', *Lancet*, 347: 1789–1792.

Theeboom, M., De Knop, P. and Weiss, M. R. (1995) 'Motivational climate, psychological responses, and motor skill development in children's sport: a field-based intervention study', *Journal of Sport and Exercise Psychology*, 17: 294–311.

Vealey, R. S. (2001) 'Understanding and enhancing self-confidence in athletes', in R. N. Singer, H. A. Hausenblas and C. M. Janelle (eds) *Handbook of Sport Psychology* (2nd edn), New York: Wiley.

Vealey, R. M. and Chase, M. A. (2008) 'Self-confidence in sport', in T. S. Horn (ed.) *Advances in Sport Psychology* (3rd edn), Champaign, IL: Human Kinetics.

Vealey, R. S., Hayashi, S. W., Garner-Holman, M. and Giacobbi, P. (1998) 'Sources of sport-confidence: conceptualization of instrument development', *Journal of Sport and Exercise Psychology*, 20: 54–80.

Wang, C. K. J. and Biddle, S. J. H. (2007) 'Understanding young people's motivation towards exercise', in M. S. Hagger and N. L. D. Chatzisarantis (eds) *Intrinsic Motivation and Self-Determination in Exercise and Sport*, Champaign, IL: Human Kinetics.

Weiss, M. R. (2000) 'Motivating kids in physical activity', *The President's Council on Physical Fitness and Sports Research Digest*, 3: 1–7.

Weiss, M. R. and Ferrer-Caja, E. (2002) 'Motivational orientations and sport behavior', in T. S. Horn (ed.) *Advances in Sport Psychology* (2nd edn), Champaign, IL: Human Kinetics.

Weiss, M. R., Smith, A. L. and Theeboom, M. (1996) 'That's what friends are for: children's and teenagers' perceptions of peer relationships in the sport domain', *Journal of Sport and Exercise Psychology*, 18: 347–379.

Wells, M. S., Ellis, G. D., Arthur-Banning, S. and Roark, M. (2006) 'Effect of staged practices and motivational climate on goal orientation and sportsmanship in community youth sport experiences', *Journal of Park and Recreation Administration*, 24: 64–85.

INDEX